# DOCUMENT-BASED ASSESSMENT

**Second Edition**

## Activities

**Authors**

**Marc Pioch, M.A.Ed.**

**Jodene Smith, M.A.**

**Contributing Authors**

Cynthia Boyle
Blane Conklin, Ph.D.
Jeanne Cummings Dustman, M.A.Ed.
James A. Percoco
Kathleen Vest, M.A.Ed.

**Consultants**

**Lindsay Casserly, M.A.Ed.**
AP History Teacher & IB Coordinator
Trabuco Hills High School

**Erin Maguire, M.A.Ed.**
Social Science Department Chair
El Toro High School

**Carrie Ferguson, M.A.Ed.**
Middle School Teacher
Journey School

**Publishing Credits**

Corinne Burton, M.A.Ed., *Publisher*
Emily R. Smith, M.A.Ed., *VP of Content Development*
Véronique Bos, *Creative Director*
James Anderson, M.S.Ed., *VP of Digital Product Development*
Robin Erickson, *Art Director*
Melissa Laughlin, *Editor*
Dani Neiley, *Assistant Editor*
Lee Aucoin, *Senior Graphic Designer*
Walter Mladina, *Photo Researcher*

**Image Credits:** p.3 (top) Library of Congress [LC-USZC4-1421]; p.3 (second from top) Huntington Art Gallery, University of Texas; p.3 (bottom) Library of Congress Geography and Map Division [G3300 1802 A7]; p.5 (bottom) LOC [LC-USZ62-61636]; p.5 (bottom right) LOC [LC-DIG-ppmsca-34695]; p.7 (top) LOC [LC-USZ62-23602]; p.7 (middle), p.11 (bottom), p.121 (right), p.253 (left), p.259 (left), p.259 (right), p.261 (left), p.261 (right), p.265, p.273, p.279, p.289 (top) U.S. National Archives; p.7 (bottom) Evening star; p.8 (left) Library of Congress [LC-USZ62-94941]; p.8 (right) Library of Congress [LC-DIG-ggbain-21677]; p.9 courtesy Emily Smith; P.10, bottom Library of Congress [LC-USZ62-21637]; p.21, p.197 Independence National Historical Park Collection; p.27, p.239 The Illustrated London News, May 15, 1915. p.631; p.35 (left) Library of Congress [LC-USZ62-120467]; p.35 (right) Courtesy Wendy Conklin; p.41, p.45 (left) chippix/Shutterstock; p.47 (left) Library of Congress [LC-USF33-031096-M5]; p.47 (right) Peter Titmuss/Shutterstock; p.49 LOC [LC-USZ62-127508]; p.51 Library of Congress [LC-USZC4-2791]; p.53 (left) Library of Congress [LC-USZ62-137257]; p.53 (left) Library of Congress [LC-USZC4-2135]; p.53 (right) United States Air Force; p.57 (left) Library of Congress [LC-USZC4-2997]; p.69 Vermont Election Division; p.73 Inna Felker/Shutterstock; p.75 Bradley Hebdon/iStock; p.79, p.83 Colin/Wikimedia Commons; p.82 Delbars/Shutterstock; p.85 Library of Congress [LC-USZ62-100172]; p.89, p.95 (top) Winterthur Museum Library; p.93 (left), p.96 Library of Congress [C-USZC2-4907]; p.93 (right) Library of Congress [LC_USZ62_120464]; p.95 (bottom) Library of Congress [LC-DIG-ppmsca-22925]; p.101 alexmak72427/iStock; p.103 (left) Bettman/Getty Images; p.103 (right) Library of Congress [LC-DIG-highsm-44463]; p.109 National Gallery of Art; p.113 (left) Library of Congress [LC-USZ62-31149]; p.113 (right) Library of Congress [LC-DIG-pga-05339]; p.119 The Library Company of Philadelphia; p.121 (left) Library of Congress [LC-DIG-pga-12360]; p.125 Library of Congress [LC-USZ62-5243]; p.127 Library of Congress [LC-USZCN4-37]; p.129 Records of the U.S. House of Representatives; p.131 (left) Library of Congress [LC-USZC4-3616]; p.131 (right) Library of Congress [LC-DIG-ppmsca-39879]; p.133, p.136 National Anthropological Archives; p.141 Library of Congress [LC-USZ62-1286]; p.143 Library of Congress [LC-DIG-ppmsca-18444]; p.155 Bule Sky Studio/Shutterstock; p.157 Bibliothéque Nationale de France; p.159 (top) Dallas Museum of Art; p.167 Spencer Sutton/Science Source; p.187 (top) Museo dell'Opera Metropolitana del Duomo; p.187 (bottom) Sistine Chapel collection; p.189 Lejeune collection; p.195 Fernando G. Baptista/National Geographic; p.199 (right), p.205 Library of Congress Print and Manuscript Division; p.209 The Thomas Jefferson Papers at the Library of Congress; p.217 Library of Congress [LC-DIG-nclc-01581]; p.219 Library of Congress Rare Book & Special Collections Division; p.221 (right) Library of Congress [LC-DIG-det-4a27975]; p.223 Corbis/VCG via Getty Images; p.227 (right) Sicnag/Flickr; p.233, p.235 (left) Everett Historical/Shutterstock; p.235 (right) Getty Images; p.237 Library of Congress [LC-DIG-ppmsca-40039]; p.237 (bottom) National Museum of Health and Medicine; p.241 World History Archive/Alamy; p.243 Library of Congress [LC-USZ62-99040]; p.249 Harry S. Truman Library and Museum; p.253 (right) Granger; p.255 Library of Congress [LC-USE6-D-005446]; p.257 Army Center for Military History; p.263 Library of Congress Geography and Map Division; p.271 Library of Congress [LC-DIG-ppmsca-47143]; p.275 (left) Library of Congress [LC-DIG-ppmsca-03128]; p.275 (right) Bettmann Archive/Getty Images; p.285 Lyndon Baynes Johnson Library & Museum; p.289 (bottom) Library of Congress [LC-DIG-ppmsca-04295]; all other images from iStock and/or Shutterstock

**Standards**

Copyright © 2010 National Council for the Social Studies
© Copyright 2010. National Governors Association Center for Best Practices and Council of Chief State School Officers. All rights reserved.
© 2014 Mid-continent Research for Education and Learning
© Copyright 2007–2019 Texas Education Agency (TEA). All Rights Reserved.
© 2019 TESOL International Association
© 2018 Board of Regents of the University of Wisconsin System
© 2019 International Society for Technology in Education (ISTE), iste.org. All Rights Reserved.

A division of Teacher Created Materials
5482 Argosy Avenue
Huntington Beach, CA 92649-1039
www.tcmpub.com/shell-education
**ISBN 978-0-7439-6437-1**
© 2020 Shell Educational Publishing, Inc.

The classroom teacher may reproduce copies of materials in this book for classroom use only. The reproduction of any part for an entire school or school system is strictly prohibited. No part of this publication may be transmitted, stored, or recorded in any form without written permission from the publisher.

Website addresses included in this book are public domain and may be subject to changes or alterations of content after publication of this product. Shell Education does not take responsibility for the future accuracy or relevance and appropriateness of website addresses included in this book. Please contact the company if you come across any inappropriate or inaccurate website addresses, and they will be corrected in product reprints.

# Table of Contents

© Shell Education

# Building Bridges with Document-Based Assessments

Greek writer Nikos Kazantzakis wrote, "Teachers are those who use themselves as bridges, over which they invite their students to cross; then having facilitated their crossing, joyfully collapse, encouraging them to create bridges of their own." History is also a bridge—a bridge between the present and the past, with the beginning plans for building bridges to a better future.

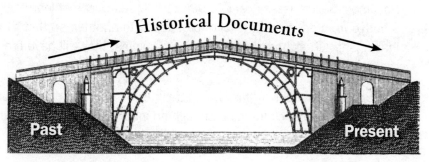

With *Document-Based Assessment Activities*, students engage in historical thinking as they connect with the past through a variety of historical documents, including written documents, paintings, photographs, maps, and more.

As students venture into more-advanced history classes, they will encounter assessment activities that are often completely new to them. These activities require them to analyze historical documents and write articulately about them. Achieving mastery with these types of assessments can be a long process. This can be frustrating for both students and teachers. *Document-Based Assessment Activities* presents these types of assessments with a scaffolded framework aimed at students of all levels. Using this approach, teachers can gradually build students' skills and the confidence they need to gain mastery.

This resource encourages students to explore their families, communities, nation, and the world at large. Students will think like historians to investigate the past. They will also learn life skills as they consider what it is like to be in someone else's shoes, developing empathy for the people whose names and stories they've only read about. Students do more than encounter history. They engage in history and they interpret history, whether it is comparing automobiles one hundred years apart or imagining the life of a Civil War soldier.

# Building Bridges with Document-Based Assessments *(cont.)*

*Document-Based Assessment Activities* will foster a love of learning with a love of history. It will construct a bridge from one year or level of proficiency to another, so that by the time students reach Advanced Placement (AP) exams and other rigorous exams, they will have the confidence and tools to meet the challenge.

Through the activities in this book, students will ask and answer compelling questions, analyze historical documents, approach learning through an inquiry lens, and gradually hone their historical-thinking skills to achieve mastery with document-based assessments.

"These lessons take history out of the dustbin and place it front and center for students where they can wrestle with the demands of a rich and rigorous educational experience.

"By holding history in their hands, students will intellectually connect with the past while at the same time seeing the relevance of whatever historical narrative they happen to be studying."

—James A. Percoco, Historian, Educator, Author

# Thinking Like a Historian

## Why Use Primary Sources?

Primary sources provide students with insight into individual perspectives from the past (Levstik and Barton 2005). To understand history, students must understand the motives and actions of people. Primary sources can provide these explanations. Sam Wineburg believes that history is a tool that changes how people think. As new primary sources are discovered, sometimes the accounts of history change. He states that history should promote discernment, judgment, and caution to avoid repeating the mistakes of the past (2001).

For more than 20 years, Wineburg's research has shown that students do not typically engage in the same processes as historians unless they have explicit instruction on how to do so (1991). Primary sources help students develop research skills that lead to analyzing sources and forming opinions.

Using primary sources offers students the opportunity to act and think as historians. Viewing historic photographs, studying written documents, and reading the comments and opinions of individuals from the past will bring history alive for students. This book, with its many primary sources and other historical documents and support materials, allows both teachers and students to expand their study of history beyond the textbook and classroom.

## Building Historical-Thinking Skills

According to the position statement of the National Council for the Social Studies (NCSS), "There is a profound difference between learning about the actions and conclusions of others and reasoning one's way toward those conclusions. Active learning is not just 'hands-on,' it is 'minds-on'" (2016, 182). Current AP social studies courses are designed to help students develop historical-thinking skills and reasoning processes, which they are assessed on in the AP exams. National and state standards also highlight the importance of building these historical-thinking skills across grades K–12.

In this resource, these skills and processes have been synthesized into five main historical-thinking skills: make connections, use evidence, consider the source, set the scene, and think across time. These five skills naturally overlap and intertwine with one another, allowing students to develop and apply some or all these skills in each lesson. The following descriptions detail each skill and how they are developed in this resource to help students think like historians.

# Thinking Like a Historian *(cont.)*

## Building Historical-Thinking Skills *(cont.)*

### Make Connections

"The challenge of history is to recover the past and introduce it to the present" (Thelen 1989). For many students, history is nothing more than a collection of dates and unconnected events. But historians love to make connections, and the possibilities of making connections throughout history are endless. Paul Sargent, an AP history teacher and blogger, briefly explains the importance of making connections to his incoming students through a video. He uses the Arab Spring, which was a series of pro-democracy uprisings in the Middle East in the early 2010s, as an example. Sargent explains that historians drew comparisons between the Arab Spring and the 1848 revolts in Europe, where people took to the streets asking for more democracy. Making these types of connections helps historians to better understand both historical and current events. By learning how to make connections as historians do, students will gain deeper understandings of history and how it is relevant and connected to their lives today.

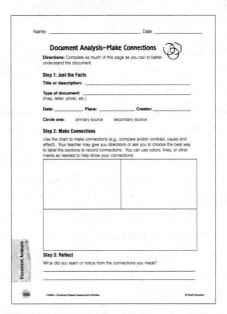

This document-analysis sheet focuses students on making connections among documents and between historical events and their lives.

### In This Resource

The lessons in this resource engage students in discussions and activities that teach and challenge them to make connections to their own lives. They'll also be asked to make connections among the past and present; the documents they analyze; and people, places, and events in history. They will find and explain similarities and differences among these things and examine cause-and-effect relationships.

Students can make connections between people in the past and themselves.

# Thinking Like a Historian *(cont.)*

## Building Historical-Thinking Skills *(cont.)*

### Use Evidence

Behind every document is a story, and historians use primary sources to piece together that story. Mark Krug, a professor of education in history and social studies at the University of Chicago, once said, "The historian and the detective have much in common" (1967). Detectives listen to testimonies, uncover evidence, and explore motives to expose the truth. Detectives rarely solve a case with just one piece of evidence. For example, they do not interview only one person at the crime scene. They want to hear the accounts from *all* possible witnesses because some of these accounts will differ, depending on the witnesses.

Historians treat history in the same manner. The only way to know what happened in the past is to study the *evidence* from that historical time period. "People leave behind both direct and indirect evidence of their ideas; these expressions of their perspectives form the basis for historical interpretations" (Levstik and Barton 2005, 171). Since historians cannot interview the dead, they analyze the evidence that the deceased left behind. Teachers must provide evidence with which students can analyze and create their own interpretations of history.

This document-analysis sheet guides students to find and use evidence as they analyze documents.

### In This Resource

The lessons in this resource challenge students to find and use evidence to discuss and answer document-based questions. Students must find proof in the documents to support the conclusions they draw. In the more complex document-based assessments, students have to use evidence to form and support thesis statements to answer document-based questions.

This example shows how students can embed evidence in their DBQ essays.

# Thinking Like a Historian (cont.)

## Building Historical-Thinking Skills (cont.)

### Consider the Source

Historians approach their work differently from other academics. For example, a mathematician is focused on the accuracy of a proof or equation, while a historian cares very much about who wrote something, when they wrote it, and for what purpose. To understand history, scholars must interpret the evidence they find. To understand the evidence, they must consider the source of the evidence. Written history is an interpretation of an event by the person who wrote it—be it the historian or the creator of the primary source. According to Levstik and Barton, "no historical account is complete" because the person who recorded the account was selective in their use of the facts and details (2005, 7). All recorded history has some form of bias. The recorder of the account has personal motives and a distinct viewpoint. Therefore, it takes more than just one account to verify the truth. Even then, the truth is not certain.

This document-analysis sheet helps students think about the point of view of the author.

In today's world, it is unwise to accept one reporter's account of an event as the truth. If the news reporter was not there when the event happened, they can give only a secondary account of the event by relying on information from sources at the scene. Similarly, people should not rely on textbooks alone for the full story of an event, and no one should rely on just one primary source for the complete facts. Historians search for other primary sources that either corroborate or conflict with the evidence they have.

### In This Resource

Throughout these lessons, students are asked to *consider the source*. During their initial analysis of documents in these lessons, students ask themselves questions, such as: *Who made this? What was their point of view? Why was it made?* and *Is the source reliable?* As students' historical-thinking skills strengthen, they begin corroborating evidence by looking at multiple sources. They will ask: *What do other sources say? Where else can I look?* and *What sources are most reliable?*

These annotations demonstrate the importance of recognizing bias.

# Thinking Like a Historian (cont.)

## Building Historical-Thinking Skills (cont.)

### Set the Scene

When trying to interpret evidence and piece together stories, historians must also examine the setting and historical contexts surrounding the evidence. They consider the circumstances and motivations surrounding the documents being investigated. This is when historians and students begin to form their own interpretations of history. When students analyze primary sources, they begin to really understand what it was like to live during a previous time period. This is where they imagine the setting of the past, which Wineburg calls *contextualization* (2001). Setting the scene and understanding the background of historical documents will help students to put historical events and attitudes into perspective, to think progressively, and to walk in the shoes of their ancestors.

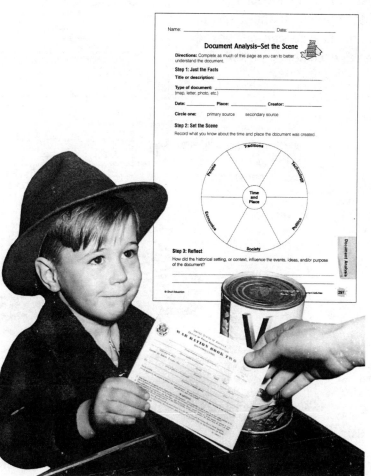

This document-analysis sheet encourages students to focus on what was happening in history at the time of a document's creation.

### In This Resource

During their analysis of the documents in these lessons, students ask themselves questions, such as: *When and where was this document created? What was it like to be alive in the past? What was different and what was the same? How would someone have viewed this event back then? What else was going on during this time and in this place?* and *How would these things have influenced the content of this document?*

Understanding the time perod is critical when analyzing a document such as this.

# Thinking Like a Historian *(cont.)*

## Building Historical-Thinking Skills *(cont.)*

### Think Across Time

Looking beyond one particular time and place is essential to interpreting history, and to do so, historians must use chronological reasoning. They think about what came before, what came after, and how people and events across time fit together, relate, and interact. According to the Public History Initiative at UCLA, "Without a strong sense of chronology—of when events occurred and in what temporal order—it is impossible for students to examine relationships among those events or to explain historical causality. Chronology provides the mental scaffolding for organizing historical thought" (n.d.).

These skills require historians to combine their abilities so they can make connections and set the scene to see and understand stories across time and far-reaching themes. The connections extend further as they begin to recognize patterns in history and draw conclusions based on where in the span of time the documents originated.

### In This Resource

The lessons in this book challenge students to find and use evidence to discuss and answer document-based questions. They will find proof in the documents to support the conclusions they draw. In the higher levels, students will use evidence to form and support thesis statements to answer document-based questions.

This document-analysis sheet challenges students to look for continuity and change across time.

Students can compare images across different time periods to discover far-reaching issues in history.

# Thinking Like a Historian *(cont.)*

## Student Historians in the Digital Age

The importance of building historical- and critical-thinking skills in students is paramount to helping students navigate and interpret the vast array of information available to them at the click of a button. We live in a time when anyone can be an author and write whatever they choose. Finding reputable sources of information has become a daunting task. It can be difficult to discern fact from fiction or reality from sarcasm and understand multiple points of view. The issue is no longer about finding information. The issue now is what we do with the information we find (Wineburg 2018). No matter the paths students take with their continued education and careers, the lessons in this resource will equip them with the skills necessary to become responsible, well-informed members of society who can interpret and analyze new information with discerning eyes.

## Using Historical-Thinking Skills in Standardized Tests

As students apply their historical-thinking skills to document-based assessments, they practice answering a variety of question types found on many standardized tests and AP exams. Described here are the most-common question types used throughout this resource.

### Selected-Response Questions

A selected-response question provides options for students from which they must "select" the correct response. These could be multiple-choice, matching, or true/false questions. These types of questions can be harder to write well but are easier to evaluate.

### Constructed-Response Questions

A constructed-response question does not give answer options to students. There is often more than one way to answer these types of questions and students must *construct* the answers themselves. The answers need to be hand scored and often allow for a range of acceptable responses. They can be simple, short-response questions, requiring students to fill in the blank (if no word bank is given), make lists, or answer in a few concise sentences. They can also be more complex extended-response questions, requiring students to write paragraphs or essays. Items such as performance tasks, presentations, and portfolios can also be considered constructed-response assessments.

AP exams refer to these types of questions as *free-response* questions. There are three types of constructed-response questions on AP exams: short-answer question (SAQ), document-based question (DBQ), and long-essay question (LEQ). The SAQs ask students to look at historical developments and processes for different time periods with the help of primary and secondary sources. For the DBQs and LEQs, students are also asked to develop arguments based on evidence. Some of that evidence must come from the historical documents included within a DBQ.

### In This Resource

Throughout these lessons, students will answer multiple-choice questions. They will also answer different types of constructed-response questions. They begin with answering short-response questions in a few sentences. Then, they build up their skills to answer extended-response questions in the form of DBQ essays. (See pages 19–20 for more information about DBQs.) The historical-thinking skills students develop through the activities in this resource can be applied to answer all types of selected- or constructed-response questions.

# How to Use This Resource

## Leveled Document-Based Assessment Sections

This resource is organized into four levels. This scaffolded approach to teaching historical thinking and analysis skills can be applied across grades K–12. Teachers can begin at any level and progress at a pace that best meets the needs of their students and supports their curriculum. By the end of this book, students will be more prepared for advanced social studies classes and standardized state tests so their time can be spent going deeper into the content rather than learning the process of analyzing documents.

### Preliminary Document-Based Assessments

- 3 units with 3 lessons per unit
- then and now themes
- student analysis includes simple images
- 2 questions per student page
- simple document analysis graphic organizers

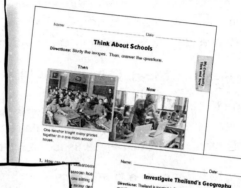

### Beginning Document-Based Assessments

- 4 units with 4 lessons per unit
- student analysis includes written documents and images
- 2–3 questions per student page
- DBQ discussions for each unit
- simple document analysis graphic organizers

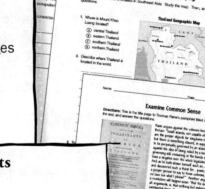

### Intermediate Document-Based Assessments

- 5 units with 2–4 lessons per unit
- student analysis includes written documents and images
- 2–3 questions per student page
- DBQ for each unit; 2–4 documents
- complex document analysis and essay graphic organizers

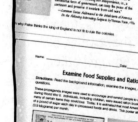

### Advanced Document-Based Assessments

- 7 units, 5–7 lessons per unit
- student analysis includes complex written documents and images
- 2–3 questions per student page
- DBQ for each unit; 5–7 documents
- complex document analysis and essay graphic organizers

    © Shell Education

# How to Use This Resource *(cont.)*

## Topic-Based Units

Units centered around key social studies topics in each section can be used during or at the end of classroom units of study related to the topics. This will enhance social studies curriculums and encourage students to synthesize their knowledge and understanding of the topics to answer the questions. The units can also be used as additional practice with document-based assessments unrelated to what is actively being covered in class. In this case, additional background information may be needed for students.

Units cover the following topics:

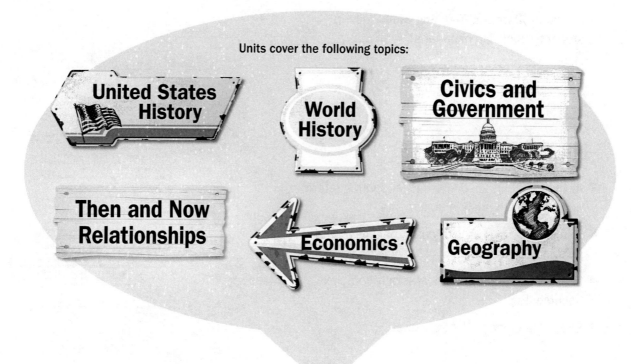

**United States History**

**World History**

**Civics and Government**

**Then and Now Relationships**

**Economics**

**Geography**

Preliminary Units

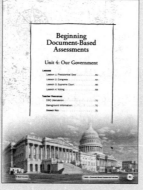

Beginning Units

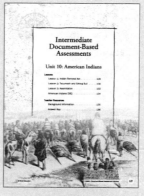

Intermediate Units

Advanced Units

# How to Use This Resource *(cont.)*

## Lessons

Each lesson has one easy-to-follow teacher page and one student activity page. Students will also use various graphic organizers to help them analyze documents and plan their DBQ essays.

### Teacher Lesson Guides

All the lesson guides in this book are broken down into clear, concise, and easy-to-use steps. This simple and consistent format will facilitate smooth transitions for teachers and students as they progress from one document-based assessment level to the next.

- Focus on **Historical-Thinking Skills** to help students think like historians.

- **Activate** background knowledge, spark interest, and prepare to analyze documents.

- **Analyze** documents with quick, engaging activities and discuss thought-provoking guiding questions.

- Learn **How To** interpret increasingly complex documents.

- **Extend** learning to the next level.

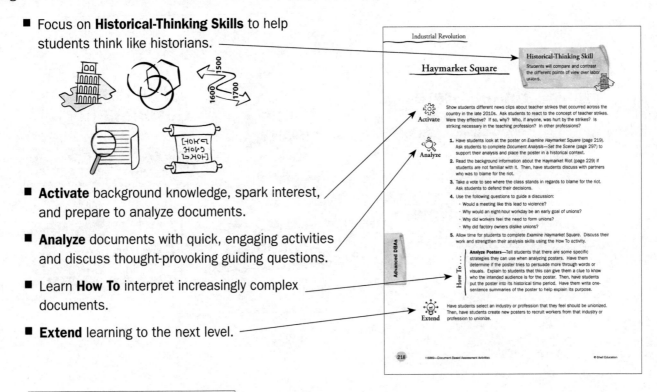

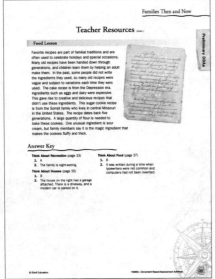

### Teacher Resource Pages

Additional background information and answer keys for the lessons are at the end of each unit. The background information provides teachers with information about the documents and relevant historical context at a quick glance. Teachers can share this information with their students as needed.

# How to Use This Resource (cont.)

## Lessons (cont.)

### Student Activity Pages

- A caption or brief description of each document and its source encourages students to consider the source of every historical document.

- A variety of document types engages students with diverse interests, backgrounds, and abilities.

- Constructed-response questions about each primary source assess students' historical-thinking and document-analysis skills.

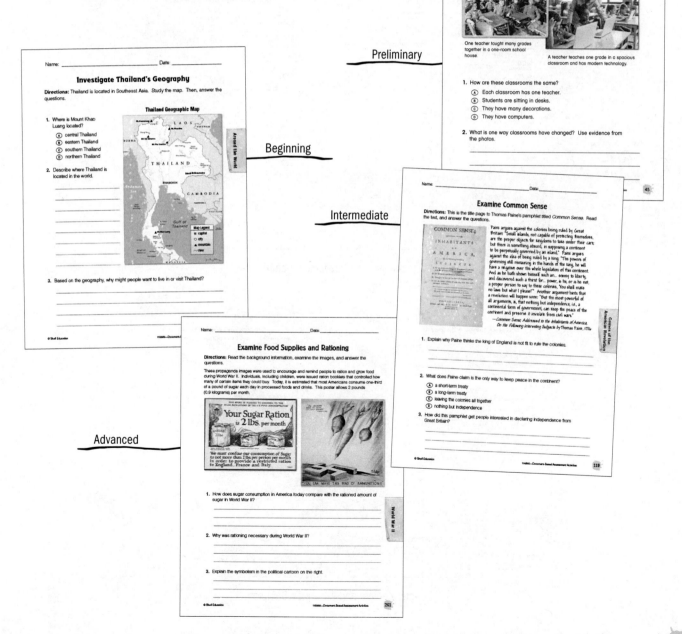

Preliminary

Beginning

Intermediate

Advanced

# How to Use This Resource (cont.)

## Lessons (cont.)

### Document-Analysis Sheets

- Students analyze each document with guiding questions and prompts that help them interpret the documents.

- Students apply historical-thinking skills in an organized, easy-to-follow way.

- Students use these pages repeatedly to build proficiency.

- These reproducible pages are located on pages 292–295.

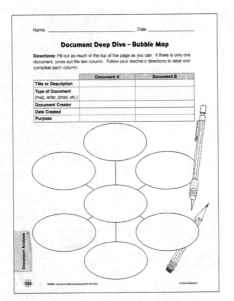 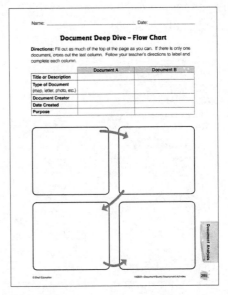

Preliminary and Beginning Samples

 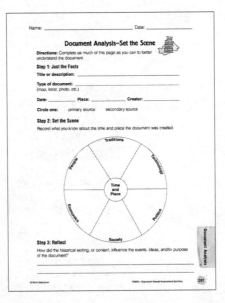

Intermediate and Advanced Samples

# How to Use This Resource (cont.)

## Lessons (cont.)

### Document-Based Questions

The DBQ represents a "real world" or authentic assessment. There are two parts to a DBQ. In the first part, students read and analyze passages, charts, graphs, photographs, and other visuals. They are asked to respond to short, scaffolded questions based on the individual documents. Then, in the DBQ task, students must draw on the material from the documents and their own knowledge to prepare answers that demonstrate their skills in comprehension, evaluation, and synthesis. Students may be asked to make comparisons and analogies, apply knowledge to the given data, take positions on issues or problems, support their conclusions, explore multiple perspectives on an event or issue, and/or apply historical analyses.

The concept of DBQs is introduced to students in the Beginning level section of this resource. In that section, DBQs are presented as discussion questions that students unpack and answer together with their teacher. As students progress to the Intermediate and Advanced levels, they answer DBQs in cohesive, well-supported essays.

### Beginner DBQs

By introducing DBQs in the form of meaningful discussions in small- or whole-group settings, students can become familiar with these types of questions in a supportive, low-risk environment. This will build students' confidence to tackle the more complex essay tasks in the subsequent sections.

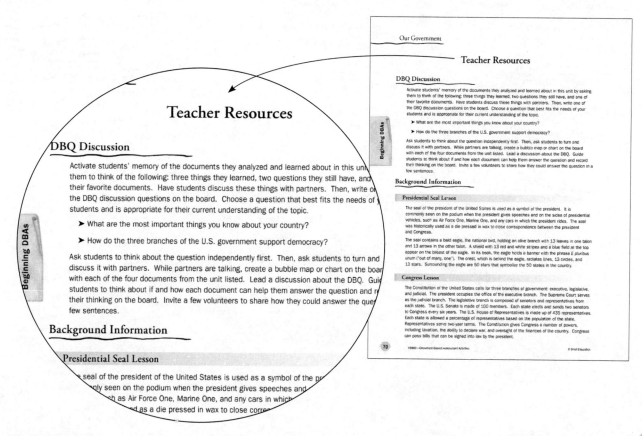

# How to Use This Resource *(cont.)*

## Lessons *(cont.)*

### Document-Based Questions *(cont.)*

#### Intermediate and Advanced DBQs

As students develop their essay-writing skills, they must reference an increasing number of documents. They will begin with two documents and build up to seven. Students will be most successful with these essays when given at the end of a unit of study on the related topic.

- Two essay tasks allow students to choose which DBQ to answer.

- Specific guidelines are given for each question to further aid student responses.

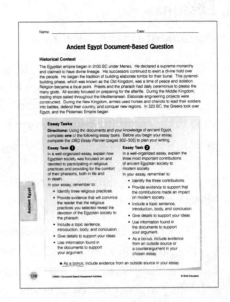

#### DBQ Essay Planner

Graphic organizers are provided on pages 302–304 to help students plan, organize, and write their essays.

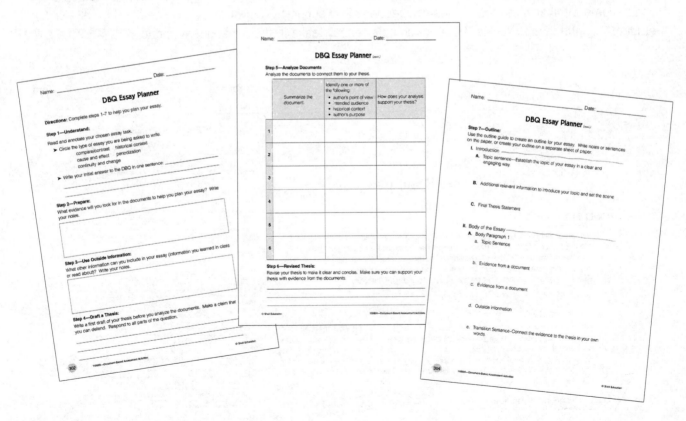

# How to Use This Resource *(cont.)*

## Digital Resources

Lesson resources can be shared through cloud-sharing services, displayed on interactive whiteboards, or printed and distributed to students. Projecting documents while students are analyzing them allows for whole-class discussions. At times, projecting full-color versions may be more beneficial than copying them on black-and-white copiers. When making copies, it is recommended to push the photo button on the copier for better image quality. (See page 311 for more details about accessing and using the digital resources.)

### How the Digital Resources Are Organized

When first accessing the digital resources, you will find the following folders:

- Preliminary DBAs
- Beginning DBAs
- Intermediate DBAs
- Advanced DBAs
- Teacher Resources

The content in each section folder includes the following components:

- student reproducibles for each lesson
- primary source images that can be projected

The Teacher Resources folder includes:

- reproducible for *Ask Questions Like a Historian Lesson* (pages 28–29)
- additional lesson resources, including graphic organizers, rubrics, and a list of source information for each historical document

# Standards Correlations

Shell Education is committed to producing educational materials that are research and standards based. To support this effort, this resource is correlated to the academic standards of all 50 states, the District of Columbia, the Department of Defense Dependent Schools, and the Canadian provinces. A correlation is also provided for key professional educational organizations.

## How to Find Standards Correlations

To print a customized correlation report for your state, visit our website at **www.tcmpub.com /administrators/correlations** and follow the online directions. If you require assistance in locating or printing correlation reports, please contact the Customer Service Department at 1-800-858-7339.

## Standards Overview

The Every Student Succeeds Act (ESSA) mandates that all states adopt challenging academic standards that help students meet the goal of college and career readiness. While many states already adopted academic standards prior to ESSA, the act continues to hold states accountable for detailed and comprehensive standards. Standards are designed to focus instruction and guide adoption of curricula. They define the knowledge, skills, and content students should acquire at each grade level. Standards are also used to develop standardized tests to evaluate students' academic progress. State standards are used in the development of our resources, so educators can be assured they meet state academic requirements.

### NCSS Themes and C3 Framework

The lessons in this book are aligned to the NCSS themes and the C3 Framework. The information listed on pages 24–27 describe the processes and thinking presented throughout the lessons.

### Content Standards

Each year, McREL International analyzes state standards and revises its standards compendium to produce a compilation of national standards. The social studies content presented throughout the lessons support a wide range of content standards ranging from grades K–12. The standards listed on page 23 describe the social studies content presented throughout the units.

### ISTE Standards

The International Society for Technology in Education (ISTE) standards provide guidelines for the knowledge and skills needed to succeed in the twenty-first century. The lessons in this book support the ISTE standards for students.

# Standards Correlations (cont.)

## Social Studies Standards

The lessons in this book focus on key social studies standards for grades K–12. This chart shows which lesson(s) align with each learning area.

| Standard | Unit(s) |
|---|---|
| Understands family life now and in the past. | Families Then and Now (pgs. 31–39) |
| Understands the history of a local community and how communities in North America varied long ago. | Communities Then and Now (pgs. 41–49), People in the Past (pgs. 85–96) |
| Understands how democratic values came to be, and how they have been exemplified by people, events, and symbols. | Our Country Then and Now (pgs. 51–59), Money (pgs. 97–108), Our Government (pgs. 61–71) |
| Understands selected attributes and historical developments of societies in Africa, the Americas, Asia, and Europe. | Around the World (pgs. 73–84), World Cultures (pgs. 151–163) |
| Understands the development and major characteristics of civilization in ancient Egypt. | Ancient Egypt (pgs. 165–179) |
| Understands how European society experienced political, economic, and cultural transformations between 1450 and 1750. | The Renaissance (pgs. 181–196) |
| Understands the politics, economy, and society of colonial America and the eventual causes of the American Revolution. | Life in the Colonies (pgs. 109–116), Causes of the American Revolution (pgs. 117–126) |
| Understands the events, people, and ideas that influenced the ideas established by the Constitution. | Constitution and New Government (pgs. 197–214) |
| Understands the United States territorial expansion affected relations with external powers and Native Americans. | American Indians (pgs. 127–136) |
| Understands the course and character of the United States Civil War. | Civil War (pgs. 137–149) |
| Understands how the Industrial Revolution changed American lives and led to regional tensions. | Industrial Revolution (pgs. 215–232) |
| Understands the causes, course, and global consequences of World War I. | World War I (pgs. 233–250) |
| Understands the causes and course of World War II and the character of the war at home and abroad. | World War II (pgs. 251–270) |
| Understands the struggle for racial and gender equality and for the extension of civil liberties. | Civil Rights Movements (pgs. 271–290) |

# Standards Correlations *(cont.)*

## Document-Based Assessments

The lessons and activities in this book encourage students to practice multiple historical-thinking skills. However, each lesson focuses on one historical-thinking skill, allowing teachers to be purposeful in their instruction. These charts show the NCSS theme and historical-thinking skill focus of each lesson.

### Preliminary Document-Based Assessments

| Unit | NCSS Theme | Lesson | Historical-Thinking Skill Focus |
|---|---|---|---|
| Families Then and Now (pages 31–39) | Time, Continuity, and Change | Recreation | Make Connections |
| | | Houses | Use Evidence |
| | | Food | Set the Scene |
| Communities Then and Now (pages 41–49) | Time, Continuity, and Change | Transportation | Make Connections |
| | | Schools | Use Evidence |
| | | Helpers | Make Connections |
| Our Country Then and Now (pages 51–59) | Time, Continuity, and Change | Places | Make Connections |
| | | People | Use Evidence |
| | | Symbols | Think Across Time |

### Beginning Document-Based Assessments

| Unit | NCSS Theme | Lesson | Historical-Thinking Skill Focus |
|---|---|---|---|
| Our Government (pages 61–71) | Power, Authority, and Governance | Presidential Seal | Set the Scene |
| | | Congress | Make Connections |
| | | Supreme Court | Think Across Time |
| | | Voting | Consider the Source |
| Around the World (pages 73–84) | People, Places, and Environments | African Safaris | Use Evidence |
| | | Thailand's Geography | Set the Scene |
| | | London's Architecture | Make Connections |
| | | Australian Barbecue | Use Evidence |
| People in the Past (pages 85–96) | Time, Continuity, and Change | Log Cabins | Set the Scene |
| | | Fashion Long Ago | Consider the Source |
| | | Indigenous People | Use Evidence |
| | | Getting Around Town | Think Across Time |
| Money (pages 97–108) | Production, Distribution, and Consumption | Currency—Quarters | Consider the Source |
| | | Paper Money | Use Evidence |
| | | Prices | Make Connections |
| | | Currency Exchange | Use Evidence |

© Shell Education

# Standards Correlations (cont.)

## Document-Based Assessments (cont.)

### Intermediate Document-Based Assessments

| Unit | NCSS Theme | Lesson | Historical-Thinking Skill Focus |
|---|---|---|---|
| Life in the Colonies (pages 109–116) | People, Places, and Environments | Colonial Seals | Make Connections |
| | | Farms and Plantations | Use Evidence |
| Causes of the American Revolution (pages 117–126) | Power, Authority, and Governance | Common Sense | Set the Scene |
| | | The Boston Massacre | Consider the Source |
| | | Declaration of Independence | Think Across Time |
| American Indians (pages 127–136) | Culture | Indian Removal Act | Think Across Time |
| | | Tecumseh and Sitting Bull | Set the Scene |
| | | Assimilation | Use Evidence |
| Civil War (pages 137–149) | Power, Authority, and Governance | Missouri Compromise | Set the Scene |
| | | Fugitive Slave Act | Make Connections |
| | | Emancipation Proclamation | Make Connections |
| | | Civil War Amendments | Think Across Time |
| World Cultures (pages 151–163) | Culture | Roman Routes and Aqueducts | Set the Scene |
| | | Chinese Armor | Use Evidence |
| | | The Importance of Zero | Set the Scene |
| | | Mesoamerican Civilizations | Make Connections |

# Standards Correlations (cont.)

## Document-Based Assessments (cont.)

### Advanced Document-Based Assessments

| Unit | NCSS Theme | Lesson | Historical-Thinking Skill Focus |
|---|---|---|---|
| Ancient Egypt (pages 165–179) | Culture | The Great Pyramid of Giza | Set the Scene |
| | | Herodotus | Consider the Source |
| | | Hieroglyphic Writing | Make Connections |
| | | Obelisks | Make Connections |
| | | Egyptian Gods | Use Evidence |
| The Renaissance (pages 181–196) | Culture | Da Vinci's Notes | Make Connections |
| | | Renaissance Churches | Set the Scene |
| | | Medieval and Renaissance Art | Make Connections |
| | | Brunelleschi's Dome | Think Across Time |
| | | Commerce in Venice | Set the Scene |
| Constitution and New Government (pages 197–214) | Power, Authority, and Governance | The Articles of Confederation | Set the Scene |
| | | Congressional Representation | Make Connections |
| | | Article II of the Constitution | Consider the Source |
| | | The Three-Fifths Compromise | Use Evidence |
| | | Federalists vs. Anti-Federalists | Make Connections |
| | | Approving the Constitution | Use Evidence |
| Industrial Revolution (pages 215–232) | Science, Technology, and Society | Child Labor | Think Across Time |
| | | Haymarket Square | Set the Scene |
| | | Changes in Communications | Make Connections |
| | | Thomas Edison | Use Evidence |
| | | Time Line of Inventions | Think Across Time |
| | | Transportation | Make Connections |

# Standards Correlations *(cont.)*

## Document-Based Assessments *(cont.)*

### Advanced Document-Based Assessments *(cont.)*

| Unit | NCSS Theme | Lesson | Historical-Thinking Skill Focus |
|---|---|---|---|
| World War I (pages 233–250) | Global Connections | Trench Warfare | Use Evidence |
| | | Poisonous Gas | Consider the Source |
| | | The *Lusitania* | Set the Scene |
| | | Communications | Make Connections |
| | | Role of Airplanes | Set the Scene |
| | | Writing Home | Use Evidence |
| World War II (pages 251–270) | Global Connections | Women at Work | Use Evidence |
| | | Contributions of Minorities | Set the Scene |
| | | 442nd Regiment | Set the Scene |
| | | Reusing and Recycling | Make Connections |
| | | Food Supplies and Rationing | Use Evidence |
| | | D-Day | Make Connections |
| | | War Bonds | Consider the Source |
| Civil Rights Movement (pages 271–290) | Civic Ideals and Practices Power, Authority, and Governance | Police Report | Think Across Time |
| | | Protests | Make Connections |
| | | Literacy Tests | Set the Scene |
| | | Letter to the President | Consider the Source |
| | | Freedom Riders | Make Connections |
| | | Dr. King | Use Evidence |
| | | Civil Rights Act of 1964 | Make Connections |

# Ask Questions Like a Historian Lesson

To warm up your students to the idea of using historical-thinking skills to analyze documents, complete this activity shortly after the school year begins.

1. As a homework assignment, have students, with the help of a family member or adult, look through souvenirs of their lives (e.g., photographs, letters, certificates, diaries, newspaper clippings, birth certificates, library cards, report cards). Have each student select a primary source document to share with the class.

2. Once students have brought their selected documents to class, begin the analysis with a simple gallery walk. Ask students to place their documents on their desks. Then, have students walk around the room to observe all the documents their classmates brought in. After a few minutes, have students return to their seats and share any observations they made.

3. Distribute copies of *Using Historical-Thinking Skills* (page 29), and read through the questions, modeling how you might answer them. You can have students use this page in one of two ways. They can write answers to the questions on separate sheets of paper, or they can work with partners to discuss their responses. Be sure to point out to students that depending on the documents they have, they may or may not be able to answer every question.

   - If you're working with elementary students, they may need more guidance in each of the thinking skills. Instead of completing this activity in one day, you can work with each of the five historical-thinking skills one at a time. In the digital resources, you'll find five separate pages with the historical-thinking questions leveled for younger students. Students can work in pairs or as a whole group to answer the guiding questions for their documents. (See page 311 for more information.)

4. After students have written or discussed the questions and completed their reflections, have them share their reflections with the class or in small groups.

5. As an extension to this activity, have groups of students make posters for the historical-thinking skills. They can add to these posters throughout the year. As students complete the lessons in this resource, they can refer back to this activity and make connections to the historical-thinking skills they will continue to develop.

Once you have prepared your students with an introduction to these historical-thinking skills, you will be well on your way to introducing them to the work of historians as they make valid inquiries into the past.

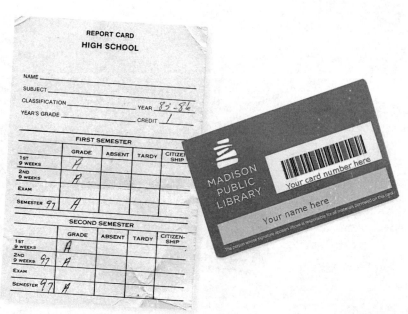

Name: _____ Date: _____

# Using Historical-Thinking Skills

**Directions:** It's time to practice using historical-thinking skills! Use the questions to analyze a document from your life. You can discuss the questions with a partner or write the answers on separate sheets of paper.

## Make Connections

- ► How is this document connected to you and your family?
- ► Do you have or know of similar documents from the past or today? If so, how do they compare?
- ► What comparisons can you make about your document and those of your classmates?

## Use Evidence

- ► What does this document reveal about you or your life?
- ► What does this document reveal about the time and place it was created?
- ► What evidence is there to come to these conclusions?
- ► What other documents might corroborate this evidence?

## Consider the Source

- ► Who created this document?
- ► Why was this document created?
- ► Who was the intended audience for this document?
- ► How can you determine if the author or creator had a particular point of view?

## Set the Scene

- ► When and where was this document created?
- ► Describe yourself at the time this document was created.
- ► What other important things were going on at the time and place this document was created?

## Think Across Time

- ► Create a time line of your life with at least five important events. Then, add this document to the time line. How does this document fit into the story of your life?
- ► How is this document related to your life today?
- ► What, if any, lasting effects has the document had on you or others?

## Reflection

Imagine someone in the very distant future discovers your document. What would they learn about you and the time and place the document is from?

# Discussing Historical Documents

When studying historical documents, it is important for students to discuss, debate, and deliberate higher-order questions. Discussions provide a vehicle to address the many English language arts standards that exist within the realm of social studies. These discussion methods can be adapted to fit students' needs and your teaching style and preference.

## Turn and Talk

This method takes little to no planning, is relatively low risk for students, and can be done at any level. Have each student "turn and talk" to a person next to them about the provided guiding questions or observations they have about documents.

## Concentric Circles

This discussion method allows student to discuss many questions with different people. Have students form two circles with equal numbers of students. Have one circle stand inside the other, facing each other. Have each student partner with the person across from them. Ask a question for partners to discuss. After a set amount of time, ask one of the circles to move one person to the right. Ask another question for new partners to discuss. Continue having the same circle rotate to new partners as many times as you choose.

## Poster Walk Discussion

This method takes more planning, but it can elicit interesting discussions. Set out posters around the room, each with a historical document and a question. Have a group of students start at each of the posters. Ask students to read the questions, discuss their thoughts, and write their responses on the posters. Then, have groups rotate to the next poster until they have had a chance to visit each one, add their thoughts, and respond to other groups' comments.

## Socratic Seminar Style Discussion

This type of discussion is student-driven and emphasizes the importance of referring to documents to guide discussions. Have one student begin by responding to an open-ended question or asking their own question. The discussion continues "popcorn" style or in a circle. Ask students to share responses to others' questions, add to others' thinking, or articulate new thoughts and questions. Remind students to constantly refer back to the document to guide their comments and questions.

## Online Discussion Resources

Online discussion tools allow students, especially those reluctant to share verbally, to contribute written comments or questions to a class discussion. Here is a list of suggested tools for online discussions:

- Google Classroom—Teachers or students can pose questions and others can comment.
- Padlet.com—Students can comment with digital sticky notes (anonymously if you choose).
- NowComment.com—Teachers or students can upload a document and have others comment digitally.

# Preliminary Document-Based Assessments

## Unit 1: Families Then and Now

**Lessons**

**Teacher Resources**

# Recreation

**Historical-Thinking Skill**

Students will compare and contrast photographs of family recreation from different time periods.

**Activate**

Tell students that recreation is what people do for fun. Ask students what they like to do for recreation.

**Analyze**

1. Have students look at the photographs on *Think About Recreation* (page 33). Ask them to complete the *Document Deep Dive—Venn Diagram* (page 292) graphic organizer to support their analysis. Have students label their Venn diagrams with the headings *Then* and *Now*. Model how to line up similar observations from each photograph across from each other in the Venn diagram.

2. Have students code their Venn diagram observations according to the following categories: *P* for people, *O* for objects, and *A* for actions.

3. Use the following questions to guide a discussion:
   - What is the same about what the families are doing? What is different?
   - How are the families dressed for their outings?
   - What evidence is there that the *Then* photograph is older?
   - Do these photos show what all families in the past and today do for recreation? Why or why not?

4. Allow time for students to complete *Think About Recreation*. Discuss their work and strengthen their analysis skills using the How To activity.

**How To . . .**

**Analyze Images Closely**—Tell students that a magnifying glass is a tool that can be useful for analyzing details in images. Provide students with magnifying glasses, and have them look at the photographs on *Think About Recreation*. Encourage students to work in a sequence manner to review the photographs. For example, students can work from right to left and from top to bottom. Discuss any details that can be seen with a magnifying glass that could not be seen as easily without it.

**Extend**

Have students generate a list of recreational activities. Ask students to think about recreational activities they like to do. Have students choose recreational activities they have not done but would like to try. Ask students to draw pictures of themselves doing those activities.

Name: _____ Date: _____

# Think About Recreation

**Directions:** Study the images.  Then, answer the questions.

### Then

Long ago, families dressed up when they went out.

### Now

Today, families often dress in casual clothes when they go out.

**1.** What is the same in both photos?

   Ⓐ Families are enjoying being outside.

   Ⓑ Photos were taken in a forest.

   Ⓒ Families have pets with them.

**2.** What is the family in the *Now* photo doing?

_____

_____

_____

**Preliminary DBAs**

# Houses

**Historical-Thinking Skill**

Students will find evidence in photos of houses that show they are from different time periods.

**Activate**

Ask students to name buildings in which people can live (e.g., house, condominium, apartment). Then, have students think specifically about houses and name features those buildings typically have (e.g., doors, windows, roof, landscaping). List those features on the board.

**Analyze**

1. Have students look at the photographs on *Think About Houses* (page 35). Ask them to complete the top section of *Document Deep Dive—Bubble Map* (page 294) to support their analysis.

2. Ask students to annotate the pictures by circling and/or writing notes about features of houses. Ask students to look for evidence that one of the houses is older. Have students write the word *evidence* in the center circle of their bubble maps. In the outer circles, have students write the evidence they found that the house on the left is old and the house on the right is more modern.

3. Use the following questions to guide a discussion:

   · Which of the houses looks older?

   · What evidence in the pictures makes you think that one house is older and one house is newer?

   · Do these pictures represent all homes in the past and today? Why or why not?

4. Allow time for students to complete *Think About Houses*. Discuss their work and strengthen their analysis skills using the How To activity.

**How To . . .**

**Analyze Images Closely**—Tell students that one way to analyze photographs is to divide them into halves or quarters. This helps focus attention on smaller aspects of the photograph. Demonstrate for students how to use two index cards to cover ¾ of one of the photographs so that only one quarter is showing. Move the index cards around to reveal other quarters of the photograph. Repeat with the second photograph. You can also project the images and look at the sections together as a class.

**Extend**

Ask students if they think all older houses were made of wood and if all modern houses are made of stone. Challenge them to find examples of modern wood houses and older stone houses. Discuss what other evidence reveals what time period they are from.

Name: _____ Date: _____

# Think About Houses

**Directions:** Study the images. Then, answer the questions.

### Then

This house has many features.
It was built of wood.

### Now

This house was built in the suburbs.

1. The houses from *Then* and *Now* are different in this way:

   (A) The newer house is made of wood.

   (B) The older house has a large porch.

   (C) Both houses have driveways.

2. What evidence is there to support that the house on the right is modern?

   _____

   _____

   _____

# Food

## Historical-Thinking Skill

Students will analyze how recipes are influenced by the time periods in which they were written.

**Activate**

Ask students to tell you about their favorite foods. Do they know the ingredients in these foods? Do they know how they are made? Have they ever helped make the foods?

**Analyze**

1. Have students look at the recipes on *Think About Food* (page 37). Ask them to complete *Document Deep Dive—T-Chart* (page 293) to support their analysis. Have students label their T-charts with the headings *Differences* and *Reasons*.

2. Lead a discussion about the differences between the two recipes. Have students list these differences on their charts. Then, discuss some of the reasons for these differences. For example, the *Then* recipe was handwritten because computers or typewriters had not yet been invented or were not common. Guide students to think of how the time period these recipes were written in influenced how they were written and what they included. (If appropriate, explain some of the context of the Great Depression, from which the cake recipe came.)

3. Use the following questions to guide a discussion:
   · How would someone know when the cake recipe was done?
   · Are there any unusual ingredients in the recipes?
   · Which recipe would be easier to follow?

4. Allow time for students to complete *Think About Food*. Discuss their work and strengthen their analysis skills using the How To activity.

**How To . . .**

**Close Read Documents**—Tell students that when analyzing two texts, they can look for similar components to compare. Have students name the components of the recipes: title, ingredients, and steps. Ask them to name any other features of the text that stand out (e.g., the cake recipe is handwritten and the cookie recipe is typed). Have students highlight the features of the recipes in the same colors to help make comparisons.

**Extend**

Have students create flow maps that show the steps to follow in both recipes. Show students how to list one step in a box and then add an arrow that points to the next step. This will repeat until all the steps are followed. Compare the number of steps. Alternatively, have students bring in family recipes to share and create flow maps for.

# Think About Food

**Directions:** Study the images.  Then, answer the questions.

### Then

Depression Cake

| | |
|---|---|
| 2 c. raisins
4 c. cold water | stew together until only 2 cups liquid is left, let cool |
| 2 c. sugar
4 T. shortening | cream together, add raisins |
| 2 t. soda
pinch salt
4 c. flour
4 t. cinnamon
2 t. nutmeg | sift together, add to other ingredients and bake in loaf |

\* makes 2 loaves

Recipes were not always written down. When they were, they often were not very specific.

### Now

**Sorrell Family Sugar Cookies**

| | |
|---|---|
| 2 cups of sugar | 1 tsp. baking soda |
| 1 cup of shortening | 1 tsp. baking powder |
| 1 cup of sour cream | 1/4 tsp. salt |
| 3 eggs | 5 cups flour |
| 1 tsp. vanilla | |

Stir together the first five ingredients.  Then, mix with the remaining ingredients.  Chill for 30 minutes.  Roll out dough and cut shapes.  Bake at 350° for 10 min.

Newer recipes are more specific.

**1.** How are the recipes different?

   Ⓐ  The *Then* recipe has sugar.  The *Now* recipe does not.

   Ⓑ  The *Now* recipe uses eggs.  The *Then* recipe does not.

   Ⓒ  The *Then* recipe is baked.  The *Now* recipe is not.

**2.** Why was the *Then* recipe handwritten?

_____

_____

_____

# Teacher Resources

## Background Information

### Recreation Lesson

Many families take time for recreation and do things for fun depending on where they live. Some families spend time hiking, visiting parks, picnicking, biking, or just playing. Long ago, families dressed up when they went out. The *Then* image shows a family at the park. The father is getting ready to take a photograph of his wife and daughter. To take the picture, he must look down into the box-like camera from up above. This picture was taken in the early 1900s. Women wore long dresses, and men wore bowler hats and suits. The *Now* image shows families at a popular viewpoint. The family in the foreground is taking a "selfie" with a camera phone.

### Houses Lesson

The architecture of houses has changed over the years. The picture of the old house shows the folk Victorian style of architecture, which was popular in the late 1800s and early 1900s. Houses in this style were ornate with elaborate trim and decorative woodwork. They often had bay windows and porches. The roofs were often steep and shingled. There was usually a single-car garage detached and located behind the house. Houses near one another often had different builders. The picture of the new house shows a modern family dwelling built with new materials. Houses built in the 1960s to the present are often categorized as neo-eclectic houses. This means that their design may be influenced by a combination of historic styles using modern materials. The house in the picture is made of sandstone. When this picture was taken, this house was just one year old. It is in a suburb near Austin, Texas. Houses built in the suburbs are often built in tracts, or designated areas of land, by the same builder. The houses tend to have a similar look to them.

# Teacher Resources *(cont.)*

## Food Lesson

Favorite recipes are part of familial traditions and are often used to celebrate holidays and special occasions. Many old recipes have been handed down through generations, and children learn them by helping an adult make them. In the past, some people did not write the ingredients they used, so many old recipes were vague and subject to variations each time they were used. The cake recipe is from the Depression era. Ingredients such as eggs and dairy were expensive. This gave rise to creative and delicious recipes that didn't use these ingredients. This sugar cookie recipe is from the Sorrell family who lives in central Missouri in the United States. The recipe dates back five generations. A large quantity of flour is needed to bake these cookies. One unusual ingredient is sour cream, but family members say it is the magic ingredient that makes the cookies fluffy and thick.

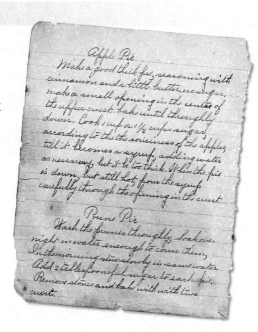

## Answer Key

**Think About Recreation** (page 33)
1. A
2. The family is sight-seeing.

**Think About Houses** (page 35)
1. B
2. The house on the right has a garage attached. There is a driveway, and a modern car is parked on it.

**Think About Food** (page 37)
1. B
2. It was written during a time when typewriters were not common and computers had not been invented.

© Shell Education

# Preliminary Document-Based Assessments

## Unit 2: Communities Then and Now

**Lessons**

# Transportation

**Historical-Thinking Skill**
Students will compare and contrast photographs of automobiles from different time periods.

**Activate**

Ask students to name as many modes of transportation as they can. Make a list on a sheet of chart paper. Ask students who has traveled using each mode of transportation by showing hands.

**Analyze**

1. Have students look at the photographs on *Think About Transportation* (page 43). Ask them to complete the top section of *Document Deep Dive— Venn Diagram* (page 292) to support their analysis.

2. Ask students to list the names of the main features of an automobile, such as: wheels, body, and windows. Have students briefly describe the parts for each automobile. Then, ask them to include the features in their Venn diagrams.

3. Use the following questions to guide a discussion:

   · What does the older car have or not have that makes it look older?

   · What does the newer car have that the older car does not? Why?

   · What has not changed in the two cars? What has changed?

   · Do these photos represent all cars from the past and today? Why or why not?

4. Allow time for students to complete *Think About Transportation*. Discuss their work and strengthen their analysis skills using the How To activity.

**How To . . .**

**Annotate Images**—Tell students that when they compare images of two similar items, it is often useful to focus on parts of the items and annotate them. For example, have students focus on the wheels of the automobile by circling the wheels in each image. Discuss the similarities and differences of the wheels. Continue comparing and contrasting other parts of the automobile. Encourage students to write question marks where they have questions.

**Extend**

Tell students to ask their parents and grandparents about cars they remember from their youth. If they can find pictures of these cars, have students bring them to school. Analyze and discuss any pictures students find.

Preliminary DBAs

Name: _____ Date: _____

# Think About Transportation

**Directions:** Study the images. Then, answer the questions.

**Then**

This is a Ford Model T. It was one of the first cars that people could afford. The first cars broke down often and had to be pushed to start.

**Now**

Today, cars are reliable. People can travel far. They can move at fast speeds with few problems.

**1.** What is one way cars have changed?

(A) They need gasoline.

(B) They have steering wheels.

(C) They can go faster.

(D) They have engines.

**2.** Why are the people pushing the *Then* car?

_____

_____

Preliminary DBAs

# Schools

## Historical-Thinking Skill

Students will find evidence in photos of classrooms that show they are from different time periods.

**Activate**

Have students draw pictures about what they like best about their classroom. Tell students what school was like when you were a child. Point out things that were similar to and different from today's classrooms.

**Analyze**

1. Have students look at the photographs on *Think About Schools* (page 45). Ask them to complete *Document Deep Dive—T-Chart* (page 293) to support their analysis. Have students label their T-charts with the words *Then* and *Now*. Ask them to document what they see in each photograph. Model how to line up similar observations from each photograph across from each other in the T-chart.

2. Ask students to review the T-chart to find evidence that one photograph is older and one photograph is newer. Have students circle evidence that tells about the time period from which the photographs were taken. Discuss how the details in the photographs help determine the time period.

3. Use the following questions to guide a discussion:

   · How does the furniture tell about the time periods the photographs were taken?

   · What evidence is there that more than one grade was in the *Then* classroom?

   · Why would so many grades need to be in one classroom?

   · Would you like to be a student in a one-room school house?

4. Allow time for students to complete *Think About Schools*. Discuss their work and strengthen their analysis skills using the How To activity.

**How To . . .**

**Find the Details**—Tell students that photographs usually show people, places, or things. Sometimes, a photograph will show all three. Explain that one way to find important details in a photograph is to focus on each category separately. Guide students to focus on the people in each photograph and discuss what they see. Repeat with the places and things.

**Extend**

Have students compare their classroom with the *Now* photograph. What things are the same? What things are different? Tell students that the photograph was taken not too many years ago. What types of things have already changed in this brief amount of time? What might change in the future?

© Shell Education

Name: _____ Date: _____

# Think About Schools

**Directions:** Study the images.  Then, answer the questions.

**Then**

One teacher taught many grades in a one-room school house.

**Now**

A teacher teaches one grade in a big classroom with modern technology.

1.  How are these classrooms the same?

    Ⓐ  Each classroom has one teacher.
    Ⓑ  Boys are wearing ties.
    Ⓒ  They have many chalkboards.
    Ⓓ  They have computers.

2.  What is one way classrooms have changed?  Use evidence from the photos.

    _____

    _____

    _____

**Preliminary DBAs**

# Helpers

**Historical-Thinking Skill**

Students will compare and contrast photographs of mail carriers from different time periods.

**Activate**

Have students share their experiences with sending and receiving mail. Ask students why someone would send mail. Discuss other methods for communicating. Ask students if they would rather receive a letter in the mail or an email. What makes receiving a letter in the mail special?

**Analyze**

1. Have students look at the photographs on *Think About Helpers* (page 47) and complete *Document Deep Dive—Venn Diagram* (page 292) to support their analysis. Explain that they will use this page to compare and contrast the photographs.

2. Ask students to list the names of the main features of mail carriers they see, such as clothing, bags, or modes of transportation, and write them on the board. Have students briefly describe each feature of the mail carriers in both photographs. Ask students to include information about these features in their Venn diagrams.

3. Use the following questions to guide a discussion:
   - What is the same about mail carriers then and now? What is different?
   - How does a mail carrier carry all the mail that needs to be delivered?
   - Why are horses and trucks needed in addition to a mail carrier walking a neighborhood?
   - Why do you think mail is carried or delivered differently now? How do you think it will change in the future?

4. Allow time for students to complete *Think About Helpers*. Discuss their work and strengthen their analysis skills using the How To activity.

**How To . . .**

**Analyze Images Closely**—Tell students that when they compare images of two similar items, it is often useful to focus on similar parts of the images and mark them on their papers. Have students circle the mail on each photograph. Discuss the similarities and differences of the mail and where it is. Continue circling, comparing, and contrasting other parts of the image.

**Extend**

Have students write letters to people and mail them. Encourage students to ask the people to whom they are sending the letters to reply with letters so your students receive mail as well.

Name: _____ Date: _____

# Think About Helpers

**Directions:** Study the images.  Then, answer the questions.

**Then**

A mail carrier in a rural area delivers mail by horse.

**Now**

A mail carrier drives a mail truck in a suburb.

1. What is the same in the two photos?

   (A) Mail is an expensive way to communicate.

   (B) The mail carriers wear the same uniform.

   (C) A mail carrier takes mail to people.

   (D) Horses are used to help deliver mail.

2. Tell two things about how the mail is delivered in the *Now* photo.

   _____

   _____

   _____

# Teacher Resources

## Background Information

### Transportation Lesson

In the early years of the twentieth century, automobiles were handmade and very expensive. They were referred to as *horseless carriages*. Only wealthy people could afford cars. It was Henry Ford's goal to develop an automobile that middle-class Americans could afford. In 1908, he did just that. At his automobile plant in Detroit, Michigan, Henry Ford began the production of his first 1908 Ford Model T. At first, production was slow. Then, in 1913, Henry Ford used the concept of an assembly line to increase production and lower the cost of his cars. Henry Ford built 15 million Model T automobiles using this production method. It allowed him to produce the cars more efficiently and sell them at a lower cost, making them more affordable for consumers.

Automobiles built by Ford Motor Company are made and sold today, but now, there are also automobiles from many other manufacturers from all around the world. Many different models are available from the same manufacturer, making for many choices when purchasing an automobile.

### Schools Lesson

Many years ago, schools were different from how they are today. As the country grew, small rural communities developed. These communities could not afford large schools, yet the children needed to be educated. Schools were often established in small one- or two-room buildings without electricity or indoor plumbing. There was often one teacher, and children of various ages learned together. The one-room schoolhouse is a tradition in some societies. Many outstanding citizens were educated in this type of school. Many schools today are large and have multiple classrooms for each grade level. Modern technology is now available to schools and is used to support learning.

    © Shell Education

# Teacher Resources *(cont.)*

## Helpers Lesson

The Pony Express was a mail service in which mail was carried by horseback from St. Joseph, Missouri, to Sacramento, California. About 400 horses were purchased to stock the Pony Express, and riders got a fresh horse every 10–15 miles (16–24 kilometers). Before the Pony Express, mail to California had to go by stagecoach, wagon, or the longest route—by ship. The official end of the Pony Express was when the telegraph was completed on October 24, 1861.

Mail carriers still work together to help deliver the mail. They use trucks and planes to get mail from city to city. The mail is sorted in local post offices and delivered to mailboxes at homes and businesses by mail carriers.

## Answer Key

**Think About Transportation** (page 43)
1. C
2. Early automobiles were not reliable and often had to be push-started.

**Think About Schools** (page 45)
1. A
2. Classrooms have one grade. They are larger (either fewer children or larger rooms). Students have access to technology.

**Think About Helpers** (page 47)
1. C
2. Now, the mail is taken by truck to a neighborhood. The mail carrier puts the mail in his truck and then drives to deliver it to a mailbox by a house.

© Shell Education

# Preliminary Document-Based Assessments

## Unit 3: Our Country Then and Now

# Places

## Historical-Thinking Skill

Students will compare and contrast photographs of Yellowstone National Park from different time periods.

**Activate**

Ask students if they have ever visited a national or state park. Discuss the difference between national and state parks and neighborhood parks with playgrounds.

**Analyze**

1. Have students look at the photographs on *Think About Places* (page 53). Ask them to complete *Document Deep Dive—Venn Diagram* (page 292) to support their analysis. Model how to line up similar observations from each photograph across from each other in the Venn Diagram.

2. Then, ask students to code what they observed according to the following categories: *P* for people, *O* for objects, and *A* for actions.

3. Have students circle one or two differences they think are the most important.

4. Use the following questions to guide a discussion:
   - What is the same in both photographs? What is different?
   - What can you infer from the number of people in each photograph?
   - Why was a sidewalk installed?

5. Allow time for students to complete *Think About Places*. Discuss their work and strengthen their analysis skills using the How To activity.

**How To . . .**

**Analyze Images Closely**—Tell students that one way to analyze photographs is to divide them into halves or quarters. This helps focus attention on smaller aspects of the photograph. Demonstrate for students how to use two index cards to cover three-fourths of one of the photographs so that only one quarter is showing. Move the index cards around to reveal other quarters of the photograph. Repeat with the second photograph.

**Extend**

Have students think of places in their cities that they think are special and would like to protect from change. Discuss possible ways to make that happen. Discuss how the areas might change if they are not protected.

Name: _____ Date: _____

# Think About Places

**Directions:** Study the images.  Then, answer the questions.

**Then**

People visited Old Faithful in Yellowstone in 1853.

**Now**

People visit Old Faithful in Yellowstone today.

1. What can you tell about Old Faithful from the photos?

   Ⓐ Old Faithful erupts about every 90 minutes.

   Ⓑ The area around Old Faithful has not changed.

   Ⓒ People enjoy watching the geyser erupt.

   Ⓓ The geyser does not erupt anymore.

2. What improvements have been made to help people view the geyser?

   _____

   _____

   _____

© Shell Education

# People

## Historical-Thinking Skill

Students will find evidence in images of people that show they are from different time periods.

**Activate**

Ask students what they know about soldiers today. Ask if they know anyone who is currently serving in the military. Identify the branches of the military: army, navy, air force, marine corps, and coast guard.

**Analyze**

1. Have students look at the images on *Think About People* (page 55). Ask them to complete the *Document Deep Dive—Bubble Map* (page 294) to support their analysis. Ask them to fill in the top part of the page as much as they can. Tell students they will look for evidence to support the claim that uniforms have stayed the same in many ways. In the center of their bubble maps, have students write *evidence uniforms have stayed the same.*

2. Have students circle evidence on their analysis sheets to show the parts of a soldier's uniform that have stayed the same through time. Ask them to write the evidence they find in the outside circles of their bubble maps.

3. Use the following questions to guide a discussion:
   - How have the uniforms changed?
   - What is similar about the uniforms? Why would these things be similar?
   - What evidence is there for the setting each group of soldiers is in?
   - What can you not learn from these images?

4. Allow time for students to complete *Think About People*. Discuss their work and strengthen their analysis skills using the How To activity.

**How To . . .**

**Make Inferences**—Tell students that when they look at a photograph, there is usually more to be learned that is not explained. This is called making inferences or drawing conclusions. Ask students to share how they know when someone is happy, or angry, even if the person doesn't tell them. Explain that students can make inferences by using what they already know and clues from the photograph. They can ask questions, such as: *What are the people doing? How do I know? What are the clues? Are there other possibilities than what I am thinking?*

**Extend**

Invite members of the military or a member of a local veteran's group to visit the class and share their uniforms if they have one or part of one. Have students write thank you letters to the soldiers.

    © Shell Education

Name: _____ Date: _____

# Think About People

**Directions:** Study the images.  Then, answer the questions.

**Then**

soldiers during the
American Revolution

**Now**

armed forces in a combat zone

1. Based on the images, what can you tell both uniforms have in common?

   Ⓐ Both uniforms include boots.

   Ⓑ Both uniforms were heavy.

   Ⓒ Both uniforms have many buttons.

   Ⓓ Both uniforms are camouflaged.

2. What evidence is there that the *Now* soldiers use new technology?

   _____

   _____

**Preliminary DBAs**

# Symbols

## Historical-Thinking Skill

Students will examine how and why the American flag design has changed over time.

**Activate**

Take a walking trip to view the flag on display on the flag pole at the front of the school. Say the Pledge of Allegiance. Discuss why the school displays the flag in front of it.

**Analyze**

1. Have students look at the images on *Think About Symbols* (page 57). Ask them to begin completing *Document Deep Dive—Flow Chart* (page 295) to support their analysis. Have students complete as much of the top of their activity sheets as they can.

2. Guide students to record how the flag design has changed over time. In the first box, have students draw or describe the flag in 1777 and why it looked as it did. In the last box, have students describe or draw the flag today and why it looks as it does. For the two middle squares, research as a class two other times in history when the flag design has changed (e.g., 1795 and 1912). Have students label and describe the flags in the boxes chronologically.

3. Use the following questions to guide a discussion:
   - What is the same on both flags?
   - What is different? Why would the number of stars change?
   - How do the changes to the flag reflect changes going on in the United States?
   - If another state was added to the United States, how would the flag probably change?

4. Allow time for students to complete *Think About Symbols*. Discuss their work and strengthen their analysis skills using the How To activity.

**How To . . .**

**Annotate Documents**—Tell students that a good way to analyze documents is to annotate them. One way to do this is to write comments and questions directly on the paper. Model doing this for students. Then, ask students to write at least two comments and two questions on or around the images. Encourage students to draw lines to or circle the areas of the images they are commenting on.

**Extend**

Have students design flags that represent themselves or the class. Encourage them to have at least three things on their flags that show symbolism. Have students share their flags with each other.

Name: _____ Date: _____

# Think About Symbols

**Directions:** Study the images.  Then, answer the questions.

**Then**

The 13 stars represent the 13 original states.  A flag with this design was first flown in 1777.

**Now**

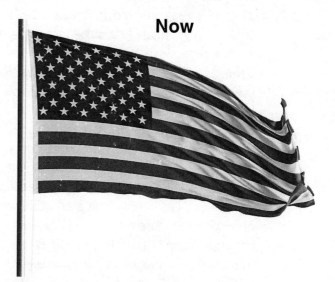

The 50 stars represent the 50 states. This flag design has been in use since 1960.

1.  How are the flags alike?

    Ⓐ  The number of stars has not changed.

    Ⓑ  The number of stripes has not changed.

    Ⓒ  George Washington ordered both flags.

    Ⓓ  They were made by the same person.

2.  What can you tell about the United States by looking at how the flag has changed over time?

    _____

    _____

    _____

# Teacher Resources

## Background Information

### Places Lesson

Exploration of the area that became Yellowstone National Park began as early as 1797 when explorer and geographer David Thompson wrote about a place that he called "Yellow Stone." In 1806, members of the Lewis and Clark expedition reported that they saw a volcano and that it sounded like thunder. In 1870, an expedition led by the Montana Surveyor General Henry Dana Washburn explored the area. Yellowstone, located in Wyoming and named for its yellow-colored rock, was the world's first national park. Because Yellowstone is a spectacular area with a variety of wildlife and more than 10,000 geysers, hot springs, and fumaroles, people wanted to protect it so that everyone could enjoy its

beauty. In 1872, President Ulysses S. Grant signed into law a bill that made Yellowstone a national park. The Yellowstone River flows through the park and creates two impressive waterfalls. The river has cut a large canyon through the yellow-colored rock. For many years, few people could visit Yellowstone because it was difficult to get there. As more people owned cars, the roadways across the United States expanded. The park became a popular place to visit. As a national park, Yellowstone is protected and regulated by the government.

### People Lesson

The earliest militia can be traced to citizens who took it upon themselves to protect their settlements against outsiders, either other settlers or native tribes. Through the years, the military has changed both in appearance and in methods of warfare. During the time of the Revolutionary War, soldiers of the Continental Army wore uniforms like those pictured in the first image. They were decorative and formal in appearance. Their hats were made of leather or fur. Hand-held weapons were usually muskets and rifles that had to be reloaded after each firing. Rifles and muskets had long barrels to which a bayonet could be attached.

The second picture shows soldiers in action today. They are dressed for combat, and their uniforms are comfortable and enable them to move easily. Their hats are made of hard material that offers maximum protection. Today, soldiers wear different types of uniforms for various kinds of duty. Weapons today are high-powered and technically complex. Soldiers also use modern technology, including computers and drones, to help them do their jobs.

# Teacher Resources (cont.)

## Symbols Lesson

The Second Continental Congress established the first official flag on June 14, 1777. Their Flag Resolution established "That the flag of the thirteen United States be thirteen stripes, alternate red and white; that the union be thirteen stars, white in a blue field representing a new constellation." There are many questions about who designed the first American flag. Many people think that Betsy Ross was the person responsible for sewing the first flag, but this cannot be confirmed. However, this account is so well known that the flag is commonly called the Betsy Ross flag. This version of the flag was first flown in 1777.

The design on the flag of the United States has changed over the years. The current flag is the 27th version of the flag. It has 13 red and white stripes which represent the 13 original colonies. There are also 50 five-pointed white stars on a field of blue in the upper left-hand corner. The stars represent each of the 50 states in the country.

## Answer Key

**Think About Places** (page 53)
1. C
2. Sidewalks have been built. Benches have been added. Many more people come to see Old Faithful erupt.

**Think About People** (page 55)
1. A
2. The *Now* soldiers have cameras on their helmets.

**Think About Symbols** (page 57)
1. B
2. The number of states has increased.

© Shell Education

# Beginning Document-Based Assessments

## Unit 4: Our Government

**Lessons**

**Teacher Resources**

# Presidential Seal

**Historical-Thinking Skill**

Students will identify how the symbols on the presidential seal represent the United States.

**Activate**

Ask students to name symbols of the United States. Record students' ideas on a sheet of chart paper. Ask guiding questions as needed to help students recall the number of original states, the current number of states, and the national bird of the United States.

**Analyze**

1. Have students look at the image on *Investigate the Presidential Seal* (page 63). Ask them to complete the top section of *Document Deep Dive—T-Chart* (page 293) for the *Document A* column only. Have students label their T-charts with the headings *Images/Words* and *Symbolism*.

2. Ask students to think about what they know about the United States and what its founding ideas are. Explain that thinking about these things can help them better understand the symbolism of the seal. If they were told that the image of the eagle was for a new video game, they would probably have different ideas about the symbolism. Ask students to record the images and words they see on the U.S. presidential seal and the possible symbolism of these things. Have students discuss their findings and symbolism ideas with partners.

3. Use the following questions to guide a discussion:
   - What does the phrase *E pluribus unum* mean in English? How does that phrase relate to the United States? (Allow students to do some research to find the answer.)
   - What numbers are represented on the seal? How do the numbers relate to the United States?
   - Why is the eagle holding an olive branch and arrows?

4. Allow time for students to complete *Investigate the Presidential Seal*. Discuss their work and strengthen their analysis skills using the How To activity.

**How To . . .**

**Find and Understand Symbolism**—Tell students that when they analyze symbolic images, it's important to remember that everything in the image may represent something. Have students name the objects that repeat on the seal: stars, circles, arrows, and leaves. Have students return to their T-charts and write the number of objects on the seal next to the words they wrote. Discuss the context of the numbers 13 and 50.

**Extend**

Show or have students research images of the seal of the vice president of the United States, the back of a half-dollar coin, or the Great Seal of the United States. Discuss the similarities and differences. Have students compare them to the presidential seal.

Name: _____  Date: _____

# Investigate the Presidential Seal

**Directions:** Study the image, and answer the questions.

This seal is used to represent the president.

1. What is one place where the 13 original states are symbolized on the seal?

   Ⓐ the words on the banner

   Ⓑ the arrows the eagle is holding

   Ⓒ the words around the outside of the seal

   Ⓓ the circle made from stars

2. Why are there 50 stars in a circle on the seal?

   _____

   _____

3. Describe the possible symbolism of something the eagle is holding or doing. Explain why this symbolism would make sense.

   _____

   _____

   _____

## Congress

**Historical-Thinking Skill**

Students will compare and contrast diagrams of the chambers of the Senate and the House of Representatives.

Beginning DBAs

**Activate**

Ask students what they know about the leaders of our country. Identify the president as one of the leaders. However, guide the discussion to include how else the people are represented. Discuss with students how laws are made and who makes them.

**Analyze**

1. Have students look at the diagrams on *Investigate Congress* (page 65). Ask them to complete the top section of *Document Deep Dive—Venn Diagram* (page 292) to support their analysis.

2. For the Venn diagram, have students write *Senate* and *House* at the top of the circles. Then, have them list observations from each diagram in the correct place. Students can also list other similarities and differences they know about the Senate and the House not shown in the diagrams.

3. Use the following questions to guide a discussion:

   · How many seats are in each chamber? How does the number of seats relate to each state?

   · Why do the House and the Senate have a different number of seats?

   · What is similar about the two diagrams?

4. Allow time for students to complete *Investigate Congress*. Discuss their work and strengthen their analysis skills using the How To activity.

**How To . . .**

**Analyze Images Closely**—Tell students that when they compare images of two similar items, it is often useful to focus on similar parts of the images. In the diagrams of the chambers of Congress, students can focus on the number of seats, the arrangements of the seating area, and the front and back of the chambers. Discuss the similarities and differences of each component.

**Extend**

Locate diagrams of the current Congress with the seats marked for each political party. Discuss which party has more representation in the House of Representatives and in the Senate. Look at the representation from other sessions of Congress. Discuss why the representation changes.

Name: _____ Date: _____

# Investigate Congress

**Directions:** These are floor plans of the chambers of the House of Representatives and the Senate. The House has 435 members. The Senate has 100 members. They are both located at the U.S. Capitol building. Study the images, and answer the questions.

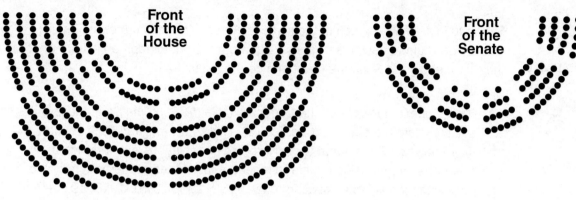

Our Government

1. What can you tell by comparing the two diagrams?

   (A) where the representatives from each state sit

   (B) how often congress meets

   (C) which group has more members

   (D) how many representatives each state has

2. What is similar about the seating arrangements for both diagrams?

   _____

   _____

   _____

3. What is a reason for some of the differences between the House and the Senate chambers?

   _____

   _____

   _____

# Supreme Court

## Historical-Thinking Skill

Students will analyze a chart showing the length of tenure on the Supreme Court and consider the influences of U.S. history and life span trends.

**Beginning DBAs**

### Activate

Show students a photograph of the justices currently sitting on the Supreme Court. Ask them to describe what they can from the photograph and share what they know about the Supreme Court and courts in general.

### Analyze

1. Have students look at the chart on *Investigate the Supreme Court* (page 67) and complete the *Document Deep Dive—Flow Chart* (page 295) to support their analysis. Explain that they will record observations about trends they see in the graph. Ask students to label the four boxes at the bottom of the page with the following dates, in order: 1789–1850, 1851–1910, 1911–1970, 1971–present.

2. Ask students to write what they notice about the tenure of the Supreme Court justices for each of these time periods. (If students are new to looking at graphs like this, you may choose to strengthen their skills with the How To activity before they complete their graphic organizers.)

3. Use the following questions to guide a discussion:
   - What patterns do you notice in the graph?
   - Think about what was happening in the United States before and around 1789. Why would the time on the Supreme Court be so short?
   - Why might the length of tenure be longer in more recent years?

4. Allow time for students to complete *Investigate the Supreme Court*. Discuss their work and strengthen their analysis skills using the How To activity.

### How To . . .

**Read Graphs**—Tell students that when reading a graph, it is important to begin by understanding what it is representing. Identify the title of the graph with students. Remind students to be sure they understand each of the words or receive clarification. For example, students may need assistance understanding the word *average*. Next, identify the *x*-axis and *y*-axis with students. Ensure students understand what is being represented in each place. Finally, look at the data in the graph, and discuss what the graph shows.

### Extend

Have students compare the graph showing average years on the Supreme Court with the terms *lengths* and *limits* in the other branches of government. Discuss the impact of not having a term limit on the Supreme Court.

    © Shell Education

# Investigate the Supreme Court

**Directions:** Study the graph. Then, answer the questions.

**Average Years on the Supreme Court from 1789 to 2006**

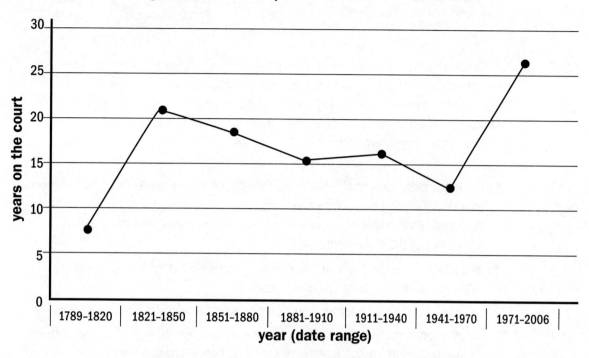

1. What can you tell about the Supreme Court from 1821–1850 by looking at the graph?

   Ⓐ Justices spent 15.2 years on the court.

   Ⓑ Years on the Supreme Court were longer overall than the time period before that.

   Ⓒ No new justices were appointed to the Supreme Court.

   Ⓓ The tenure on the Supreme Court was the highest it has ever been.

2. Describe what happened to the average years on the court from 1851–1880.

   _____

   _____

3. Compare the data from the beginning of the Supreme Court to the most recent years.

   _____

   _____

# Voting

**Historical-Thinking Skill**

Students will analyze an election ballot to think about how and why the ballot was used.

Beginning DBAs

**Activate**

Ask students a question for which they have to vote. Have students close their eyes and raise their hands to indicate their choices. Count the number of votes. Discuss with students how voting for an office, such as voting for a president, takes place when so many people need to vote. Discuss the desire for privacy when voting for important offices.

**Analyze**

1. Have students look at the ballot on *Investigate Voting* (page 69). Ask students to complete *Document Deep Dive—Bubble Map* (page 294) to support their analysis. Ask students to complete their bubble maps with details they notice about the document.

2. Ask students to think about when, why, and how a ballot is used. Use the following questions to guide a discussion:

   - Why is a voting ballot an important piece of American Democracy?

   - How does modern technology influence how people vote and how votes are collected and counted? Why is that important in an election?

   - Why are the offices listed in this order?

   - What would happen if only one person is listed for an office?

   - What things do people consider when choosing a candidate?

3. Allow time for students to complete *Investigate Voting*. Discuss their work and strengthen their analysis skills using the How To activity.

**How To . . .**

**Read Complicated Documents**—Tell students some documents have headings that can help the reader better understand the information on the document. Draw students' attention to the gray areas on the ballot. Note the bold print indicating the office being voted for. Have students identify each office listed on this ballot. Discuss how the header makes reading this document easier.

**Extend**

Choose something for the class to vote on (how to spend a free 20 minutes of class, which story to read, etc.). Work together to create ballots for the vote. Have students vote using their ballots. Follow through with the results of the election.

# Investigate Voting

**Directions:** Voters mark their choices for elected officers on a ballot. Study the ballot. Then, answer the questions.

1. Name two offices being voted on using this ballot.

_____

_____

2. How would a voter vote for someone who is not on the ballot?

_____

_____

# Teacher Resources

## DBQ Discussion

Activate students' memory of the documents they analyzed and learned about in this unit by asking them to think of the following: three things they learned, two questions they still have, and one of their favorite documents. Have students discuss these things with partners. Then, write one of the DBQ discussion questions on the board. Choose a question that best fits the needs of your students and is appropriate for their current understanding of the topic.

➤ What are the most important things you know about your country?

➤ How do the three branches of the U.S. government support democracy?

Ask students to think about the question independently first. Then, ask students to turn and discuss it with partners. While partners are talking, create a bubble map or chart on the board with each of the four documents from the unit listed. Lead a discussion about the DBQ. Guide students to think about if and how each document can help them answer the question and record their thinking on the board. Invite a few volunteers to share how they could answer the question in a few sentences.

## Background Information

### Presidential Seal Lesson

The seal of the president of the United States is used as a symbol of the president. It is commonly seen on the podium when the president gives speeches and on the sides of presidential vehicles, such as Air Force One, Marine One, and any cars in which the president rides. The seal was historically used as a die pressed in wax to close correspondence between the president and Congress.

The seal contains a bald eagle, the national bird, holding an olive branch with 13 leaves in one talon and 13 arrows in the other talon. A shield with 13 red and white stripes and a blue field at the top appear on the breast of the eagle. In its beak, the eagle holds a banner with the phrase *E pluribus unum* ("out of many, one"). The crest, which is behind the eagle, radiates lines, 13 circles, and 13 stars. Surrounding the eagle are 50 stars that symbolize the 50 states in the country.

### Congress Lesson

The Constitution of the United States calls for three branches of government: executive, legislative, and judicial. The president occupies the office of the executive branch. The Supreme Court serves as the judicial branch. The legislative branch is composed of senators and representatives from each state. The U.S. Senate is made of 100 members. Each state elects and sends two senators to Congress every six years. The U.S. House of Representatives is made up of 435 representatives. Each state is allowed a percentage of representatives based on the population of the state. Representatives serve two-year terms. The Constitution gives Congress a number of powers, including taxation, the ability to declare war, and oversight of the finances of the country. Congress can pass bills that can be signed into law by the president.

Beginning DBAs

# Teacher Resources *(cont.)*

## Supreme Court Lesson

The Supreme Court is within the judicial branch, one of the three branches of government. It helps keep the executive and the legislative branches in balance. The Supreme Court is the highest court in the United States. It was established in Article III, Section 2 of the Constitution. It states that these judges "hold their office during good behavior." This means they are appointed for life unless they are impeached and convicted. Court cases decided by lower courts can be appealed to the Supreme Court. The decision of the Supreme Court is the final decision. Nine justices or judges serve on the Supreme Court. They are appointed by the president of the United States. The justices serve lifetime appointments. This means the judges continue to serve until they resign or die.

## Voting Lesson

In the United States, citizens choose their government leaders by voting. The people who get the most votes win. They get to be the leaders. Government leaders are chosen in elections. In elections, citizens who are at least 18 years old can vote. Votes are marked on ballots. Although many methods have been used for voting in the past, modern ballots are marked with a tool that makes a dot. The marked ballots are then taken to scanners and counted. Many other ballots are completely digital. Votes are counted and recorded by computers. Ballots are kept secret. This is so people can vote honestly. They do not have to worry about what others will think.

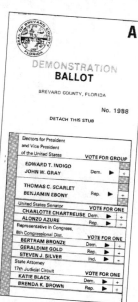

## Answer Key

**Investigate the Presidential Seal** (page 63)
1. B
2. The 50 stars are symbols of the 50 states in the United States.
3. Answers should include the possible symbolism of something related to what the eagle is holding or doing and a reason why this symbolism makes sense for the presidential seal of the United States.

**Investigate Congress** (page 65)
1. C
2. The seating in both diagrams is arranged in a semi-circle.
3. One reason there are differences is because they have different numbers of people. The Senate has 100 members. Two members are from each state. The House has 435 representatives with different numbers from each state.

**Investigate the Supreme Court** (page 67)
1. B
2. The length of tenure declined in that time period.
3. The length of tenure rose by almost 20 years.

**Investigate Voting** (page 69)
1. Example: The office of president and state senator are being voted on.
2. The voter would fill in the bubble next to the Write-In line and write the name of the person they want to vote for.

© Shell Education

# Beginning Document-Based Assessments

## Unit 5: Around the World

**Lessons**

**Teacher Resources**

# African Safaris

**Historical-Thinking Skill**

Students will use evidence from the photograph to make inferences about an African safari.

Beginning DBAs

**Activate**

Ask students to name animals that can be found around where they live. Then, ask students to name animals they can only see in a zoo. Record this list on the board or a sheet of chart paper. Have students identify which of these animals live in Africa. Tell students that many people travel to Africa and go on safaris to see these animals because it is the only place they can be seen in the wild. Which animals would they hope to see on safari?

**Analyze**

1. Have students look at the photograph on *Investigate African Safaris* (page 75). Ask them to complete *Document Deep Dive—T-Chart* (page 293) to support their analysis. First, have them complete as much of the top of the page as they can. Then, have students label their T-charts with the words *Inference* and *Evidence*. (If students are new to making inferences, you may choose to strengthen their skills with the How To activity before they complete the chart.)

2. Provide students with the following example: *Inference—The people on the safari are excited to see a lion; Evidence—They are all standing up taking photographs to document the experience.* Then, ask students to work with partners to write two more inferences and the evidence for each. Ask volunteers to share their T-charts.

3. Use the following questions to guide a discussion:
   - How do you know the people are interested in the lion?
   - Why are the people staying in the vehicle?
   - Which vehicle would you prefer to be in?

4. Allow time for students to complete *Investigate African Safaris.* Discuss their work and strengthen their analysis skills using the How To activity.

**How To . . .**

**Make Inferences**—Tell students that when they look at a photograph, there is usually more to be learned that is not explained. This is called making inferences or drawing conclusions. Ask students to share how they know when someone is happy, or angry, even if the person doesn't tell them. Explain that students can make inferences by using what they already know and clues from the photograph. They can ask questions, such as: *What are the people doing? How do I know? What are the clues? Are there other possibilities than what I am thinking?*

**Extend**

Have students choose a person in the vehicle in the photograph and write a journal entry from that person's perspective about what they saw on the safari.

    © Shell Education

Name: _____ Date: _____

# Investigate African Safaris

**Directions:** This is a photo from a safari in South Africa. Many people visit certain countries in Africa to go on safaris. They see animals in the wild that they can't see anywhere else in the world. Study the image. Then, answer the questions.

1. What is the main reason why these people would go on safari?

    Ⓐ to hike

    Ⓑ to see wild animals

    Ⓒ to sleep in tents

    Ⓓ to wear safari clothing

2. What evidence is there in this picture to support your answer to the first question?

    _____

    _____

    _____

3. How do you know these vehicles are good for going on safaris?

    _____

    _____

# Thailand's Geography

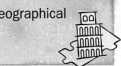

### Historical-Thinking Skill
Students will identify geographical features in Thailand.

**Activate**

Show students a map of the world, and ask them to identify the seven continents. Point to Asia, and ask students to name as many countries as they can in Asia. Tell students that today, they will be looking at a map of a country in Asia.

Beginning DBAs

**Analyze**

1. Have students look at the map on *Investigate Thailand's Geography* (page 77). Ask students to complete *Document Deep Dive—Bubble Map* (page 294) to support their analysis. At the bottom of their bubble maps, have students record the features and characteristics they see on the map. Tell students they can add their own bubbles if they need more room.

2. Ask students to annotate the following features of the map: *M* for mountain, *R* for river, and *C* for city. Ask students to analyze the relationship between the mountains, rivers, and parks.

3. Use the following questions to guide a discussion:
   - What is the purpose of the small map in the corner?
   - What might be some effects of having so much coastline?
   - What geographic features can you find in Thailand?
   - How would the shape of Thailand be a benefit and a challenge?

4. Allow time for students to complete *Investigate Thailand's Geography*. Discuss their work and strengthen their analysis skills using the How To activity.

**How To . . .**

**Read a Map**—Tell students that when looking at a map, they should first orient themselves by reading the title of the map or the caption. Then, they should look for any tools that will help them read the map, such as a map key or distance scale. Ask students to identify the main purpose of the map. Is it to show geography, agriculture, roads, etc.? Ask students to identify main features of the map, which are often identified on a map key: cities, mountains, national parks, rivers, and other bodies of water.

**Extend**

Place students into smaller groups, and have each group research an aspect of Thailand, such as weather, religion, language, or wildlife. Have groups report back to the whole class about what they learned.

Name: _____ Date: _____

# Investigate Thailand's Geography

**Directions:** Thailand is located in Southeast Asia. Study the map. Then, answer the questions.

**1.** Where is Mount Khao Luang located?

- (A) central Thailand
- (B) eastern Thailand
- (C) southern Thailand
- (D) northern Thailand

**2.** Describe where Thailand is located in the world.

_____

_____

_____

_____

_____

_____

**Thailand Geographic Map**

**3.** Based on the geography, why might people want to live in or visit Thailand?

_____

_____

_____

_____

# London's Architecture

**Beginning DBAs**

## Historical-Thinking Skill

Students will compare and contrast features of structures seen in the London skyline.

**Activate**

Name a city, such as New York or Paris, and ask students to identify structures they know of in that city (Empire State Building, Eiffel Tower, etc.). Tell students that buildings and other structures that are visible from far away often help people identify the city in photographs.

**Analyze**

1. Have students look at the architectural features in the photograph on *Investigate London's Architecture* (page 79). Ask them to complete *Document Deep Dive—T-Chart* (page 293) to support their analysis. Have students label their T-charts with the words *Structure* and *Features*. Ask students to document what they see in the photograph to support each heading. Point out and ask students to label Big Ben and the London Eye. Have students make up a name for other structures, such as "triangle building" for the pointed skyscraper behind Big Ben, or have them write numbers or letters on the photograph and in the chart to identify other structures.

2. Ask students to review the features listed in the T-chart and code the features: *O* for older buildings, and *M* for modern buildings. Ask students to identify features similar in older buildings and features similar in modern buildings.

3. Use the following questions to guide a discussion:
   - How do the materials and designs reflect the time period in which the different structures were made?
   - Why would Big Ben and the London Eye be so tall?
   - What do the contrasting styles of buildings tell you about London?
   - What can you infer about a city that has both older and more modern buildings?

4. Allow time for students to complete *Investigate London's Architecture*. Discuss their work and strengthen their analysis skills using the How To activity.

**How To . . .**

**Analyze an Image Closely**—Tell students that a magnifying glass is a tool that can be useful for analyzing details in images. Provide students with magnifying glasses, and have them look at the photograph. Encourage students to work in a sequence manner to review the photograph. For example, students can work from right to left and from top to bottom. Discuss any details that can be seen with the magnifying glass that cannot be seen as easily without it. Have students add any new observations to their T-charts.

**Extend**

Have students look at a photograph of the skyline of another metropolitan city and either repeat the same activity as they did above or compare and contrast that city's skyline with London's skyline.

    © Shell Education

Name: _____ Date: _____

# Investigate London's Architecture

**Directions:** London is a very old city. It is also one of the most modern cities. Study the image. Then, answer the questions.

1. What can you learn from looking at this photo?

   Ⓐ London has both old and new architecture.

   Ⓑ London has only old buildings.

   Ⓒ All the buildings in London are tall.

   Ⓓ The buildings in London are very spread out.

2. Describe Big Ben, the large clock tower.

   _____

   _____

   _____

3. Both Big Ben and the London Eye sit along the River Thames. What conclusions can you draw about the River Thames?

   _____

   _____

   _____

# Australian Barbecue

Beginning DBAs

### Historical-Thinking Skill

Students will use evidence from the photograph to tell about a way food is cooked in Australia.

**Activate**

Ask students to tell about foods their families like to eat. Prompt students to think about how those foods are prepared. Is the food served raw or is it cooked? How is it cooked? Are other people invited to share in the meal? Are the foods or preparation styles related to any family or cultural traditions?

**Analyze**

1. Have students look at the photograph on *Investigate Australian Barbecue* (page 81) and complete *Document Deep Dive—T-Chart* (page 293) to support their analysis. Have students label their T-charts with the words *Inference* and *Evidence*. On their activity sheets, they will document what they can infer from what they see in the photograph.

2. In the *Inference* column, encourage students to write what they learn or can conclude from the photograph. In the *Evidence* column, ask students to explain what evidence in the photo led them to that inference. For example, the lines on the meat are from the grill because they are the same as the grill lines, and it is clear the food is hot because tongs are being used and there is a flame. Discuss student findings.

3. Use the following questions to guide a discussion:
   · How are the foods being cooked? How do you know?
   · How do you know the foods have been seasoned?
   · What could you likely conclude about the weather during a barbecue? Why?
   · What else could the barbecue tradition tell you about Australian culture?

4. Allow time for students to complete *Investigate Australian Barbecue*. Discuss their work and strengthen their analysis skills using the How To activity.

**How To . . .**

**Infer with Your Senses—**Review the five senses with students: hearing, seeing, smelling, tasting, and touching. Tell students that when analyzing a source, often more than just the sense of seeing can be used. Explain that this is a perfect photograph to use the sense of smell and hearing to make inferences. Remind students that an inference is something that is not directly stated but can be figured out or concluded. Prompt students with questions that require them to infer with the sense of smell, hearing, taste, or touch.

**Extend**

Have students make menus of food items they enjoy eating with their families. Encourage students to include pictures of the foods and even recipes to go with their menu items. Then, have students discuss what can be learned about them or their families from their menus.

Name: _____ Date: _____

# Investigate Australian Barbecue

**Directions:** Meat and vegetables are common at a barbie, or barbecue, in Australia. Study the image. Then, answer the questions.

1. How is the food prepared?

   (A) in an oven

   (B) on the stove

   (C) in a microwave

   (D) on a grill

2. Why would the food have to be watched closely as it cooks?

   _____

   _____

   _____

3. How might the weather in Australia influence the tradition of an outdoor barbecue?

   _____

   _____

   _____

# Teacher Resources

## DBQ Discussion

Activate students' memories of the documents they analyzed and learned from in this unit by asking them to think of the following: three things they learned, two questions they still have, and one of their favorite documents. Have students discuss these things with partners. Then, choose a question that best fits the needs of your students and is appropriate for their current understanding of the topic. Write your chosen DBQ on the board.

➤ What are the most important things you know about people and places around the world?

➤ How can geography influence the look, feel, or culture of a place?

Ask students to think about the question independently first. Then, ask students to turn and discuss it with partners. While partners are talking, create a display web or chart listing each of the four documents from the unit. Lead a discussion about the DBQ. Guide students to think about it and how each document helps them answer the question. Record their thinking on the web or chart. Invite a few volunteers to share how they could answer the question in a few sentences.

## Background Information

### African Safaris Lesson

The landscape in many parts of Africa is grassland called *savannas*. These savannas are home to animals such as elephants, zebras, lions, giraffes, as well as many other types of animals. People from around the world come to Africa to see these animals. The trip they take through the grasslands is called a *safari*.

Not that long ago, people would go on safari to hunt for these animals. They would kill the animals and bring back the heads as trophies. Now, most areas where these animals live are protected. It is illegal to hunt in national parks. Now, people go on safari to see the animals. Some people like to photograph them and the land. Safaris are an important part of tourism in Africa. Billions of dollars a year are spent to take safaris. This is good for the African economy.

© Shell Education

# Teacher Resources *(cont.)*

## Thailand's Geography Lesson

Thailand is located in Southeast Asia. Around 68 million people live in Thailand. About half of the people live in urban areas, and the other half live in rural areas. Agriculture is an important part of the economy. Thailand has many rice fields, and rice is an important export.

Most of the people in Thailand are Buddhist. Thailand is well-known for its Buddhist temples and statues.

Thailand has many forests. The forests are home to tigers, elephants, and leopards. There are also many beaches and islands. Rain is very common between May and September. In 2004, there was an earthquake in the Indian Ocean. The earthquake triggered a large tsunami that hit Thailand. Many people died and a lot of damage was done to towns along the coast.

## London's Architecture Lesson

London is the capital of England. It is one of the main metropolitan cities in the world. It has been an important city for centuries.

Two distinct features of the London skyline show both modern and older architecture. Big Ben is the large clock tower that sits along the River Thames. It was built in 1859 and is 315 feet (96 meters) tall. It is a well-known feature of London. It has been designated as a UNESCO World Heritage Site. This means it will be conserved for future generations to enjoy.

Another feature of the London skyline is the London Eye. It also sits along the River Thames. This Ferris wheel started taking passengers in 2000 and stands 443 feet (135 meters) tall. Visitors can take rides in the London Eye to see views of the London skyline.

## Australian Barbecue Lesson

Barbecuing is a popular method of cooking in Australia. Putting meat on the *barbie*, as it is called there, means to cook it outdoors over fire. Meats that are barbecued are cooked at a low temperature for longer periods of time. When foods are cooked this way, the seasonings and smoke from the fire are absorbed into the meat. The meat becomes very tender. Meats that are typically used include: beef, pork, lamb, and sometimes even kangaroo! Vegetables can also be cooked over the fire. But barbecuing is more than just cooking the meat. It allows family and friends to socialize around mealtime.

# Teacher Resources *(cont.)*

## Answer Key

### Investigate African Safaris (page 75)

1. B
2. The jeeps are stopped and people are taking pictures of lions.
3. The one vehicle is designed with open sides so that people can see better. The other vehicle has protections on the top and sides, but passengers can easily see.

### Investigate Thailand's Geography (page 77)

1. C
2. Thailand is located in Southeast Asia. It is surrounded by the countries of Cambodia, Laos, Burma, and Malaysia.
3. Thailand has many beaches, islands, forests, and mountains. People enjoy visiting these types of places.

### Investigate London's Architecture (page 79)

1. A
2. The tall clock tower is a four-sided rectangular prism that comes to a point at the top. There is a clock on each side. It is attached to another building.
3. The river must be an important part of London since two well-known sites are located along it.

### Investigate Australian Barbecue (page 81)

1. D
2. The foods are cooked over a fire and may burn if they are not watched carefully.
3. Most barbecues are outside, so if it is raining, people won't be able to cook their food properly.

© Shell Education

**Beginning DBAs**

# Beginning Document-Based Assessments

## Unit 6: People in the Past

**Lessons**

**Teacher Resources**

# Log Cabins

Historical-Thinking Skill

Students will think about the time period of an image to better understand the context.

**Beginning DBAs**

**Activate** Show students a map of the United States. Discuss where much of the population lived during the early history of the United States. Review with students what happened as the population grew and the various reasons for moving west.

**Analyze**

1. Have students look at the image on *Investigate Log Cabins* (page 87). Ask students to begin *Document Deep Dive—Bubble Map* (page 294) to support their analysis. Ask students to first complete as much of the top of the page as they can.

2. Identify Missouri on the map of the United States. If possible, display a map of the Louisiana Purchase, and identify where Missouri is in the purchased territory. Review how people got from one place to another during that time and discuss what life was like. In their bubble maps, ask students to write what they know about the United States during the time period of westward expansion (setting, motivations, available materials, lifestyle, etc.).

3. Use the following questions to guide a discussion:
   - What is each person in the photo doing?
   - Why would logs be a good resource for building this home?
   - What would be some positives and negatives of this type of lifestyle?
   - How does the image represent common themes and/or ideas about this time period?

4. Allow time for students to complete *Investigate Log Cabins*. Discuss their work and strengthen their analysis skills using the How To activity.

**How To . . .**

**Analyze an Image**—Tell students that one way to analyze photographs is to divide them into halves or quarters. This helps focus attention on smaller aspects of the image. Demonstrate for students how to use two index cards to cover three-fourths of the image so that only one quarter is showing. Move the index cards around to reveal other quarters of the image. Encourage students to annotate the different parts of the image by circling or making notes about details.

**Extend** Have students find pictures of other styles of homes in magazines or on the internet, including urban, rural, and suburban examples. Compare those homes to the log cabin. Discuss the reasons for these differences.

 © Shell Education

Name: _____ Date: _____

# Investigate Log Cabins

**Directions:** This Missouri family built their own house in 1820.  Study the image. Then, answer the questions.

1. Why were logs probably used to construct this house?

   (A) There were many trees available to use as materials.

   (B) The people only knew how to build houses out of trees.

   (C) The people did not know how to build with other materials.

   (D) The logs were easy to stack and cheap to purchase.

2. What conclusions can be drawn by the number of people in the image and the size of the house?

   _____

   _____

   _____

3. Why would this house and the activities the people are doing not be typical today?

   _____

   _____

   _____

# Fashion Long Ago

**Historical-Thinking Skill**

Students will evaluate the reliability of a catalog to represent the clothing styles of a time period.

**Beginning DBAs**

**Activate**

Ask students to identify how people get their clothes today. Where do they go? How do they know what everyone will be wearing? How do they know the price of each item?

**Analyze**

1. Have students look at the image on *Investigate Fashion Long Ago* (page 89). Ask students to complete *Document Deep Dive—T-Chart* (page 293) to support their analysis. Ask students to think about whether a Sears catalog would be a good source of information about women's fashion long ago. Then, ask students to label their T-charts with the headings *Reliable* and *Not Reliable*.

2. Lead a discussion about the reliability of a Sears catalog to represent the clothing styles from this time period. Discuss who may have used the catalog and how, the types of items Sears would put in the catalog (e.g., practical, frivolous, both), and what would happen in future catalogs if items didn't sell well. Then, ask students to consider how these things and others might affect the reliability of the source. Have them complete their T-charts with information to support each column.

3. Use the following questions to guide a discussion:
   - How do the clothing styles compare to today?
   - How does the catalog compare to catalogs today?
   - What inferences can you make and what evidence supports your inferences?
   - Why would a written description of each clothing item be necessary?
   - Where else could you learn about women's fashion during this time?

4. Allow time for students to complete *Investigate Fashion Long Ago*. Discuss their work and strengthen their analysis skills using the How To activity.

**How To . . .**

**Read Catalogs**—Draw students' attention to the numbers under each person shown in the image. Then, refer students to the description boxes on the page. Have students identify where the numbers match. Tell students that when the numbers correspond, that is how they will know which box describes which clothing item and the pricing information too.

**Extend**

Have students create their own catalog pages of clothes (or other items) they would like to order. Have them include pictures, descriptions, and pricing. Have students share their catalogs.

Name: _____ Date: _____

# Investigate Fashion Long Ago

**Directions:** This image is from a 1912 catalog.  Study the image.  Then, answer the questions.

1. What is true about this catalog page?

   Ⓐ It shows the style all women wore at this time.

   Ⓑ Each person is showing the dress in the same pose.

   Ⓒ The picture was taken with a camera.

   Ⓓ The picture is hand drawn.

2. Describe the general look of the dresses on this page.

   _____

   _____

3. What is one reason this catalog would not be a good source for understanding all fashion at that time?

   _____

   _____

   _____

# Indigenous People

**Historical-Thinking Skill**

Students will use evidence from an image to support the idea that Inuits long ago were resourceful in the harsh environment they lived in.

**Beginning DBAs**

**Activate**

Have students close their eyes, and ask them to imagine a place that is very, very cold with ice and snow as far as the eye can see. Then, ask students to imagine living in that place and using only the resources they can find. Tell them that they will learn more about the Inuit people and how they lived.

**Analyze**

1. Have students look at the image on *Investigate Indigenous People* (page 91). Ask students to complete *Document Deep Dive—T-Chart* (page 293) to support their analysis. Have students label their T-charts with the headings *Item* and *Natural Resource*. On this page, ask students to document the items (sleds, boots, etc.) they see in the photograph and the natural resources they would have been made of.

2. Have students review their T-charts and find evidence that the Inuit lived in a harsh environment and were resourceful. Ask each student to write a one- or two-sentence summary at the bottom of the page, telling about the types of places the Inuit lived and how they used natural resources.

3. Use the following questions to guide a discussion:
   - What can you tell about the family from this image?
   - Why are dogs shown in the image?
   - What types of clothing are the people wearing?
   - What can you tell about how the family travels?

4. Allow time for students to complete *Investigate Indigenous People*. Discuss their work and strengthen their analysis skills using the How To activity.

**How To . . .**

**Analyze Images Closely**—Tell students that photographs usually show people, places, or things. Sometimes, an image will show all three. Explain that one way to closely analyze a photograph is to focus on each category separately. Guide students to focus on the people in the image and discuss what they see. Repeat with the places and things.

**Extend**

Ask students to think about the natural resources that are available in the area where they live. How would students be able to survive using only those natural resources? What would be easy? What would be more challenging? How would the environment affect the clothing, food, and ways to get around?

Name: _____ Date: _____

# Investigate Indigenous People

**Directions:** The Inuit people use resources found where they live to survive.  Study the image.  Then, answer the questions.

1.  What can you tell about people in the picture?

    (A) They are going swimming.
    (B) They live in houses made of wood.
    (C) They live in a place that is cold.
    (D) They travel in cars.

2.  Name two items in the picture.  How would they help the people?

    _____

    _____

3.  How is the way the baby is being carried evidence that the Inuits are resourceful in a harsh environment?

    _____

    _____

    _____

# Getting Around Town

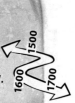

**Historical-Thinking Skill**

Students will identify the causes and effects of the invention of the automobile on people's abilities to travel in the early twentieth century.

**Activate**

Take a quick poll, and ask students how they got to school today. Identify the benefits and drawbacks of each type of transportation used. Ask students to imagine a time when horses were used exclusively for getting around. Have them think about the effects from when the first few automobiles were on the roads.

**Analyze**

1. Have students look at the photographs on *Investigate Getting Around Town* (page 93). Ask students to complete the top of *Document Deep Dive—Flow Chart* (page 295) to support their analysis. Have students label their charts *Transportation Across Time*. Then, have them label the boxes in this order: *Long Ago, Early 1900s, Today, In the Future*. Ask students to draw or write words to describe transportation that correlate to each box. Explain that the *Long Ago* and *Early 1900s* box should describe transportation shown in the photos.

2. Use the following questions to guide a discussion:

   · Why would horses and automobiles be on the same street?

   · Who owned the automobiles? Why didn't everyone own one?

   · Why would someone want to invent automobiles? How were they an improvement to the types of transportation that came before?

   · Why are few or no horses on the streets today?

3. Allow time for students to complete *Investigate Getting Around Town*. Discuss their work and strengthen their analysis skills using the How To activity.

**How To . . .**

**Analyze Images Closely**—Tell students that a magnifying glass is a tool that can be useful for analyzing details in images. Provide students with magnifying glasses, and have them look at the photographs. Encourage students to work in a sequence manner to review the photographs. For example, students can work from left to right and from top to bottom. Remind students to look at the vehicles, the people driving the vehicles, and the effects on the surrounding area. Discuss any new information students noticed.

**Extend**

Ask students to think about how they will get around in the future. Discuss the following questions with students: *What technologies are being developed right now that may affect how we get around? What will happen to older methods of transportation as newer ones become available?*

**Beginning DBAs**

Name: _____ Date: _____

# Investigate Getting Around Town

**Directions:** Automobiles were introduced during the early part of the twentieth century. When they first came out, they were very expensive. Study the images. Then, answer the questions.

1. How were the car and horse-drawn carriages the same?

    Ⓐ They both were unreliable.

    Ⓑ They were both very expensive.

    Ⓒ Everyone had access to both.

    Ⓓ They both took people where they wanted to go.

2. Why did some people have cars and some people still have horse-drawn carriages in the early 1900s?

    _____

    _____

    _____

3. What assumptions can you make about the people in the carriage and in the car?

    _____

    _____

# Teacher Resources

## DBQ Discussion

Activate students' memories of what they did and learned in this unit by giving them one minute to makes lists of as many things as they can related to the unit. Have students share and discuss their lists with partners. Then, choose a question that best fits the needs of your students and is appropriate for their current understanding of the topic. Write the chosen DBQ on the board.

➤ How were people different long ago? How were they the same?

➤ How have advances in technology affected changes in society, both positively and negatively?

Ask students to think about the question independently first. Then, ask students to turn and discuss it with partners. While partners are talking, create a display web or chart listing each of the four documents from the unit. Lead a discussion about the DBQ. Guide students to think about if and how each document can help them answer the question. Record their thinking on the web or chart. Invite a few volunteers to share how they could answer the question in a few sentences.

## Background Information

### Log Cabins Lesson

Pioneers are the people who moved west to settle land in the 1800s. Log cabins were a common style of home they built. The houses were constructed by using lengths of trunks of trees. Notches were cut out at each end of the log and were interlocked with other logs to form the four walls of the cabin. Mud or clay was used to seal the cracks between the logs to make the walls more weatherproof. Many log cabins also had stone fireplaces in them. The fireplaces were used for cooking and heat.

Pioneer homes were usually small—consisting of only one room. Sometimes, families would hang blankets to form walls to divide the room further. Multiple families or extended families would often live together until they were able to build their own log cabins.

Beginning DBAs

# Teacher Resources (cont.)

## Fashion Long Ago Lesson

Beginning DBAs

The Sears catalog was a common source for purchasing goods in households in the United States for decades. The roots of the catalog can be traced back to 1886 when Richard Sears printed an advertisement for watches and jewelry. At that time, many people were moving west because of the Homestead Act of 1862. The expanding railroad and postal systems made ordering things by mail very convenient for people who lived where stores were sparse. From the catalog, people could order a wide range of items, including sewing machines, bicycles, clothing, and eye glasses.

The catalog continued to expand what it offered and eventually became known as the "Wish Book." The holiday catalogs were especially popular as children all over the United States made Christmas wish lists based on the pictures in the catalog.

The Sears catalog is also known for the number of celebrities that either appeared in the catalog or who launched their careers by posing in it. The last Sears catalog was printed in 1993.

## Indigenous People Lesson

The Inuit have lived in the polar region for many centuries. There is a lot of snow and ice in this region, and it is very cold. The resources there are scarce. Inuit made clothes from animal fur. They often had to leave their homes to hunt and fish. Due to the harsh weather conditions, this travel was very difficult, but the Inuit found ways. They traveled across the snow and ice in sleds. The sleds had rails that could easily go along the snow and ice. Dogs often pulled the sleds. When they were away from their homes, they built igloos. Igloos are huts built with blocks of ice. The Inuit went in them to stay warm.

There are many Inuit people living today. Many of them still live in the polar regions. Some of them have moved to cities. Although some Inuit have maintained a lifestyle similar to their ancestors, many of them have adapted to more modern ways of life.

# Teacher Resources *(cont.)*

## Getting Around Town Lesson

In the early part of the twentieth century, many things were changing. People were spreading out all across the country. New technologies were developed to bring electricity and phones into people's homes. Methods of transportation were changing too. Prior to this time, people got around by horse and carriage. Trains, trollies, and subways were other means of public transportation. But these ways had limitations. They had specific stops and times. They sometimes did not provide a direct way to get to where people wanted to go.

In 1885, Karl Benz built the first gasoline automobile in Germany. Shortly after, Henry Ford began building automobiles in the United States. He used an assembly line to build the automobiles faster. This also made them more affordable. But they were not affordable to everyone at first. There was a time when city streets were filled with both horse-drawn buggies and carts as well as automobiles. Automobiles allowed people to get around town faster. They also allowed people to go places more quickly and directly.

## Answer Key

### Investigate Log Cabins (page 87)

1. A
2. The family who lives here is probably composed of an extended family. The house is small, so the family spends time outside too.
3. Because of technology, there are more activities for people to do. There are parks families can go to for entertainment, and they can play video games inside their homes.

### Investigate Fashion Long Ago (page 89)

1. D
2. The dresses would be considered formal today. The skirts are very long and most have long sleeves.
3. It is only showing clothing from one store, so it would not give people an idea of all the women's fashion at the time.

### Investigate Indigenous People (page 91)

1. C
2. The woman is wearing snowshoes that help her move around on the snow easier. There is a sled which could also be used for transportation along the snow.
3. The woman is carrying the baby on her back. The baby is wrapped up and it appears that the wrapping is part of the woman's clothes.

### Investigate Getting Around Town (page 93)

1. D
2. Cars were still new and very expensive. Not everyone could afford a car at first.
3. These people were probably wealthier than others who did not have either. The car was probably more expensive, so those people may be wealthier.

# Beginning Document-Based Assessments

## Unit 7: Money

# Currency—Quarters

## Historical-Thinking Skill

Students will assess the reliability of a quarter as a source for understanding important aspects of the United States.

**Activate**

Flip a quarter, and ask students, "Heads or tails?" Discuss with students why we call one side of a coin *heads* and the other side *tails*. (A head is shown on one side, and a tail is the presumed opposite of a head.)

**Analyze**

1. Have students look at the images on *Investigate Currency—Quarters* (page 99). Ask them to complete *Document Deep Dive—T-Chart* (page 293) to support their analysis. Have students label their T-charts with the headings *Words* and *Images*. Ask them to document what they see in the images to support each heading.

2. Explain to students that documents and artifacts are often influenced by the people who create them and by the purpose for which they are created. Discuss with students what would have been the purpose of the quarter's design and how it might look different if someone else designed it.

3. Use the following questions to guide a discussion:
   - What do the words and images on the quarter symbolize?
   - Do the designs on the backs of quarters represent things that are important to everyone in that state?
   - What other images or words could possibly represent the United States?
   - Would you visit a place based on what you see on their currency? Why or why not?

4. Allow time for students to complete *Investigate Currency—Quarters*. Discuss their work and strengthen their analysis skills using the How To activity.

**How To . . .**

**Read Text on Images**—Tell students that to completely understand a document, they must understand all the parts of the document. Although there are not many words or images on quarters, each item was chosen for significance to our country or the state it represents. Provide resource ideas for how students can understand words such as *liberty* and *E pluribus unum* (e.g., internet, dictionaries, consulting experts). Ask students to highlight any words and confirm their meanings with one of the resources mentioned.

**Extend**

Provide students with other U.S. coins and coins from around the world. Ask them to analyze those coins and compare what they see to their findings from the quarter.

Beginning DBAs

Name: _____ Date: _____

# Investigate Currency–Quarters

**Directions:** The front of the quarter shows George Washington. There are many designs for the back of a quarter. The eagle was commonly shown before 1999. Since then, the design has changed to celebrate important places in the United States. The back also shows the year the coin was made. Study the images. Then, answer the questions.

**Front**

**Back**

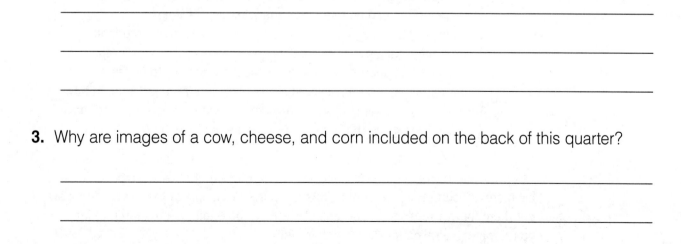

1. What can you tell about Wisconsin from the back of this quarter?

    (A) The capital of Wisconsin is Madison.

    (B) Wisconsin has very flat land.

    (C) Farming is important in Wisconsin.

    (D) Wisconsin is east of Minnesota.

2. Describe the front of the quarter.

    _____

    _____

    _____

3. Why are images of a cow, cheese, and corn included on the back of this quarter?

    _____

    _____

    _____

# Paper Money

## Historical-Thinking Skill

Students will examine currency of the United States.

**Activate**

Ask students to describe what happens when they go the store and want to buy something. Discuss the need for money in our society. How do we get it? What is it used for? What is the difference between real money and money from a game? Ask students how they would know if money was real money or fake money, such as money from a board game.

**Analyze**

1. Have students look at the images on *Investigate Paper Money* (page 101). Ask students to complete the top section of *Document Deep Dive—Bubble Map* (page 294) to support their analysis. Have students look for evidence that the bill in the photograph is real U.S. money and not fake money or money from a different country. Have them circle any clues they find.

2. Have students write the word *evidence* in the center circle of their bubble maps. In the outer circles, ask students to write the evidence they found that the bill is currency of the United States. Pair students, and have them discuss their findings with each other.

3. Use the following questions to guide a discussion:
   · What do the symbols on the bill have in common?
   · What other denominations of bills do you know about? Which of these is common and/or uncommon?
   · Why do countries need different designs on their currencies?

4. Allow time for students to complete *Investigate Paper Money*. Discuss their work and strengthen their analysis skills using the How To activity.

**How To . . .**

**Analyze Images Closely**—Tell students that a magnifying glass is a tool that can be useful for analyzing details in images, especially those as complex as U.S. currency. Provide students with magnifying glasses, and have them look at the photographs. Encourage students to work in a sequence manner to review the photographs. For example, students can work from left to right and from top to bottom. Discuss any details that can be seen with the magnifying glass that cannot be seen as easily without it.

**Extend**

Ask students to look for design elements on currency that make counterfeiting a bill more difficult. Have students circle the parts in the image that were purposely put there for this reason. Encourage students to do additional research to learn how people determine if bills are counterfeit.

    © Shell Education

Name: _____ Date: _____

# Investigate Paper Money

**Directions:** The hundred-dollar bill was redesigned in 2013. It includes advanced technology to combat counterfeiting. Study the images. Then, answer the questions.

1. What is the most prominent feature on the front of the hundred-dollar bill?

   (A) the number 100
   (B) the bald eagle
   (C) a picture of Benjamin Franklin
   (D) the dollar sign

2. What forms of security do you see that can help prevent counterfeiting?

   _____

   _____

   _____

   _____

# Prices

**Beginning DBAs**

**Historical-Thinking Skill**

Students will compare and contrast menus to make inferences about the value of money both long ago and today.

**Activate**

Generate conversation by asking students to identify ways they spend their money. Do they spend their money on wants or needs?  How do they know what they want to spend their money on?  How do they learn if those things go on sale?

**Analyze**

1. Have students look at the advertisements on *Investigate Prices* (page 103). Ask students to complete the top section of *Document Deep Dive—Venn Diagram* (page 292) to support their analysis.  Then, ask them to use the Venn diagram to compare and contrast the advertisements.

2. Ask students to choose a few items to create a meal from both advertisements.  How much does each meal cost?  Which is more expensive? Why?  What does that tell about the value of money today versus long ago?

3. Use the following questions to guide a discussion:
   - Is there a difference between how many items are shown on the advertisement?  Which is easier to read?
   - Why are most of the menu items from today more expensive?  What does that tell about the value of money?
   - Which is more appealing, the handwritten menu or the one with photographs?

4. Allow time for students to complete *Investigate Prices*.  Discuss their work and strengthen their analysis skills using the How To activity.

**How To . . .**

**Read Advertisements**—Identify the pricing on the advertisements as well as the quantities.  Note with students that some of the pricing includes multiple items.  Help students calculate the price difference between a meal from each menu.

**Extend**

Ask students to create menus for a restaurant 50 years in the future.  How much does each item cost?  Why?  Then, lead a discussion about the concept of inflation.

Name: _____  Date: _____

# Investigate Prices

**Directions:** Study the images. Then, answer the questions.

**1.** What is the same about these advertisements?

    Ⓐ They only advertise fruits and vegetables.

    Ⓑ They give one price for many items together.

    Ⓒ They show photos of the food.

    Ⓓ They are both written by hand.

**2.** How do the menus compare? What are the reasons for the differences and the similarities?

_____

_____

_____

_____

# Currency Exchange

Beginning DBAs

> **Historical-Thinking Skill**
>
> Students will use evidence from a currency rate chart to identify currency and exchange rates for countries around the world.

**Activate**

Show students a dollar bill. Ask them what they can use money for. Then, ask if they can use a U.S. dollar in another country. Why or why not? Tell students that today, they will learn about what they would have to do to spend money in another country.

**Analyze**

1. Have students look at the chart on *Investigate Currency Exchange* (page 105). Ask students to complete the top section of *Document Deep Dive—Bubble Map* (page 294) to support their analysis.

2. Have each student choose one country from the chart to focus on. Have them color it with a highlighter. In the center circle of their bubble maps, ask students to write the names of the countries they chose. Then, ask them to write details about their countries' currency in the outer circles of their bubble maps. If they have extra circles, tell students they can write questions or research what the currency looks like.

3. Pair students so that each student in the pair has a different country. Have students compare the information in their bubble maps. Which student can get more currency for a dollar in the country they chose?

4. Use the following questions to guide a discussion:
   - What other countries also call their currency *dollars*?
   - Which currency gives the best value for converting to a U.S. dollar? The worst?
   - Why would countries have their own currency?

5. Allow time for students to complete *Investigate Currency Exchange*. Discuss their work and strengthen their analysis skills using the How To activity.

**How To . . .**

> **Read Charts**—Tell students that the title and/or captions of a chart is the first thing they should read. Have them circle the title on their charts. Tell students that it is important to understand how a chart is organized. Guide students to identify the headings. Explain how the information in each column aligns to the heading. Identify the country names in the first column. Tell students that all the information in that row is for the country at the beginning of the row.

**Extend**

Have students choose a country's currency to research. Have students use a currency converter on the internet to practice converting a U.S. dollar. Have students find images of the currency to compare and contrast with a U.S. dollar.

Name: _____ Date: _____

# Investigate Currency Exchange

**Directions:** This chart shows the exchange rate for currencies of different countries. Study the chart. Then, answer the questions.

**Exchange Rate of Foreign Currency to U.S. Dollars on June 30, 2019**

| Country | Currency Name | Foreign Currency to $1 |
|---|---|---|
| Argentina | peso | 42.69 |
| Germany | euro | 0.88 |
| Iceland | krona | 124.52 |
| India | rupee | 68.60 |
| Japan | yen | 107.73 |
| South Korea | won | 1,154.45 |
| United Kingdom | pound | 0.79 |

1. In which country does the U.S. dollar have the largest exchange rate?

   Ⓐ India
   Ⓑ South Korea
   Ⓒ Iceland
   Ⓓ France

2. Describe how the exchange rate chart is organized into columns.

   _____

   _____

   _____

3. Pretend you are going on a trip to India. Tell about what would happen if you exchanged one U.S. dollar.

   _____

   _____

   _____

# Teacher Resources

## DBQ Discussion

Activate students' memories of what they did and learned in this unit by giving them one minute to makes lists of as many things as they can related to the unit. Have students share and discuss their lists with partners. Then, choose a question that best fits the needs of your students and is appropriate for their current understanding of the topic. Write the chosen DBQ on the board.

➤ What are some of the different types of money in the past and today?

➤ How and why has money changed over time and from place to place?

Ask students to think about the question independently first. Then, ask students to turn and discuss it with partners. While partners are talking, create a display web or chart listing each of the four documents from the unit. Lead a discussion about the DBQ. Guide students to think about if and how each document can help them answer the question. Record their thinking on the web or chart. Invite a few volunteers to share how they could answer the question in a few sentences.

## Background Information

### Currency—Quarters Lesson

The quarter is a coin issued by the United States Mint. It is worth a quarter of a dollar, or 25 cents. The quarter is known as the *George Washington* quarter because a profile of the first president appears on the front, or obverse, of the coin. This side of the coin is also commonly called the *head*. The reverse or back side of the coin is commonly called the *tail*. For decades, it featured the eagle, which is a symbol of the United States. Although the design on the back of the quarter has changed, the words *E pluribus unum* appear on every quarter. The words mean "out of many, one."

In 1999, the U.S. Mint began changing the designs on the backs of quarters in a program called the *50 State Quarters*. Each year, new designs were issued to honor five different states. That program ended in 2009 and ended up including the District of Columbia and other territories. In 2010, a new program began. It is called the *America the Beautiful Quarters* program. The program commemorates beautiful places in the United States, such as national parks and other national sites.

# Teacher Resources (cont.)

## Paper Money Lesson

Countries issue money called *currency* that citizens can use to buy and sell things. In the United States, the main currency is the dollar. There is a symbol used to show the dollar called the *dollar sign*. It looks like this: $.

A dollar can be divided into smaller currency called *cents*. In the United States, currency smaller than a dollar is usually coins, such as pennies, nickels, dimes, or quarters. There is a dollar coin, but it is not commonly used.

Dollar bills are printed on paper. Bills issued in the United States include the one, two, five, ten, twenty, fifty, and one-hundred dollar bills. Each bill has a different design on both the front and back. Because bills are printed, they have historically been easier to counterfeit than coins. Measures have been put into place to try to combat this problem. Fine details are included in the designs that make them hard to replicate. Bills, which were traditionally only printed in green, are now printed in many colors. Holograms are also on bills as well as strips embedded in the bills. All these efforts make it more difficult for people to produce counterfeit money.

The U.S. dollar is one of the most used currencies all over the world. It is widely accepted even in other countries.

## Prices Lesson

People work to earn money. They use the money they earn to buy goods and services. There is a lot of competition to get people to spend their money. One way companies try to get consumers to choose their goods and services is by advertising and offering deals. There are many ways to advertise. Newspapers, television, radio, and the internet are some of the ways. Many restaurants post signs and menus on the street or in windows.

Food is a good that everyone needs. There is a lot of competition among companies to try to get consumers to shop at their stores. Prices have also changed significantly. This is because the value of money has changed.

# Teacher Resources *(cont.)*

Beginning DBAs

## Currency Exchange Lesson

Currency is the money that is used in a country. Most countries have their own currency. In the United States, the currency is the dollar. Some countries accept a U.S. dollar to use to pay for goods or services, but most places require the currency of their own country. In this case, a traveler would have to exchange their money for the currency of the country. This can be done at a bank or other business that handles currency exchange. Usually, people can exchange currency in places such as airports, train stations, and travel agencies. Exchanges usually have signs posted that show the exchange rates for each country's currency.

## Answer Key

### Investigate Currency—Quarters (page 99)
1. C
2. The front of the quarter has a profile picture of George Washington. The word *Liberty* appears on the left side of the quarter, and the phrase *In God We Trust* appears on the right side of the quarter.
3. The cow, cheese, and corn are important parts of Wisconsin's economy.

### Investigate Paper Money (page 101)
1. C
2. There is a ribbon down the front of the bill that is a security protection. There are many detailed images that would make it hard to duplicate. There is also a watermark that can be seen on both sides (not visible in the image, but students may know that Franklin's face can be seen when held to the light).

### Investigate Prices (page 103)
1. B
2. The prices overall are higher in the newer menu. This is because the purchasing value of money has gone down. Both of the ads offer people special deals. This is because people in the past and today like good deals.

### Investigate Currency Exchange (page 105)
1. B
2. The exchange rate chart has countries listed in one column and the currency name in the next column. Then, it has the rate of exchange in the last column.
3. To go on a trip to India, you would have to exchange U.S. dollars for rupees. In exchange for one U.S. dollar, you would receive 68.60 rupees.

# Intermediate Document-Based Assessments

## Unit 8: Life in the Colonies

**Lessons**

**Teacher Resources**

# Colonial Seals

## Historical-Thinking Skill

Students will draw conclusions about the economic, political, and social life in the New England, Middle, and Southern colonies from the historical context of the time.

**Intermediate DBAs**

### Activate

Show students a topographical map of the United States, and ask them to find Massachusetts, Pennsylvania, and Virginia. Discuss some of the geographic features of each of the areas as well as the weather. Google Earth™ is an excellent resource for studying the geography of these areas.

### Analyze

1. Have students look at the images on *Examine Colonial Seals* (page 111). Ask them to complete *Document Analysis—Set the Scene* (page 297) to support their analysis.

2. Ask students to list what they see in each seal on the backs of their analysis sheets. Then, have them group what they have observed into the following categories: people, objects, actions, and words. For additional support, read the background information (page 115) to students, and have them check if their observations were accurate.

3. Use the following questions to guide a discussion:
   · Why did colonies have seals?
   · How do you think seals were used?
   · What can we infer about each colony from its seal?

4. Allow time for students to complete *Examine Colonial Seals*. Discuss their work and strengthen their analysis skills using the How To activity.

**How To . . .**

**Read Special Lettering**—Discuss the pronunciation of Æ with students. Then, share that *et* means "the," *de* means "of," and *u*'s look like *v*'s. Have students write the words in the seals and discuss their meanings. Then, have them write a few phrases using this style.

### Extend

Ask students to think about this question: *Based on what you already know about each colony, what else might you want to include in a seal?* Have them draw their own seals for one of the colonies.

# Examine Colonial Seals

**Directions:** Read the background information, study the images, and answer the questions.

The Massachusetts Bay Colony was founded in 1628. The seal here was used until 1686 and from 1689–1692. The Pennsylvania Colony was founded by William Penn in 1681. The Colonial Seal of Pennsylvania had parts of William Penn's own seal. The Virginia Colony was founded in 1607 by the Virginia Company. It was a joint stock company.

**Massachusetts Bay Seal**

**Pennsylvania Seal**

**Virginia Seal**

1. What images does the Massachusetts Bay Colony seal use to entice people to come to the colony?

   (A) a protective king

   (B) a friendly native in need of help

   (C) symbols of religious freedom

   (D) fields of various crops

2. What do the words and images on the seals reveal about the governing of the colonies?

   _____

   _____

   _____

3. Based on the seals, were there more similarities or differences among the colonies? Does this seem accurate from what you know about the time period?

   _____

   _____

   _____

# Farms and Plantations

**Historical-Thinking Skill**

Students will look for evidence of community and family life and geography of major regions of colonial America.

**Activate**

Show students a map of the United States. Work together to identify where the different colonial regions were—New England colonies, Middle colonies, and Southern colonies. Have them create lists of facts they remember for each region. Then, have students mingle and exchange facts to add to their lists.

**Analyze**

1. Have students look at both pictures on *Examine Farms and Plantations* (page 113). Then, ask students to complete *Document Analysis—Use Evidence* (page 299) to support their analysis. Have students choose picture A or B for the chart in step 2. Ask them to record claims or conclusions they can make about the daily life and geography of the area based on the picture. Then, they should write the evidence from the pictures to support their claims/conclusions.

2. Have students partner with someone who chose a different picture. Have them work together to connect what they learned from the pictures with possible matching colonial regions. Tell them they can write *N.E.*, *M*, and/or *S* next to each claim or conclusion they made. Ask partners to decide which colonial region they believe is represented in each picture.

3. Use the following questions to guide a discussion:
   - What are the similarities and differences between colonial farms and plantations?
   - Which colonies are known for having farms and which are known for having plantations?
   - What evidence is there of what it might be like to live in picture A?
   - What evidence is there of what it might it be like to live in picture B?

4. Allow time for students to complete *Examine Farms and Plantations*. Discuss their work and strengthen their analysis skills using the How To activity.

**How To . . .**

**Make Inferences**—Discuss and define *inference* together as a class. Then, provide the dictionary definition: "a conclusion reached on the basis of evidence and reasoning." Ask students to share the evidence they would use to make a prediction or educated guess about what it was like to live in picture A and picture B. Select two to three additional images to share with students. Have them practice making inferences based on evidence from those images.

**Extend**

Challenge students to find a third image that represents the New England colonies. Then, identify the evidence in that image to infer that it was an example of an area in New England.

**Intermediate DBAs**

Name: _____ Date:_____

# Examine Farms and Plantations

**Directions:** Read the background information, study the images, and answer the questions.

Picture A is an artist's version of a small family farm from the colonial period. Picture B is an artist's version of a plantation from the colonial period.

Picture A

Picture B

1. In which colonies did people make a living from small family farms similar to Picture A?

   (A) New England colonies      (C) Southern colonies

   (B) Middle colonies           (D) all the above

2. In which colonies did people make a living from large plantations similar to Picture B?

   (A) New England colonies      (C) Southern colonies

   (B) Middle colonies           (D) all the above

3. Describe some of the reasons for the differences between farm and plantation family lifestyles.

   _____

   _____

   _____

# Colonies Document-Based Question

## Historical Context

During 1607–1776, America was at the height of colonialism. There were 13 English colonies in the New World. Life in the colonies was different from life in Great Britain. Great Britain took care of governing the colonists and had a say in how things were run. But, the colonists had to use their resources to make a living and survive. In many ways, the colonists were much like everyone else. The colonists had opinions. They cared about their places of business. They had a system to make sure work was completed. By the time of the American Revolution, the colonies had learned to work together for a common good.

### Essay Tasks

**Directions:** Using the documents and your knowledge of colonial America, complete **one** of the following essay tasks. Before you begin your essay, complete the *DBQ Essay Planner* (pages 302–305) to plan your writing.

#### Essay Task ❶

In a well-organized essay, describe the daily life of early colonists and what they valued.

In the essay, remember to:

- Provide details about how the different colonial regions lived.

- Give examples of what each colonial region valued and why they held those values.

- Include a topic sentence, introduction, body, and conclusion.

- Give details to support your ideas.

- Use information found in at least one of the documents to support your argument.

#### Essay Task ❷

Select one of the three colonial regions: New England, Middle, or Southern. In a well-organized essay, explain why that region would be the best place to live in colonial America.

In the essay, remember to:

- Identify and describe the region you are selecting.

- Compare and contrast life in the region you select to the other two regions.

- Include a topic sentence, introduction, body, and conclusion.

- Give details to support your ideas.

- Use information found in at least one of the documents to support your argument.

★ As a bonus, include evidence from an outside source in your essay.

# Teacher Resources

## Background Information

### Colonial Seals Lesson

Seals have been used throughout history. They proved to people that letters were real. In the past, many people were not able to read and write. Those people needed to know that the document's contents were real. A wax imprint of a king or a leader's coat of arms was made by pressing a ring in hot wax. This impression was then used to seal the document and make sure it was authentic.

The Massachusetts Bay Colony Seal was used from about 1629 to 1684. On the seal, the American Indian makes a peaceful sign with his arrow pointing down. He is saying, "Come over and help us." This could show the purpose of the colony as well as the hopes for trade. The Latin phrase around the seal says, "Seal of the Society of Massachusetts Bay in New England."

The Charter of Pennsylvania was given by Charles II of England to William Penn. It stated that the first Great Seal of Pennsylvania would contain the Penn family's coat of arms, which is in the center. This seal was used until the American Revolution.

The Seal of Virginia was the seal of the Virginia Company of London. It was the joint stock company that founded the colony. Then, it became a crown colony in 1624. The seal places King James in the center to honor him. The Latin phrase around the seal means "the seal of your rule over Great Britain and France."

### Farms and Plantations Lesson

In the New England colonies, farming was limited to small family farms. The climate was cold, and there was a short growing season. They used the sea for fishing and commerce. Family farms usually had gardens and produced small crops, just enough so that families were almost self-sufficient. Any extra produce or goods were sold at markets or traded for other goods families needed. Crops and livestock were similar to those in England and included wheat, barley, oats, cattle, swine, and sheep.

The middle colonies also had family farms. These family farms were more productive than those of New England because of the climate. They were known as the breadbasket colonies because they produced the most grain in all the colonies.

In the Southern colonies, the warmer climate allowed for a much longer growing season. The Southern colonies mostly produced cash crops, such as rice and tobacco, to sell for a profit. Large plantations developed, especially along rivers used as highways to transport the crops. Slave labor was used, which generated a profit for enslavers. The Southern colonies also had small family farms for those who could not afford large property tracts or enslaved people. Cotton did not become profitable in this region until after the cotton gin was invented in 1793 by Eli Whitney.

Intermediate DBAs

# Teacher Resources *(cont.)*

## Answer Key

### Examine Colonial Seals (page 111)

1. B

2. Students should mention that the Virginia Seal reveals governing by the crown, the Pennsylvania Seal reveals governing by the proprietor, William Penn, and the Massachusetts Bay Seal reveals governing by the people.

3. There were more differences based on the seals mostly in the founding of the colonies. In particular, Pennsylvania being a proprietorship indicated more independence.

### Examine Farms and Plantations (page 113)

1. D

2. C

3. Students should mention that small farms relied heavily on large families to work the farm together to survive. On plantations, enslaved people became an important economic factor for the cash crops in the South.

### Colonies Document-Based Question (page 114)

Refer to pages 306–307 for the DBQ Rubrics.

Intermediate DBAs

# Intermediate Document-Based Assessments

## Unit 9: Causes of the American Revolution

**Lessons**

**Teacher Resources**

# Common Sense

**Historical-Thinking Skill**

Students will assess the circumstances that brought about the "shot heard 'round the world."

**Activate**

Lead students in a discussion of what it means to have common sense. Then, prompt students to discuss why Thomas Paine titled this particular pamphlet *Common Sense*. Have students list the events that the colonies experienced that might have led Thomas Paine to write this pamphlet.

**Analyze**

1. Have students look at and read the original page of *Common Sense* and the transcription on *Examine Common Sense* (page 119). Ask students to complete *Document Analysis—Set the Scene* (page 297) to support their analysis.

2. Then, ask students to read the words of Paine a couple times with partners and discuss the points or claims he tried to make. Have them list these things on the backs of their papers. Then, ask them to organize those claims and decide which arguments and points of views they can trust and which they should question. Have students share their ideas with the class.

3. Use the following questions to guide a discussion:
   - Where was this document published?
   - What is the author's point of view?
   - What was going on at the time that made the author feel this way?
   - Why does the author say it is "absurd" for Great Britain to rule the colonies?

4. Allow time for students to complete *Examine Common Sense*. Discuss their work and strengthen their analysis skills using the How To activity.

**How To . . .**

**Critically Evaluate an Argument**—Learning how to analyze and critically evaluate arguments will help students make better arguments and strengthen their points of view. Ask students to think about times in their lives where they were trying to make a point to someone else. On separate sheets of paper, have students write their arguments and use bullets to provide the evidence that supports their side. Have students share their arguments and supporting evidence with partners. Ask partners to rate the supporting evidence on a scale of 1 to 5 (5 being most convincing and 1 being not convincing at all).

**Extend**

Have students respond to Thomas Paine and his arguments in *Common Sense* by writing editorials for a newspaper or a news website. Ask students to identify biases and points of views and show how they weaken the argument Thomas Paine is making.

# Examine Common Sense

**Directions:** This is the title page to Thomas Paine's pamphlet titled *Common Sense*. Read the text, and answer the questions.

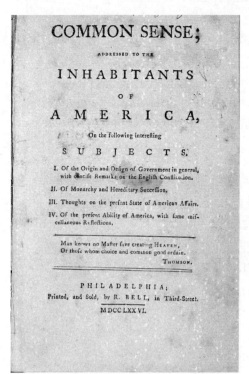

Paine argues against the colonies being ruled by Great Britain: "Small islands, not capable of protecting themselves, are the proper objects for kingdoms to take under their care; but there is something absurd, in supposing a continent to be perpetually governed by an island." Paine argues against the idea of being ruled by a king: "The powers of governing still remaining in the hands of the king, he will have a negative over the whole legislation of this continent. And as he hath shown himself such an... enemy to liberty, and discovered such a thirst for... power, is he, or is he not, a proper person to say to these colonies, 'You shall make no laws but what I please!'" Another argument hints that a revolution will happen soon: "But the most powerful of all arguments, is, that nothing but independence, i.e., a continental form of government, can keep the peace of the continent and preserve it inviolate from civil wars."

—*Common Sense; Addressed to the Inhabitants of America, On the Following Interesting Subjects* by Thomas Paine, 1776

**1.** Explain why Paine thinks the king of England is not fit to rule the colonies.

_____

_____

_____

**2.** What does Paine claim is the only way to keep peace in the continent?

(A) a short-term treaty

(B) a long-term treaty

(C) leaving the colonies all together

(D) nothing but independence

**3.** How did this pamphlet get people interested in declaring independence from Great Britain?

_____

_____

_____

Causes of the American Revolution

# The Boston Massacre

## Historical-Thinking Skill

Students will analyze how the source of information can change how people interpreted the Boston Massacre.

### Activate

Show students a TV or online commercial. Discuss the point of view and the purpose of the commercial with the class. Have students analyze the commercial to find persuasive evidence from it. Ask students if they believe commercials are an example of propaganda.

### Analyze

1. Have students study the images on *Examine the Boston Massacre* (page 121). Assign one image to part of the class and the other image to the other part of your class. Let them focus on and analyze their images.

2. Have students find partners with the opposite image of the Boston Massacre, and have them compare and contrast the two images.

3. With their partners, have students complete *Document Analysis—Consider the Source* (page 298) to support their analysis of each image of the Boston Massacre.

4. Use the following questions to guide a discussion:
   - What is going on in this picture?
   - Who do you think is the aggressor in this image?
   - What is propaganda?
   - Why would Crispus Attucks's death have been depicted more predominantly in the later image than the earlier one?

5. Allow time for students to complete *Examine the Boston Massacre*. Discuss their work and strengthen their analysis skills using the How To activity.

**How To . . .**

**Identify Point of View**—Tell students there are three basic points of view: objective, first person, and third person. Understanding the point of view in a document can help identify bias and allow you to draw your own conclusions. First-person point of view is used when a person tells the story directly from their experiences using the word "I." Third-person point of view is more limited because the person can retell the story from indirect experiences. Objective point of view is used when just the facts are given without interpretation. Work with students to identify examples of each type.

### Extend

Have students research and find written commentary on the Boston Massacre at the time (see page 309 for source ideas). Discuss what evidence they find and whether it supports or conflicts with the portrayal in the images.

Intermediate DBAs

Name: _____  Date: _____

# Examine the Boston Massacre

**Directions:** Paul Revere created the left image in 1770. William L. Champney created the right image in 1855. Study the images, and answer the questions.

by Paul Revere

by William L. Champney

1. Why would the event shown in these images be called the Boston Massacre?

   _____

   _____

   _____

2. What about each of these sources makes you question the reliability?

   _____

   _____

   _____

3. How would Paul Revere's image be used as propaganda?

   Ⓐ to try and get the colonists angry so they fight the British

   Ⓑ to stir up support for the British taxes

   Ⓒ to help develop a feeling of partnership between the colonies

   Ⓓ to communicate the true story of what happened in Boston

# Declaration of Independence

Intermediate DBAs

## Historical-Thinking Skill

Students will examine the causes and effects of the Declaration of Independence.

**Activate**

Explain to students that when American towns received their copies of the Declaration of Independence in the summer of 1776, citizens read it aloud to crowds of people as a community event. Assign groups of students sentences or passages from the Declaration of Independence. Allow them to practice reading their parts aloud. Have a class performance of the lines.

**Analyze**

1. Have students study the excerpt on *Examine the Declaration of Independence* (page 123). Ask them to complete the top section of *Document Analysis— Think Across Time* (page 300) to support their analysis.

2. As a class, generate a list of seven to ten events before and during the American Revolution. Have students write the events onto scraps of paper or sticky notes. Then, in small groups, have students place the events in order. Once the order has been confirmed, students can write the events on the time lines at the bottom of their analysis sheets.

3. Use the following questions to guide a discussion:
   - How would the American Revolution have been different if certain events did not happen or if they happened in a different order?
   - What is the document's tone and purpose?
   - How would the world be different today if this document had not existed?
   - Is this document propaganda? Why or why not?
   - How might a colonist or a soldier have felt hearing this read aloud?

4. Allow time for students to complete *Examine the Declaration of Independence*. Discuss their work and strengthen their analysis skills using the How To activity.

**How To . . .**

**Identify Time Periods**—Tell students that it is possible to still know the time period of a primary source even if the date is not provided. Using context clues, such as language and vocabulary, can be one strategy. Identifying the author or creator of the primary source is another strategy. Have students look for clues of the time period in the language of this document. Then, ask students to rewrite a few sentences using modern language. Discuss what things about this document would be similar and different if it were written today.

**Extend**

Have students examine the life and philosophies of John Locke. Ask them to identify how Locke's philosophies influenced the Declaration of Independence.

© Shell Education

# Examine the Declaration of Independence

**Directions:** Read the excerpt of the Declaration of Independence, and answer the questions.

In every stage of these Oppressions We have Petitioned for Redress in the most humble terms: Our repeated Petitions have been answered only by repeated injury. A Prince whose character is thus marked by every act which may define a Tyrant, is unfit to be the ruler of a free people. Nor have We been wanting in attentions to our British brethren. We have warned them from time to time of attempts by their legislature to extend an unwarrantable jurisdiction over us. We have reminded them of the circumstances of our emigration and settlement here. We have appealed to their native justice and magnanimity, and we have conjured them by the ties of our common kindred to disavow these usurpations, which, would inevitably interrupt our connections and correspondence. They too have been deaf to the voice of justice and of consanguinity. We must, therefore, acquiesce in the necessity, which denounces our Separation, and hold them, as we hold the rest of mankind, Enemies in War, in Peace Friends.

We, therefore, the Representatives of the United States of America, . . . solemnly publish and declare, That these united colonies are, and of Right ought to be, Free and Independent states; that they are Absolved from all Allegiance to the British Crown, and that all political connection between them and the state of Great Britain, is and ought to be totally dissolved; and that as Free and Independent States, they have full Power to levy War, conclude Peace, contract Alliances, establish Commerce, and to do all other Acts and Things which Independent States may of right do.

—Declaration of Independence, July 4, 1776

Causes of the American Revolution

1. Name and describe at least one way that the colonists claim they have tried to deal with their problems with Great Britain.

   _____

   _____

   _____

2. Provide at least two reasons why this document was important in the lives of the American colonists.

   _____

   _____

   _____

3. What does the phrase "British brethren" mean in the context of this document?

   (A) British enemy          (C) British tax payers

   (B) British people         (D) British government

# American Revolution Document-Based Question

## Historical Context

In colonial America, an argument over rights turned into a war. The British collected more taxes. "Taxation without representation" became the rallying cry against Britain. Colonists began to resist British rule more and more. Getting the colonists to fight for freedom was not easy. Each colony wanted to keep its power. The colonies had their own cultures and priorities. However, they agreed to fight for liberty.

### Essay Tasks

**Directions:** Using the documents and your knowledge of the American Revolution, complete **one** of the following essay tasks. Before you begin your essay, complete the *DBQ Essay Planner* (pages 302–305) to plan your writing.

#### Essay Task ①

In a well-organized essay, describe how the colonial Patriots convinced other colonists to support the idea of independence from Great Britain.

In the essay, remember to:

- Evaluate the actions of the Patriots that persuaded others to follow them before the Declaration of Independence was written.

- Include a topic sentence, introduction, body, and conclusion.

- Give details to support your ideas.

- Use information found in the documents to support your argument.

#### Essay Task ②

In a well-organized essay, describe three protests, documents, or events that contributed to the beginning of the American Revolution.

In the essay, remember to:

- Address all key issues of the assigned task.

- Incorporate specific details that prove an understanding and knowledge of this topic.

- Include a topic sentence, introduction, body, and conclusion.

- Give details to support your ideas.

- Use information found in the documents to support your argument.

★ As a bonus, include evidence from an outside source in your essay.

© Shell Education

# Teacher Resources

## Background Information

### Common Sense Lesson

Thomas Paine was a recent British immigrant to the American colonies. He became famous when he wrote a pamphlet called *Common Sense*. This simple document was published in Philadelphia. *Common Sense* sparked the movement for the colonies to declare independence from Great Britain. In *Common Sense*, Paine writes about why the colonies should be independent. He argues that monarchies are an inefficient form of government. He shows the economic benefits the colonies would receive if they were independent. He also points out the absurdity of a small island ruling a large continent. *Common Sense* sold 150,000 copies in its first of several printings, finally reaching about half a million copies sold. Paine is credited with persuading the colonists toward independence. The Continental Congress declared independence within six months of the pamphlet's publication. Paine later wrote another inspirational work, *The Crises*. General George Washington used it to raise the morale of his troops shortly before the Battle of Trenton.

Intermediate DBAs

### The Boston Massacre Lesson

Parliament repealed the Townshend Acts, but that did not help Bostonians who had British soldiers marching in their streets. On a snowy March day in 1770, young colonial boys hurled insults at a British soldier who then knocked one of the boys down with his rifle. A crowd gathered as the boy cried out for help. The soldier called more guards over, including Colonel Thomas Preston. Soon, the crowd of about 400 men began throwing snowballs and chunks of ice at the soldiers. One soldier was hit with a club, and shortly after that, the soldiers fired into the crowd. Five colonists were killed, including Crispus Attucks, and more were wounded.

After Governor Hutchinson promised to put the soldiers on trial for murder, the city calmed down, but for a while, it was in a state of riot. Attorney John Adams decided to take the case and defend the soldiers, even though he faced opposition from many colonists, including his cousin Samuel Adams. John Adams wanted to prove that the soldiers could have a fair trial, even in Boston, and he won their case on the grounds of self-defense. He probably also helped the Sons of Liberty, including his cousin, by not introducing some evidence that may have implicated them.

The colonists called the riot the Boston Massacre. They used it as propaganda against the British. Silversmith Paul Revere created an engraving that portrayed the colonists as innocent bystanders. This image was printed in newspapers and helped convince many neutral colonists to join the Patriots' cause.

# Teacher Resources *(cont.)*

## Declaration of Independence Lesson

By June of 1776, the delegates of the Continental Congress began to debate the idea of independence that Virginia had proposed. Congress created a committee of five men to

write a document declaring independence. Thomas Jefferson was chosen from the committee to compose the main draft. When the committee presented the document to Congress, the other delegates quickly began to edit the document. Finally, on July 2, the Congress officially adopted the document.

Copies of the document were sent to printers throughout the colonies. George Washington had a copy read to his troops. The document established the reasons the colonies were justified in separating from Great Britain. Jefferson paraphrased John Locke, arguing that the duty of government is to protect natural human rights. When government fails to do so, mankind has the right to change that government.

In this excerpt, Jefferson explains that the choice for independence was a last resort. His reference to "A Prince whose character is thus marked by every act which may define a Tyrant, is unfit to be the ruler of a free people" is a reference to Niccolò Machiavelli's book *The Prince*. In *The Prince*, he argues that sometimes a prince needs to assert his power broadly for the good of the state, even if his actions are cruel. The last paragraph formally recognizes the new United States of America.

## Answer Key

### Examine Common Sense (page 119)

1. The king is an "enemy to liberty." He has a "thirst for power." He should not be allowed to tell the colonies which laws he wants them to follow.

2. D

3. Answers may include that the arguments were persuasive because they touched on the personal reasons that the British king was a poor leader. The pamphlet also stated that war was inevitable. Therefore, the people should join the cause and help fight against British rule, or they would suffer when the war began.

### Examine the Boston Massacre (page 121)

1. It is called the Boston Massacre because it happened in Boston. The picture shows unarmed people being killed, which is a massacre.

2. Students may think that Paul Revere was biased because he created the image for propaganda. William L. Champney's image was created 85 years after the event, which could also affect its reliability.

3. A

### Examine the Declaration of Independence (page 123)

1. Answers may include that the colonists claim that they "Petitioned for Redress," "warned them (British citizens) from time to time of attempts by their legislature to extend an unwarrantable jurisdiction over us," and appealed to the British citizens' "native justice."

2. Answers may include that it was important to the colonists because it reminded them and everyone else that they tried to work with Great Britain, but Great Britain refused to work with them. It shows that the colonists had a reason to declare independence. It was also important because it defined the goal that the colonists were reaching toward—full independence.

3. B

### American Revolution Document-Based Question (page 124)

Refer to pages 306–307 for the DBQ Rubrics.

© Shell Education

Intermediate DBAs

# Intermediate Document-Based Assessments

## Unit 10: American Indians

**Lessons**

**Teacher Resources**

# Indian Removal Act

## Historical-Thinking Skill

Students will examine the causes and effects of the Indian Removal Act.

### Activate

Make a copy of the image and cut the first 12 lines so they are separated from one another. Have students work with partners to rewrite the lines they are given. For example, students could abbreviate United States to U.S. to make it easier to read. Have partners read it aloud in order. Tell them that this is a bill from the U.S. government. Discuss their initial thoughts or impressions.

Intermediate DBAs

### Analyze

1. Have students study the document on *Examine the Indian Removal Act* (page 129). Ask them to complete *Document Analysis—Think Across Time* (page 300) to support their analysis. Guide students as needed to complete their time lines.

2. Have students research to find and compare and contrast two maps of American Indian tribes. The first map should identify American Indian tribes before the settlement of the American Colonies, and the second map should be of American Indian tribes today.

3. In small groups, have students summarize the effect of actions such as the Indian Removal Act on American Indian tribes.

4. Use the following questions to guide a discussion:
   - Why do you think the lines are numbered?
   - Where were the American Indian tribes living before this bill?
   - Why did the government want to move these tribes west of the Mississippi River?
   - How do the effects of this bill and other acts like it make an impact today?

5. Allow time for students to complete *Examine the Indian Removal Act*. Discuss their work and strengthen their analysis skills using the How To activity.

### How To . . .

**Use Vocabulary to Unlock a Source**—Explain to students that vocabulary in official government documents can sometimes be difficult to understand. When analyzing a document like this, they should identify key pieces of vocabulary that they do not recognize or understand. Then, using a thesaurus (book or computer), have them find the vocabulary term and look up its synonyms. Have them go back to the document and replace the unknown vocabulary with synonyms that they do know and see if that helps unlock the meaning of the document.

### Extend

Have students research both fiction and nonfiction books on the Trail of Tears. Then, have each student choose a book to read and create a presentation summarizing it for the class.

# Examine the Indian Removal Act

**Directions:** Read the background information, study the image, and answer the questions.

On May 28, 1830, President Andrew Jackson signed the Indian Removal Act. This act authorized the U.S. government to trade unsettled lands west of the Mississippi for Indian lands within U.S. states. Some tribes left their homes peacefully, but many tribes resisted the act.

> 21st CONGRESS.
> 1st SESSION.
>
> # S. 102.
>
> IN SENATE OF THE UNITED STATES.
> FEBRUARY 22, 1830.
>
> Mr. WHITE, from the Committee on Indian Affairs, reported the following bill; which was read, and passed to a second reading:
>
> # A BILL
>
> To provide for an exchange of lands with the Indians residing in any of the States or Territories, and for their removal West of the river Mississippi.
>
> 1   Be it enacted by the Senate and House of Representatives
> 2   of the United States of America in Congress assembled, That
> 3   it shall and may be lawful for the President of the United
> 4   States to cause so much of any territory belonging to the Unit-
> 5   ed States, West of the river Mississippi, not included in any
> 6   State, and to which the Indian title has been extinguished, as
> 7   he may judge necessary, to be divided into a suitable number
> 8   of districts, for the reception of such tribes or nations of Indi-
> 9   ans as may choose to exchange the lands where they now re-
> 10  side, and remove there; and to cause each of said districts to
> 11  be so described by natural or artificial marks, as to be easily
> 12  distinguished from every other.
> 1     SEC. 2. And be it further enacted, That it shall and may
> 2   be lawful for the President to exchange any or all of such
> 3   districts, so to be laid off and described, with any tribe or na-
> 4   tion of Indians now residing within the limits of any of the

**American Indians**

**1.** Why was this bill created?

_____

_____

**2.** What did this bill mean for American Indians?

(A) Tribes will be forced to share their land together with settlers.

(B) Tribes will volunteer to move west of the Mississippi River.

(C) Tribes will be forced to live west of the Mississippi River.

(D) Tribes will not go to war with settlers.

**3.** How did this change the lives of American Indians?

_____

_____

# Tecumseh and Sitting Bull

**Historical-Thinking Skill**

Students will evaluate how early state and federal policy influenced various American Indian tribes.

**Activate**

Ask students to make a list of characteristics that make someone a great leader. Write students' responses on the board, and as a class, identify the top five characteristics of a great leader. Then, explain that students will learn about two American Indian leaders, and they should see if those leaders possess these characteristics.

**Analyze**

1. Have students study the images on *Examine Tecumseh and Sitting Bull* (page 131). Ask them to work with partners to complete *Document Analysis—Set the Scene* (page 297) to support their analysis. On the front of their sheets, have students fill in their graphic organizers with everything they know about Tecumseh from the image and their own background knowledge. On the backs of their sheets, have students re-create the concept wheel and write the same type of information for Sitting Bull.

2. Use the following questions to guide a discussion:
   - Why was the portrait of Tecumseh painted?
   - Why was this photograph of Sitting Bull taken?
   - What are the points of view of the artists?
   - What are two inferences you can make about these pictures?
   - Why are these portraits historically important?

3. Allow time for students to complete *Examine Tecumseh and Sitting Bull*. Discuss their work and strengthen their analysis skills using the How To activity.

**How To . . .**

**Interpret Portraits**—Explain to students that interpreting any work of art can be difficult. When they interpret a portrait, they should look for meaning. Have them examine the following features closely: clothing; size of the portrait; other objects, animals, or symbols and what they may indicate; what the person's face or pose can reveal about the personality of the person; and the point of view of the artist. Have them use their answers to make inferences and then check additional resources to see if their interpretations were accurate. Have students practice this with other famous portraits.

**Extend**

Sitting Bull was killed on December 15, 1890, for his connection to the Ghost Dance movement. The Ghost Dance movement was a spiritual movement that prophesized the return of traditional culture. Have students organize and conduct a class debate about the Ghost Dance movement. Did it help preserve traditional American Indian culture, or did it actually bring about its end?

# Examine Tecumseh and Sitting Bull

**Directions:** Read the background information, study the images, and answer the questions.

The image on the left is a portrait of Tecumseh created from a wood block print. Tecumseh was a Shawnee Indian chief in the early 1800s. The image on the right is a photograph of Sitting Bull taken in 1885 by David Francis Barry. Sitting Bull was a leader of the Hunkpapa Lakota tribe in the late 1800s.

1. Which chief fought in the War of 1812? Which chief battled George Custer at Little Bighorn in 1876?

_____

_____

2. How were the lives and actions of these men influenced from the time and place they lived?

_____

_____

_____

3. What were these leaders trying to achieve?

_____

_____

_____

# Assimilation

## Historical-Thinking Skill

Students will draw conclusions using evidence of how early state and federal policy influenced various American Indian tribes.

**Activate**

Show students some examples of Latin roots and their meanings. See if they can determine some examples of words that use those roots. Examples: *Fac*, to make, factory, manufacturer; *aud*, to hear, audience, audition. Then, write the word *assimilate* on the board. Have student make inferences about what the root *similate* means. The root comes from *similis*, meaning "like, resembling, or of the same kind." Discuss the meaning of the word *assimilation*.

**Analyze**

1. Have students study the photographs on *Examine Assimilation* (page 133). Ask students to complete *Document Analysis—Use Evidence* (page 299) to support their analysis. Guide students as needed to complete their charts. Remind them to make some claims and/or draw some conclusions from the photos and their background knowledge. Then, they should write evidence to support what they write in the first column.

2. Have students share their charts in small groups. Ask students to give one another feedback about how strong and supportive their evidence is.

3. Use the following questions to guide a discussion and help students add to their charts:

   • What was the purpose of the Carlisle School?

   • Why were these photographs taken? How do you know?

   • What sacrifices did the children make at the school?

   • Why might it be difficult for students to return to live with their tribes?

4. Allow time for students to complete *Examine Assimilation*. Discuss their work and strengthen their analysis skills using the How To activity.

**How To . . .**

**Identify Bias**—Explain to students that bias is when something shows a preference or prejudice for or against a person or idea. As you read, see, or listen to materials, keep the following questions in mind to help you identify bias: *What facts has the creator left out? What other information is needed to understand the entire story?* Ask students to try and identify possible bias in the photographs.

**Extend**

Ask students to create lessons on language that would validate and affirm a student's home culture while helping them build an understanding of mainstream American culture.

# Examine Assimilation

**Directions:** Read the background information, study the images, and answer the questions.

These photos were taken at the Carlisle School in 1886. They show students when they entered the school and after they had been there for some time.

1. What visible changes did students at the Carlisle School go through?

    (A) They no longer used their native language.

    (B) They dressed in western clothing.

    (C) They embraced western traditions.

    (D) They were successful students.

2. What changes can you infer the students at the Carlisle School went through that you cannot see in the images?

    _____

    _____

    _____

3. Why might these photos not be considered concrete evidence of the effects of attending the Carlisle School?

    _____

    _____

    _____

American Indians

# American Indians Document-Based Question

## Historical Context

After America gained independence, settlers continued moving westward. Settlers and American Indians disagreed over land rights. The Louisiana Purchase doubled the size of the country. While the land was vast, many different American Indian tribes called much of that land home. Early on, many tribes helped settlers, including the Lewis and Clark exploration team commissioned to map out the new territory. But over time, events such as the gold rush would change their relationships forever.

**American Indians**

## Essay Tasks

**Directions:** Use the documents and your knowledge of American Indians to complete **one** of the following essay tasks. Before you begin your essay, complete the *DBQ Essay Planner* (pages 302–305) to plan your writing.

### Essay Task ❶

In a well-organized essay, describe how settlers limited the freedom of the American Indians in the 1800s.

In your essay, remember to:

- Tell about specific hardships that American Indians suffered because of American actions.

- Include information about famous individuals who tried to achieve freedom for their people.

- Include a topic sentence, introduction, body, and conclusion.

- Give details to support your ideas.

- Use information found in the documents to support your argument.

### Essay Task ❷

In a well-organized essay, support or oppose the U.S. government policies toward American Indians during the 1800s.

In the essay, remember to:

- Establish the policies that you will support or oppose.

- Include details and evidence that support your argument.

- Include a topic sentence, introduction, body, and conclusion.

- Give details to support your ideas.

- Use information found in the documents to support your argument.

★ As a bonus, include evidence from an outside source in your essay.

# Teacher Resources

## Background Information

### Indian Removal Act Lesson

Government treaties with American Indians were common. The government offered to buy land from the tribes, and this was a peaceful transaction. In some of the treaties, the government would provide such things as clothing, farming tools, food, and horses to help the American Indians live.

In 1814, the U.S. government began a new campaign to move five of the largest tribes to the West. The tribes did not want to move, but they signed the documents to make the government happy, hoping they would be allowed to retain some of their land. This was a voluntary period of movement, so most tribes still stayed in the East. They adopted some practices of white settlers to try to assimilate into society, such as large-scale farming and education practices.

In 1830, Congress passed the Indian Removal Act. This law gave the president the right to force tribes to move to the West. It affected all tribes living east of the Mississippi River, and any tribe could be moved to the newly designated Indian Territory. Indian Territory was land on the west side of the Mississippi River. It was reserved specifically for the tribes, thus the term *reservations*. The government promised the tribes that white settlers would never be allowed there.

### Tecumseh and Sitting Bull Lesson

Tecumseh was a Shawnee Indian chief who worked to organize a vast American Indian power, uniting several tribes to confront the westward migration of the United States. In August 1811, William Henry Harrison, the governor of Indian Territory, met with Tecumseh. Harrison worried about Tecumseh more than anyone else. Tecumseh's older brother, named The Prophet, had dreamed of an America that would return to the way it was before the Europeans arrived. Tecumseh worked to achieve that dream by recruiting American Indians and uniting them in his alliance. Not all American Indians supported him, and those who did not support him helped the Americans track him. Later, Tecumseh was killed at the Battle of Thames.

The Sioux was one of the most dominant tribes in the Great Plains and Rocky Mountains. A gold rush in 1874 attracted many gold seekers to South Dakota's Black Hills. However, it was sacred land to the Plains Indians and was protected by the Fort Laramie Treaty of 1868. Lieutenant Colonel George Armstrong Custer trespassed onto this land in South Dakota's Black Hills when looking for both a place to build a fort and find gold. The Sioux, along with the Cheyenne and a few other tribes, attacked Custer in southern Montana at the Battle of Little Bighorn in the summer of 1876. Sitting Bull and Crazy Horse, along with Cheyenne leader Two Moons, led the attack, killing all 250 of Custer's men except one scout. The tribes were united for this brief moment and celebrated a stunning military victory.

# Teacher Resources *(cont.)*

**Intermediate DBAs**

## Assimilation Lesson

The Carlisle School and others like it developed in an attempt to help American Indians adapt and change from their own culture to what was deemed the appropriate American culture. The Carlisle School opened in Pennsylvania in 1879. The push to educate American Indian children dates back to the first Europeans in America who worked to spread the Christian religion to the American Indians, whom they considered pagans. More than 12,000 American Indian children attended the Carlisle School between 1879 and 1918.

Once at the boarding school, American Indian children were forced to abandon all external remnants of their culture. Their hair was cut, they had to wear new clothes, and they were given new names. They were punished if they spoke in their native language. The school included both academic and vocational studies, and all students had chores to do.

Some children adapted successfully and then returned to their tribes to help them adapt. Some children ran away. Others returned to their tribes before they were indoctrinated and were sometimes referred to as the "lost people." As the American Indians from different tribes found common ground with one another, friendships developed among them. This was a rare positive effect of the boarding school that some historians say led to the Pan-Indian identity that is evident now between all tribes. Tribes anguished over losing both their children and their tribal identities.

## Answer Key

### Examine the Indian Removal Act (page 129)
1. This bill was created so that the president could force tribes to move west.
2. C
3. It might have caused wars because they had to live in new areas that were not so well defined. It might have changed what they ate because of the animals available to hunt. It may have changed their housing/clothing needs because of the differences in climate and weather.

### Examine Tecumseh and Sitting Bull (page 131)
1. Tecumseh fought in the War of 1812. Sitting Bull fought at Little Bighorn.
2. Answers will vary and should highlight the conflict between American Indians and Europeans.
3. Answers may include that both leaders wanted to preserve Indian lands and culture. They did not want to adapt to the white man's way of life or move to reservations. They worked to bring their people together to fight for the right to live as they always had.

### Examine Assimilation (page 133)
1. B
2. Answers could include religious conversion, language conversion to English only, or separating tribes so that they could not speak their traditional languages. Harsh discipline was also used.
3. Answers could include that the photos were posed portraits, and photography at the time would have required them to pose for a long period. They also seem to have the intent of showing how the students have benefited from the school. They could not show concrete evidence of the mental and emotional effects of the school.

### American Indians Document-Based Question (page 134)
Refer to pages 306–307 for the DBQ Rubrics.

# Intermediate Document-Based Assessments

## Unit 11: Civil War

**Lessons**

**Teacher Resources**

# Missouri Compromise

**Activate**

Ask students to share with partners times when they had issues with someone and they were forced to compromise. Have them share the issues or topics they compromised on and the results. What did both sides get? Were both sides happy? Did the compromise solve the issue?

**Analyze**

1. Make copies of the map on *Examine the Missouri Compromise* (page 139), and cut each copy into puzzle pieces. Place the puzzles into bags and distribute them to students. Have students work in small groups to put the puzzle together.

2. Write the words *Missouri Compromise* on the board. Ask students if they have any ideas on what the compromise would have been by looking at the map. Have students share their ideas.

3. Distribute copies of *Examine the Missouri Compromise* to students. Ask them to complete *Document Analysis—Set the Scene* (page 297) to support their analysis. Guide students as needed to add the information about the historical context around the Missouri Compromise.

4. Use the following questions to guide a discussion:
   - Were people in 1820 addressing the moral issue of slavery with the Missouri Compromise?
   - What was the Missouri Compromise?
   - What would have been a better solution?

5. Allow time for students to complete *Examine the Missouri Compromise*. Discuss their work and strengthen their analysis skills using the How To activity.

**How To . . .**

**Read Maps**—Explain to students that maps do more than teach geography. Maps show change over time and tell about the people who made them and the time periods in which they lived. The first step is to examine and identify the parts of a map. Most maps have titles and other labels, which give key information about them. The author, or source, of a map can give the reader an idea about its purpose and reason for creation. Have students circle the parts of the Missouri Compromise map that give them information and help them understand the time and place it was created.

**Extend**

Have students write newspaper articles from the perspective of Northern or Southern newspapers about the Missouri Compromise.

Name: _____ Date: _____

# Examine the Missouri Compromise

**Directions:** This map was published in 1919 by James McConnell. Study the map, and answer the questions. Look at a current map of the United States to help you.

THE MISSOURI COMPROMISE, 1820.

THE MISSOURI COMPROMISE

In 1818 Missouri asked admission to the Union as a slave state.

In 1819 there were eleven free states and eleven slave states.

For more than two years Congress debated on the question of the admission of Missouri as a slave state.

Congress was finally persuaded by Henry Clay to accept the Missouri Compromise of 1820 which provided that Missouri should enter the Union as a slave state but prohibited slavery in all other territory of the Louisiana Purchase north of 36° 30.

In 1820 Maine was admitted as a free state. Therefore, when Missouri was admitted in 1821 as a slave state, the number of free states and slave states were again equal.

The western boundary of Missouri at the time it was admitted as a state was a straight north and south line to the southern boundary of Iowa. The triangular portion between that line and the Missouri River was purchased from the Sae and Fox Indians in 1837. It was known as a the Platte Purchase.

Civil War

1. Name at least two states that were labeled as slave states on this map.

    _____

    _____

2. What is the closest free state to Missouri?

    (A) Nebraska          (C) Iowa

    (B) Illinois          (D) Tennessee

3. Look at the slave states and the free states. Although the slave states have more land area, how are the slave states and free states equal?

    _____

    _____

    _____

# Fugitive Slave Act

Historical-Thinking Skill

Students will examine differing points of view related to the Fugitive Slave Act.

**Activate**

Discuss what a political cartoon or illustration is with students. Guide students to make a connection to political memes created and shared today.

**Analyze**

1. Have students study the poster on *Examine the Effects of the Fugitive Slave Act* (page 141). Ask them to complete *Document Analysis—Make Connections* (page 296) to support their analysis. Have students label the top two columns of their graphic organizers with *Northern Perspective* and *Southern Perspective*. Have them work with partners to write ideas of what each side's reaction to the Fugitive Slave Act would be at the time it was issued.

2. Ask students to label the bottom section of their graphic organizers *Reasons*. Then, have them write reasons for the differences and similarities between the two sides.

3. Use the following questions to guide a discussion:
   - What is happening in the image?
   - How are the men dressed? Why did the artist do this?
   - Why was this illustration created and published?
   - What is the point of view of the artist?

4. Allow time for students to complete *Examine the Effects of the Fugitive Slave Act*. Discuss their work and strengthen their analysis skills using the How To activity.

**How To . . .** **Make Inferences**—Review with students that an inference is a conclusion that is reached using evidence and reasoning. Ask students what inferences can be made about the men in the drawing based on things such as their clothing, expressions, positions, and surroundings.

**Extend**

Have students research the stories of escaped enslaved people. What was their journey to freedom like? Where did they go? What was life like for those people who found freedom?

# Examine the Effects of the Fugitive Slave Act

**Directions:** This political illustration portrays the artist's views of the effects of the Fugitive Slave Act. Study the poster, and answer the questions.

**1.** What is happening in this image?

_____

_____

_____

**2.** What is the artist's purpose or message?

_____

_____

**3.** Why would the artist include the first line of the Declaration of Independence in the bottom right?

_____

_____

_____

# Emancipation Proclamation

## Historical-Thinking Skill

Students will formulate a personal interpretation of the Emancipation Proclamation to gain a better understanding of the significant moment in history.

**Activate**

Provide students with copies of the Emancipation Proclamation. Then, in small groups, have the groups rewrite the text in their own words. Allow each group to share its paraphrased versions aloud.

**Analyze**

1. Have students look at the image and read the excerpt on *Examine the Emancipation Proclamation* (page 143). Then, have them complete the top section of *Document Analysis—Make Connections* (page 296) to support their analysis.

2. Read the background information about the painting with students. Ask students to circle each item mentioned in the painting. On the bottom section of their analysis sheets, ask students to label the two columns *Painting* and *Symbolism*. Have students work in partners to list the different things they see in the painting and then write the symbolism of those things. In the bottom section of their graphic organizers, ask students to write a few sentences describing the connection these symbols have to the Emancipation Proclamation.

3. Use the following questions to guide a discussion:
   - How would Southerners view this document?
   - How would Union soldiers view this document?
   - How would enslaved people view this document?
   - Why might enslaved people not have learned about the Emancipation Proclamation right away?

4. Allow time for students to complete *Examine the Emancipation Proclamation*. Discuss their work and strengthen their analysis skills using the How To activity.

**How To . . .**

**Analyze Symbolism**—Explain to students that symbolism in art could be an action, a person, a place, a word, or an object used to represent an abstract idea. The key to understanding symbolism in visual arts is having solid background knowledge of the subject. Some symbols can be obvious. Other symbols require more effort to fully understand their meaning. Symbols can add dimension to the work's meaning. First, have students identify the symbols. Then, have them use outside resources to research their meaning and make connections.

**Extend**

Have students select another historic moment in the Civil War and create images that represent that moment. Their images should include a minimum of four symbols that are used to convey a message about the historic moment.

**Intermediate DBAs**

Name: _____ Date:_____

# Examine the Emancipation Proclamation

**Directions:** Read the background information. Then, study the painting, read the excerpt from the document, and answer the questions.

This image is based on a painting by David Gilmour Blythe. It shows Lincoln writing the Emancipation Proclamation in his study. His left hand is on a Bible that rests on a copy of the U.S. Constitution. There are busts of former presidents Andrew Jackson and James Buchanan in the image. The scales of justice are on the left and the American flag covers the window.

"That on the first day of January, in the year of our Lord one thousand eight hundred and sixty-three, all persons held as slaves within any State or designated part of a State, the people whereof shall then be in rebellion against the United States, shall be then, thenceforward, and forever free."

—*Emancipation Proclamation, January 1, 1863*

1. According to the excerpt, in what states would the enslaved people be freed?

   _____

   _____


2. The painting shows Lincoln writing the Emancipation Proclamation. List an object you can see in the painting, and explain how that object may have served as an inspiration for Lincoln as he was writing.

   _____

   _____

   _____

   _____

# Civil War Amendments

**Historical-Thinking Skill**

Students will examine the effects of the civil war and the significance of the Thirteenth, Fourteenth, and Fifteenth Amendments.

1500
1600 1700

**Activate**

Ask students to create the Twenty-Eighth Amendment to the Constitution. Students should base their amendments on issues that would be relevant in today's world. Have students write their amendments so they are clear and easy to understand. Then, have them share their amendments with the class.

**Analyze**

1. Have students read the Thirteenth, Fourteenth, and Fifteenth Amendments on *Examine Civil War Amendments* (page 145). Ask them to complete *Document Analysis—Think Across Time* (page 300) to support their analysis. Tell students to include these three amendments on their time lines. Then, work together to add any other dates they think are significant.

2. Place students into small groups, and have them use their knowledge of history to discuss what they would change, add, or delete to these three amendments.

3. Use the following questions to guide a discussion:

   · What did the Thirteen Amendment make official?

   · According to the Fourteenth Amendment, who can be a citizen?

   · Why were these amendments added in this order?

   · What are the similarities between the three amendments? How are they different?

   · How would things be different today if these amendments did not exist?

4. Allow time for students to complete *Examine Civil War Amendments*. Discuss their work and strengthen their analysis skills using the How To activity.

**How To . . .**

**Summarize to Understand**—Tell students that summarizing a primary source in their own words can help them gain a better understanding of the primary source. Explain that to summarize, they should first closely read the document. They may have to read the document more than one time. Next, they should make lists or outlines that include the main idea and any supporting details in their own words. Then, have them write their summaries using their lists, and limit their summaries to just one or two sentences. Ask students to choose one or more of the amendments to practice this skill.

**Extend**

Have students research other amendments to the U.S. Constitution that were proposed but not passed into law.

Intermediate DBAs

© Shell Education

# Examine Civil War Amendments

**Directions:** Read the background information, study the amendments, and answer the questions.

These amendments were made to the Constitution immediately after the Civil War. The Thirteenth Amendment was added in 1865. It freed the enslaved people of America. The Fourteenth Amendment defined who could be a citizen of the United States, and it was added in 1868. The Fifteenth Amendment was added in 1870, and it assured the right to vote for all citizens.

**Thirteenth Amendment Section 1**

Neither slavery nor involuntary servitude, except as a punishment for crime whereof the party shall have been duly convicted, shall exist within the United States, or any place subject to their jurisdiction.

**Fifteenth Amendment Section 1**

The right of citizens of the United States to vote shall not be denied or abridged by the United States or by any State on account of race, color, or previous condition of servitude.

**Fourteenth Amendment Section 1**

All persons born or naturalized in the United States and subject to the jurisdiction thereof, are citizens of the United States and of the State wherein they reside. No State shall make or enforce any law which shall abridge the privileges or immunities of citizens of the United States; nor shall any State deprive any person of life, liberty, or property, without due process of law; nor deny to any person within its jurisdiction the equal protection of the laws.

**Civil War**

1. Which amendment protects citizens from unjust laws by the states where they live?

   (A) Thirteenth Amendment          (C) Fifteenth Amendment
   (B) Fourteenth Amendment          (D) all the above

2. Which of these amendments refers directly to slavery? Why might one amendment refer to enslaved people while the others do not?

   _____

   _____

   _____

3. What effect did the Fourteenth and Fifteenth Amendments have on the lives of African Americans in the United States?

   _____

   _____

   _____

# Civil War Document-Based Question

## Historical Context

During the 1800s, people in the United States were divided. One of the major issues that divided the nation was slavery. Southerners did not want their ways of life changed. Enslaved people did much of the physical work on the plantations. Some people in the North did not believe that enslaved people should continue to be used. This disagreement led to many other problems in the country. Congress tried to prevent a war by compromising. But, the compromises were not enough. In the end, all the events further divided the North from the South and led to a devastating war.

## Essay Tasks

**Directions:** Using the documents and your knowledge of the Civil War, complete **one** of the following essay tasks. Before you begin your essay, complete the *DBQ Essay Planner* (pages 302–305) to plan your writing.

### Essay Task ❶

In a well-organized essay, describe the events that led up to and ultimately caused the Civil War.

In your essay, remember to:

- Tell about specific laws and events that led to tensions between the North and the South.

- Include information about famous individuals who tried to achieve freedom for enslaved people.

- Include a topic sentence, introduction, body, and conclusion.

- Give details to support your ideas.

- Use information found in the documents to support your argument.

### Essay Task ❷

In a well-organized essay, explain why the Civil War was inevitable.

In the essay, remember to:

- Write a strong thesis that establishes your argument.

- Incorporate specific details and evidence to support your argument.

- Include a topic sentence, introduction, body, and conclusion.

- Give details to support your ideas.

- Use information found in the documents to support your argument.

★ As a bonus, include evidence from an outside source in your essay.

Civil War

# Teacher Resources

## Background Information

### Missouri Compromise Lesson

By the 1800s, life in the North and the South was very different. The issue of slavery affected many parts of life, and it was important that there were an equal number of slave states and free states. New territories had formed as people settled the land in the West. Then, after they grew, the territories could become new states. When a new state was added to the Union, new representatives were added to Congress.

People in Missouri wanted their territory to become a state. Missouri could either enter the Union as a slave state or a free state. Southerners did not want Northerners to have more votes in Congress, and Northerners did not want slavery to spread farther into the West. However, there were many free state supporters who were not abolitionists. Instead, they were part of a movement called *free soil*. This movement demanded that free white people get free land. They did not like slavery because slave owners had plantations that took up most of the available land, and they took many African Americans with them wherever they settled these plantations.

In 1820, Henry Clay of Kentucky helped pass a plan in Congress that had Missouri enter the Union as a slave state. Maine would separate from Massachusetts and would become a free state. From then on, all territories above Missouri's southern border were free, and all territories below its southern border were slave states. They called this the Missouri Compromise.

### Fugitive Slave Act Lesson

More than anything, most enslaved people wanted their freedom. Some of them even risked their lives and tried to run away from their owners to achieve this goal. Enslaved people had much to lose when they ran away. Many times, they never saw their families again. If captured, enslavers would severely beat their enslaved people. In 1740, South Carolina passed a law that made it legal to kill enslaved people found away from their homes. It did not matter if the enslaved person resisted or not. In Georgia, in 1755, a law was passed that encouraged the killing of male runaways. People who returned dead enslaved men were likely to receive a much higher reward than if they returned alive women or children. Some people made their living by hunting and capturing runaways. In 1850, the Fugitive Slave Act was passed as part of the Compromise of 1850. The Fugitive Slave Act allowed slave catchers to travel into Northern free states to hunt down escaped enslaved people. It also denied fugitives who claimed to be freemen the right to a fair jury trial and put all fugitive cases under federal jurisdiction.

# Teacher Resources <sub></sub>(cont.)

## Emancipation Proclamation Lesson

Abraham Lincoln was the Republican candidate for president in 1860. One of the party's platforms was to stop the spread of slavery into new territories of the United States. When Lincoln became the sixteenth president, many people believed he would immediately abolish slavery. As a result, many Southern states seceded from the Union, and the Civil War began.

Lincoln's main goal was to keep the Union together. He had planned to leave slavery alone where it already existed, but he wanted to stop it from spreading to new states. During the Civil War, many abolitionists pushed him to do something more about slavery. Frederick Douglass, a former enslaved person and powerful orator, argued for the abolition of slavery. Some Northerners agreed and felt that freeing enslaved people was an actual military necessity. Since the Confederacy's foundation was built on the institution of slavery, the North believed it could defeat the South by dismantling slavery. This was how Abraham Lincoln was persuaded. Constitutionally, he had no power to confiscate a citizen's property; however, now that the states were in rebellion, Lincoln's powers as commander in chief of the military gave him the authority to free enslaved people to defeat the enemy.

Lincoln announced the Emancipation Proclamation shortly after the Battle of Antietam in 1862. Once he decided to emancipate enslaved people, he needed a political victory to achieve the goal successfully. In the summer of 1862, Lee's army retreated into Virginia after Antietam. President Lincoln then announced the Emancipation Proclamation, which freed only enslaved people in the states that had seceded. Enslaved people in the border states of Delaware, Maryland, West Virginia, and Kentucky were not freed. Not only did Lincoln not have the power to free those enslaved people, but also he could not risk that these states might secede if he freed them. Many enslaved people in the South did not learn of the proclamation until the Union army invaded their homes. Some enslaved people did not find out about the Emancipation Proclamation until after the war had ended.

## Civil War Amendments Lesson

When Abraham Lincoln issued the Emancipation Proclamation in 1862–63, it was only the beginning of a long road to freedom for African Americans in the United States. The Civil War was still raging. The abolition of slavery was added to the Constitution with the Thirteenth Amendment in December of 1865. But even though enslaved people were free, that did not mean that they had the full rights of citizenship. In 1856, an enslaved man named Dred Scott had sued for his freedom. He was an enslaved man living in a territory where slavery was illegal. The Supreme Court ruled against him by a vote of seven to two, saying that people of African descent could not be citizens of the United States and therefore could not sue in federal court.

The Fourteenth Amendment addressed this ruling by declaring that anyone born in the United States had all the rights and privileges of full citizenship. It also added protection against states that might attempt to curb the rights of citizens. Until this time, the Constitution did not explicitly prevent the states from passing laws that might violate the rights of citizens.

The Fifteenth Amendment specified that a citizen's right to vote could not be denied because of the person's race or color or because the person was once enslaved. The Thirteenth, Fourteenth, and Fifteenth Amendments are sometimes called the Reconstruction Amendments because they were proposed and ratified in the Reconstruction period (1865–1870) after the Civil War.

# Teacher Resources *(cont.)*

## Answer Key

### Examine the Missouri Compromise (page 139)

1. Students may list any two of the following as slave states: Missouri, Louisiana, Mississippi, Alabama, Georgia, South Carolina, North Carolina, Virginia, West Virginia (part of Virginia at the time), Maryland, Delaware, Kentucky, and Tennessee.

2. B

3. The free states and the slave states both had 12 states each. Also, students might say that while the land area is greater in the slave states, the free states had larger populations.

### Examine the Effects of the Fugitive Slave Act (page 141)

1. Four African American men are running from and being shot at by white men.

2. Answers may include the author is pro-abolition and sympathizes with fugitive slaves and free African American men who were also affected.

3. The artist was probably using the "all men are created equal" phrase as an argument against slavery.

### Examine the Emancipation Proclamation (page 143)

1. Slaves would be free in the states in rebellion against the United States—the South.

2. Objects may include the Constitution, the American flag, the scales of justice, or the busts of Andrew Jackson or James Buchanan, and students should explain how the objects they chose inspired Lincoln as he wrote.

### Examine Civil War Amendments (page 145)

1. B

2. The Fifteenth Amendment refers to slavery because it guarantees the right to vote regardless of a previous condition of servitude. The Fourteenth Amendment included enslaved people in the broad definition of citizenship because they were born here, so a specific mention of them was not needed.

3. Answers may include that the amendments made a large impact on the lives of African Americans. Full citizenship and the right to vote was granted to African Americans.

### Civil War Document-Based Question (page 146)

Refer to pages 306–307 for the DBQ Rubrics.

Intermediate DBAs

© Shell Education

# Intermediate Document-Based Assessments

## Unit 12: World Cultures

### Lessons

### Teacher Resources

# Roman Routes and Aqueducts

## Historical-Thinking Skill

Students will examine the significant individuals and achievements of Roman society.

**Activate**

Place students into groups of four to six. Provide students with four to six sheets of paper, masking tape, and small balls that roll (marbles or gumballs). Have students use their materials to build contraptions that can connect two desks, bringing the ball from one desk to the other. Allow time for planning and testing. Explain the connection between transporting a marble from one place to another to the design of Roman aqueducts.

**Analyze**

1. Have students study the pictures on *Examine Roman Routes and Aqueducts* (page 153). Have them guess the purpose of the structures. Explain the system of aqueducts, roads, and bridges that the Romans built throughout the Roman empire.

2. Have students complete *Document Analysis—Set the Scene* (page 297) to support their analysis.

3. Use the following questions to guide a discussion:
   - Why would systems of aqueducts, roads, and bridges be important to building empires?
   - How would this aqueduct system work?
   - How do you think this aqueduct system was constructed?
   - Who would use and benefit from these systems?
   - Why were these systems significant for this time and place?

4. Allow time for students to complete *Examine Roman Routes and Aqueducts*. Discuss their work and strengthen their analysis skills using the How To activity.

**How To . . .**

**Find Additional Primary Sources**—Explain to students that when they are given a primary source, no matter how detailed, it is limiting in the information it can provide. A great strategy to increase knowledge is to find additional primary sources that will add to their knowledge of the original primary source. Ask students to use the facts they gathered from the photos to begin additional research. They can use other sources of information and compare them to the photos.

**Extend**

Have students take their archeology research further by researching ecofacts of a given historical time period. Ecofacts are the environmental and organic remains of ancient ecosystems. Guide students to draw conclusions about the artifacts they research from the ecofacts discoveries.

# Examine Roman Routes and Aqueducts

**Directions:** Read the background information, study the images, and answer the questions.

The photo on the left is of a Roman aqueduct. It carried fresh water from upland streams to the city of Rome. Roman engineers designed the system. Soldiers, slaves, and prisoners of war built it. The tops of the aqueduct had a channel for the running water. Once the water arrived in Rome, it was diverted into pipes that led to homes and public buildings. The photo on the right is of a section of the Roman highway. It was paved with stones and stretched over thousands of miles.

**World Cultures**

1. What architectural form was used to add strength to the aqueduct?

   Ⓐ stone        Ⓒ arches
   Ⓑ columns      Ⓓ cement

2. Explain three ways aqueducts benefited the Roman lifestyle.

   _____
   _____
   _____

3. Why might the Romans have built paved highways?

   _____
   _____
   _____

# Chinese Armor

## Historical-Thinking Skill

Students will study sculptures for evidence of the technology, beliefs, and culture of an ancient Chinese civilization.

**Activate**

Make copies of the image on *Examine Chinese Armor* (page 155), and cut the image into four sections. Provide a quarter of the image to each student. Have them write what they observe in their quarters, what they infer, and what they wonder. Next, have students find people with the other three quarters of the image. Have them repeat the process and see if their observations, inferences, and questions change. Connect this activity to the larger issue of understanding history when we only have access to some information.

**Analyze**

1. Distribute new, uncut copies of *Examine Chinese Armor* to students. Have students complete *Document Analysis—Use Evidence* (page 299) to support their analysis. Ask students to think like archaeologists. Explain that these statues were found relatively recently in 1974. Before that, no one knew they existed. Have students use the chart on the bottom half of their sheets to write what they think about the place, time, and culture from which these sculptures came.

2. Use the following questions to guide a discussion:
   - What do you think these statues were used for?
   - How long do you think it took to create these statues?
   - Can you make any inferences about the technology, beliefs, or culture of the society that created these terra-cotta warriors?
   - How could you confirm or verify the conclusions you made about the place, time, and culture these sculptures are from?

3. Allow time for students to complete *Examine Chinese Armor*. Discuss their work and strengthen their analysis skills using the How To activity.

**How To . . .**

**Analyze Sculptures**—Explain to students that when analyzing sculptures, there are additional elements to consider because they are three-dimensional objects. Students should consider the sizes of the sculpture, and identify the medium or material(s) used. If the sculpture is historical in nature, they should examine the condition it is in and whether it is whole and undamaged or a fragment and worn. Also, students should consider the age of the subject, the pose, movement, clothing, and facial expressions to gain further insight. Have students practice using these tips on these Chinese sculptures and/or other famous historical sculptures.

**Extend**

Ask students to research other ancient Chinese inventions. Have them make lists to rank the top five inventions and defend their rankings.

Intermediate DBAs

    © Shell Education

Name: _____ Date: _____

# Examine Chinese Armor

**Directions:** Read the background information, study the image, and answer the questions.

This image is a photograph of the ancient terra-cotta warrior statues discovered in northwestern China in 1974. There were more than 8,000 full-size statues in the tomb where they were discovered.

1. What kind of protection do you see on these statues?

   (A) armor and helmets     (C) spiritual protections

   (B) weapons     (D) no protection

2. What are the warriors missing in this picture? Why might that be?

   _____

   _____

   _____

3. What does this discovery tell us about ancient Chinese society?

   _____

   _____

   _____

© Shell Education

World Cultures

# The Importance of Zero

## Historical-Thinking Skill

Students will evaluate the importance of India's contribution of the number zero in mathematics and astronomy.

**Intermediate DBAs**

**Activate**

Ask students to think about how important the number/concept of zero is in everyday life. Encourage students to share answers and write them on the board. Then, ask students to imagine life without the number/concept of zero.

**Analyze**

1. Have students study the image on *Examine the Importance of Zero* (page 157). Ask them to complete *Document Analysis—Set the Scene* (page 297) to support their analysis. Share some or all the background information (page 162) with students if they are not familiar with Brahmagupta, a famous Indian astronomer and mathematician, to help them better set the scene on their analysis sheets.

2. Use the following questions to guide a discussion:
   - Why would zero be a significant concept during this time period?
   - What other early civilizations used the concept of zero?
   - Why would someone think about a concept such as the number zero in the first place?
   - What connections are there between mathematics and astronomy?

3. Allow time for students to complete *Examine the Importance of Zero*. Discuss their work and strengthen their analysis skills using the How To activity.

**How To . . .**

**Interpret Drawings**—Drawings can reveal much more than just the subject of a drawing. Artists would sometimes begin a piece of work by sketching a simple version in ink or black chalk. Explain to students that there are many things to look for when interpreting drawings. In drawings, the artist can reveal not only information about the subject, but about themselves as well. Students should identify the time period and where the artist comes from to understand the subject better. Drawings are often connected with the history of the places in which they were made.

**Extend**

Have students work in small groups to identify inventions from different ancient civilizations that were identical or similar. Then, have them create maps of the ancient civilization's inventions using symbols and legends.

Name: _____ Date: _____

# Examine the Importance of Zero

**Directions:** Read the background information, study the image, and answer the questions.

Brahmagupta is known as the Father of Zero. He was the first to give rules to compute with zero. He wrote his most famous book in Sanskrit in AD 628. He stated that "When zero is added to a number or subtracted from a number, the number remains unchanged, and a number multiplied by zero is zero." He also made rules for dealing with positive and negative numbers.

19th century illustration of Hindu astronomer and mathematician

**World Cultures**

1. Write two equations that show a rule written by Brahmagupta related to the number zero.

_____

_____

2. What cultural elements can you identify in the drawing?

_____

_____

_____

_____

# Mesoamerican Civilizations

## Historical-Thinking Skill

Students will compare and contrast the significant social, cultural, and political features of the Maya, Inca, and Aztec societies.

### Activate

Place the three images from *Examine Mesoamerican Civilizations* (page 159) around the room and label them 1, 2, and 3. Tell students that these three primary sources show something about three different civilizations in Mesoamerica. Then, have students write the words *farming*, *sports*, *art*, *resources*, and *time* on separate sticky notes. Have them label each sticky note with the appropriate image number(s). Ask students to share and defend their answers.

### Analyze

1. Distribute copies of *Examine Mesoamerican Civilizations* to students. Ask them to use the images to complete *Document Analysis—Make Connections* (page 296) to support their analysis. For step 2, ask students to write observations and inferences about each of the three civilizations from the images. Encourage students to add other information they know about these civilizations.

2. Ask students to use four different colors to highlight or circle similarities. They can use the colors in the following way:
   - color 1: similarities among all three pictures
   - color 2: similarities among the Maya and Inca
   - color 3: similarities among the Maya and Aztec
   - color 4: similarities among the Inca and Aztec

3. Use the following questions to guide a discussion:
   - What is the most important thing on this Aztec calendar?
   - Why do you think the Inca terraced the land?
   - What connections can you make between these civilizations and the world today?

4. Allow time for students to complete *Examine Mesoamerican Civilizations*. Discuss their work and strengthen their analysis skills using the How To activity.

**How To . . .** **Compare Images**—Tell students that an easy way to compare images is to makes notes directly on the paper. They can look for similarities, circle them, and write thoughts or questions. Challenge them to find as many similarities in the photos as they can. Then, ask students to think of ways they could annotate the images to highlight differences.

### Extend

Have students make distinctions between how the different Mesoamerican civilizations ended. Then, have them summarize their findings and propose ideas of how to keep some of the traditions from those civilizations alive.

Intermediate DBAs

 © Shell Education

Name: _____ Date:_____

# Examine Mesoamerican Civilizations

**Directions:** Read the background information, study the images, and answer the questions.

The top image is of a Maya ball game called *ulama*. It revolved around religious beliefs. The bottom left photo is of Inca terraced land. The bottom right photo is of an Aztec artifact. It is one of their calendars, which depicts their sun god in the center.

**1.** How do you know that the Maya game was a serious tradition?

_____

_____

**2.** How do you know that the Inca were resourceful people?

    Ⓐ They created a great trade system with the Maya.

    Ⓑ They discovered how to build pyramids.

    Ⓒ They found ways to farm, even in the mountains.

    Ⓓ They developed many uses for gold and silver.

**3.** How does this calendar show the Aztec's dedication toward their gods and toward technology?

_____

_____

_____

# World Cultures Document-Based Question

## Historical Context

People who share the same beliefs, practices, attitudes, and values create a culture. Throughout the world and over time, civilizations have developed unique cultures. Their environments, ancestors, and needs to survive influence their cultures. Religions, philosophies, natural resources, and more also define them. There are many examples of how ancient cultures affect a society's way of life.

## Essay Tasks

**Directions:** Using the documents and your knowledge of world cultures, complete **one** of the following essay tasks. Before you begin your essay, complete the *DBQ Essay Planner* (pages 302–305) to plan your writing.

### Essay Task ❶

In a well-organized essay, identify the two most important and influential inventions from ancient civilizations.

In your essay, remember to:

- Identify the inventions, the ancient civilization that created them, and what their purposes were.

- Provide evidence to convince the reader that your selected inventions are the most important.

- Include a topic sentence, introduction, body, and conclusion.

- Give details to support your ideas.

- Use information found in the documents to support your argument.

### Essay Task ❷

In a well-organized essay, explain the lasting effects the various world cultures have had on today's society and way of life.

In your essay, remember to:

- Give examples of how the contributions of various cultures have affected our daily lives.

- Explain how the ways of life from various world cultures have affected our beliefs and ways of thinking.

- Include a topic sentence, introduction, body, and conclusion.

- Give details to support your ideas.

- Use information found in the documents to support your argument.

★ As a bonus, include evidence from an outside source in your essay.

World Cultures

# Teacher Resources

## Background Information

### Roman Routes and Aqueducts Lesson

Roman leaders were very well-organized engineers.  They were keenly aware that providing an infrastructure of roads and fresh water was extremely important in building a strong empire.  Roman leaders believed that if people could easily travel from place to place, communicate messages in a reasonable time, and have the water, food, and homes that they needed, they would be content.  A well-built road system would also make it easier to control conquered areas because soldiers could travel anywhere in the empire.

Rome built 11 major aqueducts from 312 BC to AD 226.  These aqueducts transported fresh water from mountain streams throughout the Roman Empire.  The aqueduct system included channels of stone cut through the rocks and a series of bridge-like structures with troughs running along the top.  Some of these arched structures were over 100 feet (30 meters) tall and were built of layered stone slabs and volcanic ash concrete.  This system provided enough water to serve more than a million people.  When the water reached the city limits, it flowed through lead pipes to wealthy persons' homes and to public structures.  Some of those structures were public baths (free and paid), public latrines, and fountains.  The public also benefited from a sewer system that carried away disease-causing waste.  Firefighters could also pump water through leather hoses to extinguish fires.

The Roman road system stretched over thousands of miles throughout their entire kingdom.  These paved roads allowed goods to be transported in an orderly manner.  Roads were usually about 15 feet (4.5 meters) wide and laid with smooth, flat stones.  Soldiers, enslaved people, and prisoners of war built roads.  The Romans also developed a relay system to send letters and government messages along the highway.  Messengers rode by horseback at the fastest pace possible from one station to another.  They would change horses at each station.

© Shell Education

Intermediate DBAs

# Teacher Resources *(cont.)*

Intermediate DBAs

## Chinese Armor Lesson

In 1974, farmers drilled a well in northwestern China. To their surprise, after they had drilled down through the earth some distance, their drill bit found air. The farmers had drilled through the ceiling of the massive tomb constructed by Emperor Qin Shi Huangdi. He ruled China from 247–221 BC. These farmers found more than 8,000 full-size statues inside a tomb. They saw an army of life-size men and horses.

It took over 700,000 workers more than 38 years to make the statues and tomb. Each warrior is unique. They are carved from a clay-like material called *terra-cotta*. Many people think the sculptors that worked on the tomb carved the warriors to look like their own faces. This way, the emperor would not be the only one to reach the afterlife. Each sculptor who put himself in the army would make it to the afterlife too. This was good because many of the workers were sealed inside the tomb alive. The emperor did not want them to tell people the secrets of the tomb. The remains of these tomb workers were found inside the tomb. The terra-cotta warriors are all over 6 feet (1.83 meters) tall. When they were sculpted, each soldier wore real armor and carried a real weapon. The generals are taller than their soldiers. There are infantrymen ready with their weapons. Cavalrymen are near their horses and chariots. The archers are ready to shoot down the enemy. The entire army looks as if it is marching off to battle.

## The Importance of Zero Lesson

Brahmagupta was born in AD 598 in Bhinmal, India. He spent most of his life in Bhinmal where he studied mathematics and astronomy. He eventually became the leader of the astronomical observatory at Ujjain. Ujjain was also the center of mathematics in India.

Brahmagupta's most important contribution to mathematics was the introduction of zero. He introduced that zero in the number system stood for nothing. He studied and introduced many rules of arithmetic that are still part of the mathematical theory today. He also introduced the concept of negative numbers. Brahmagupta wrote a book where he provided the formula for the area of a triangle. In addition, he expressed the rules of trigonometry, including the values of the sin function. He is also credited with introducing the formula for cyclic quadrilaterals, and he gave an accurate value of pi.

In the area of astronomy, Brahmagupta argued that Earth and the universe are round, not flat. He was the first person to use mathematics to predict the positions of the planets. He even calculated the timing of both lunar and solar eclipses. These discoveries were a major improvement in science at that time. His calculation of the length of the solar year was 365 days, 5 minutes, and 19 seconds, which is very accurate to today's calculation of 365 days, 5 hours, and 19 seconds.

# Teacher Resources *(cont.)*

## Mesoamerican Civilizations Lesson

The Maya enjoyed sporting events such as the ball court game *ulama*, which revolved around religion. The court, often shaped like an *I*, represented the world. The ball stood for the moon and the sun. The violent competition between teams was a symbol of the battle between darkness and light, or the death and rebirth of the sun. The Maya believed that playing the game would help them reap a better harvest. The players propelled the hard rubber ball from their hips into a ring to win. They wore special hip padding for protection. However, the stakes for this game were very high. Players on the losing team were sometimes killed by their opponents.

Most of the Inca lived in homes built from stucco. Those who lived in the mountains did not have enough flat land to farm, so they terraced the land and farmed on the sides of the mountains. Potatoes and corn were among their main crops. The cold, dry climate even allowed them to freeze-dry their food and store it for future use. This way, there was always enough food for everyone.

The Aztecs had sophisticated calendars that were used for various purposes. One calendar kept track of the days and recorded 365 days in a year. It helped them to know when to plant and harvest their crops. Another calendar had 260 days and was used to keep track of the rituals for the gods. The primary source pictured on page 159 was used to keep track of the five creations of the sun. The sun god is in the center of the calendar.

## Answer Key

### Examine Roman Routes and Aqueducts (page 153)
1. C
2. Answers may include that aqueducts provided running water for drinking, bathing, and sanitation; Romans did not have to haul water from springs or wells; water was readily available to put out fires.
3. Answers may include that Romans built these roads to transport goods, allow soldiers to move quickly around the empire, and send letters and government messages more quickly.

### Examine Chinese Armor (page 155)
1. A
2. They are missing weapons. Students' theories may vary and should be logical. The warrior statues were equipped with real weapons. Some were recovered. It is believed that the rest were looted after creation or have rotted away.
3. Answers may include that this discovery shows that the culture was advanced in producing protective armor for the army.

### Examine the Importance of Zero (page 157)
1. $1 + 0 = 1$; $2 \times 0 = 0$
2. Answers could include the person's clothing, hair, facial markings, tools, and position.

### Examine Mesoamerican Civilizations (page 159)
1. Based on the picture, they made sure the players had protective gear. The fact that this picture exists also suggests it was important. It was also a game that revolved around religious beliefs.
2. C
3. They honored their gods using calendars such as this one. They also kept a meticulous count of the days so they knew when to plant and harvest.

### World Cultures Document-Based Question
(page 160)
    Refer to pages 306–307 for the DBQ Rubrics.

© Shell Education

# Advanced Document-Based Assessments

## Unit 13: Ancient Egypt

**Lessons**

**Teacher Resources**

# The Great Pyramid of Giza

## Historical-Thinking Skill

Students will analyze the significant beliefs and accomplishments of Egyptian rulers.

### Activate

Ask students to think about how different cultures honor or celebrate their dead. Students can reference their own cultures or cultural stories that they know. Have students share with partners. Then, ask students to think about how they would like to be honored, and have them write their responses.

### Analyze

1. Distribute copies of *Examine the Great Pyramid of Giza* (page 167) to students. Explain that the pyramid was how ancient Egyptians honored their leaders, the pharaohs. Then, have students read the background information.

2. Have students complete *Document Analysis—Set the Scene* (page 297) to support their analysis.

3. Ask students how the tunnels and chambers inside the pyramid were constructed and which chamber was for burial of the king. In small groups, have students share their supporting evidence with one another.

4. Use the following questions to guide a discussion:
   - Why would this pyramid be chosen as one of the Seven Wonders of the World?
   - Why is a pyramid considered the perfect form for construction?
   - Why do you think Egyptian kings chose this geometric form for their tombs?
   - Why was an elaborate tomb so important to Egyptians?

5. Allow time for students to complete *Examine the Great Pyramid of Giza*. Discuss their work and strengthen their analysis skills using the How To activity.

**How To . . .**

**Understand Diagrams**—Explain to students that it is important to understand the point of view of a diagram. Is it a side view, top view, or 3-D view? How would the diagram look different from a different angle? Tell students that when they look at a diagram of a location or building, such as the Pyramid of Giza, it can be helpful to imagine themselves at that place. Ask students to look at the diagram and imagine themselves in different locations of the pyramid. Ask them to close their eyes and imagine what they would see or feel as they looked around. Discuss any new questions, observations, or understandings students have after this visualization exercise.

### Extend

Have students research and develop a presentation about other structures that were considered one of the Seven Wonders of the Ancient World.

**Advanced DBAs**

© Shell Education

# Examine the Great Pyramid of Giza

**Directions:** Read the background information, study the image, and answer the questions.

This pyramid was constructed for Pharaoh Khufu. The Greeks called him *Cheops*. It was built around 2560 BC. It is the only structure on the classical Seven Wonders of the World list that is still standing. The tomb was robbed long ago, so no mummies or artifacts have been found. The tomb had three chambers, a grand gallery, and two shaft passages. Today, we know that the shaft passages align with astrological sites. This is a modern diagram, created based on examination of the actual pyramid.

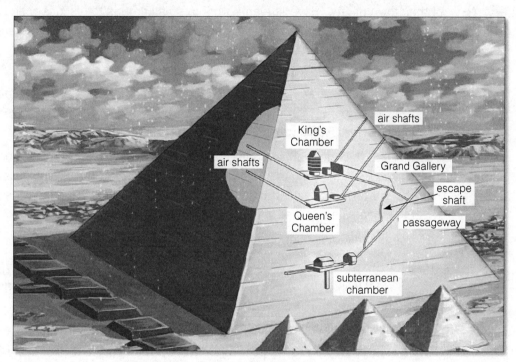

1. How is this pyramid an example of the superior engineering skills of the Egyptians?

   _____

   _____

2. What does this elaborate pyramid and tomb style reveal about the Egyptian's beliefs about death?

   _____

   _____

   _____

3. How did the time and place influence the designs of the pyramids?

   _____

   _____

   _____

# Herodotus

**Activate**

Ask students to take on the role of tour guide for their town or city. A group of tourists have arrived and want to know about the history, culture, and customs of their town or city. Have students work in small groups to discuss their ideas. Then, have one student share their story with the class as if the class were the tourists and the student was the tour guide.

**Analyze**

1. Have students read the background information and excerpt on *Examine Herodotus* (page 169). Then, ask them to complete *Document Analysis— Consider the Source* (page 298) to support their analysis.

2. Discuss the role that Herodotus had in helping people learn about ancient cultures. Tell them this source was written around 400 BC. This was 2,000 years after the Great Pyramid of Giza was constructed and during the time of the Peloponnesian War between Sparta and Athens.

3. Use the following questions to guide a discussion:
   - Why is Herodotus called the "father of history"?
   - What was Herodotus's goal for writing this? Could his purpose have influenced the information he did or did not include?
   - How do you think some of these religious rituals got started?
   - Why is the date this information was written important to consider?

4. Allow time for students to complete *Examine Herodotus*. Discuss their work and strengthen their analysis skills using the How To activity.

**How To . . .**

**Annotate Written Text**—Explain to students that annotating directly onto a document can support understanding and analysis. They can underline important parts, circle new or interesting words, and write comments and questions. Have students reread the excerpt closely with partners and practice annotating the text by underlining priestly customs and writing any thoughts or questions they have. For example, tell students they could make a note of similarities to other religious customs they know about. Then, ask students to suggest other strategies for annotating text.

**Extend**

Have students examine the other works of Herodotus and cross-reference his ideas with other evidence from history.

**Advanced DBAs**

Name: _____ Date:_____

# Examine Herodotus

**Directions:** Read the background information, read the excerpt, and answer the questions.

This is an excerpt from a history book written by Herodotus, a traveling Greek scholar, from about 440–428 BC. His goal was to chronicle the history of all the cultures surrounding the Mediterranean Sea. This excerpt focuses on the rituals that Egyptian priests performed prior to entering the sacred chamber in a temple to care for the god each day. This writing emphasizes the powerful and specialized role of priests and rituals in the society.

"They are religious to excess, far beyond any other race of men, and use the following ceremonies: They drink out of brazen cups, which they scour every day; there is no exception to this practice. They wear linen garments, which they are especially careful to have always fresh washed.... The priests shave their whole body every other day, that no lice or other impure thing may adhere to them when they are engaged in the service of the gods. Their dress is entirely of linen, and their shoes of the papyrus plant: it is not lawful for them to wear either dress or shoes of any other material. They bathe twice every day in cold water, and twice each night; besides which they observe, so to speak, thousands of ceremonies."

—Excerpt from *Histories by Herodotus*

**1.** What are the most important aspects of this ritual?

_____

_____

_____

**2.** Do you agree with this quotation from the text: "They are religious to excess, far beyond any other race of men"? Explain your answer with details.

_____

_____

_____

**3.** Explain how reliable you think Herodotus's writings are.

_____

_____

# Hieroglyphic Writing

### Historical-Thinking Skill

Students will analyze how written codes and stories reflect social conditions in Egypt.

**Activate**

Write the alphabet on the board. Underneath each letter, draw a simple symbol (e.g., @, *, +). Then, write out the word *hieroglyphics* using the code, and have students decode the word. Discuss students' experiences decoding the word.

**Analyze**

1. Have students study the image on *Examine Hieroglyphic Writing* (page 171) and look for common patterns. Does each symbol represent an object or action, or does it represent letter combination sounds?

2. Explain that many monuments and buildings in Egypt still contain this type of writing. Refer to the Rosetta Stone to remind students how we finally learned how to interpret these symbols. Explain the two different forms of Egyptian writing in the background information (page 178).

3. Ask students to complete *Document Analysis—Make Connections* (page 296) to support their analysis. Tell students to use the chart on this page to compare and contrast hieroglyphic writing with their own writing system.

4. Use the following questions to guide a discussion:
   - Do you think this writing was done on papyrus or stone?
   - Who do you think would do the writing?
   - How do you think writing systems like this evolve?

5. Allow time for students to complete *Examine Hieroglyphic Writing*. Discuss their work and strengthen their analysis skills using the How To activity.

## How To . . .

**Find Additional Sources**—Explain to students that when they are given a primary source, no matter how detailed, it is limiting in the information it can provide. A great strategy to increase knowledge is to find additional sources that will add to their knowledge and corroborate information learned from the original primary source. Ask students to practice this skill by researching to find another primary or secondary source related to Egyptian hieroglyphics. Then, have them compare the information from the two sources.

**Extend**

Have students create their own coded alphabets with keys. Then, have them create different words or messages for other students to decipher.

**Advanced DBAs**

Name: _____ Date: _____

# Examine Hieroglyphic Writing

**Directions:** Read the background information, study the image, and answer the questions.

This is an image of an Egyptian tablet showing hieroglyphic writing. Egyptians wrote inscriptions on most of their monuments, tombs, and temples to honor their gods or pharaohs. Writing on papyrus was either for business, trade, or religious reasons. There were two forms of writing: the formal hieroglyphics and the casual writing called *hieratic* that was used in business and personal communications.

1. Name at least five different images you recognize from the tablet.

   _____

   _____

2. Why would the pharaohs want to use the talents and services of trained, full-time scribes and stonemasons?

   _____

   _____

   _____

3. Why was papyrus a significant invention?

   Ⓐ Writing was quickly becoming something everyone was capable of doing.

   Ⓑ It was easier to write on, allowing for better business and personal correspondence.

   Ⓒ Writing on a paper product could keep control of the people through religion.

   Ⓓ Writing on a paper product allowed for more trade outside the empire.

# Obelisks

**Historical-Thinking Skill**

Students will appraise the social and economic framework of Egypt.

**Activate**

Display the photo of Hatshepsut's Obelisk in the Karnak temple in Luxor, Egypt, which can be found on *Examine Obelisks* (page 173). Ask students to name a national monument in Washington, DC, that is also an obelisk. Have students study the photograph and discuss what they see. This photo was chosen so that students could see the comparison between the obelisk's height and the person standing next to it. Ask students to figure out how many people would equal the obelisk's height. It is hard to tell that the structure has four sides and a square base, so explain the proportions.

**Analyze**

1. Have students re-examine the picture on *Examine Obelisks* and complete *Document Analysis—Make Connections* (page 296) to support their analysis.

2. Guide students to label their charts so they can compare and contrast the Egyptian Obelisk with the Washington Monument. Have students work with partners to complete their charts.

3. Use the following questions to guide a discussion:

   · Why do you think American architects chose to use an obelisk shape for the Washington Monument?

   · How has this obelisk remained in such good condition over time?

   · The Obelisk of Hatshepsut is about 97 feet (30 meters) high. How do you think it has stood up and stayed in place all these years?

4. Allow time for students to complete *Examine Obelisks*. Discuss their work and strengthen their analysis skills using the How To activity.

**How To . . .**

**Make Inferences**—Discuss and define the word *inference* as a class. Ask students to share the evidence they would use to make a prediction or educated guess about how this obelisk remained in such good condition over time and how it has stood up and stayed in place all these years. Select two to three additional images of ancient monuments to share with students. Have them practice making inferences based on evidence from those images.

**Extend**

Ask students to create or draw designs of monuments in honor of themselves. Their designs have to be things that could actually be created by humans. Have students explain why they chose their monuments and what they represent.

**Advanced DBAs**

Name: _____ Date: _____

# Examine Obelisks

**Directions:** Read the background information, study the image, and answer the questions.

Obelisks were carved from one large piece of granite using simple tools. This is a photo of an obelisk that is still standing in Egypt. It was designed and ordered to be built by Hatshepsut, a female pharaoh, to honor her father. This obelisk is 97 feet (30 meters) high and is the tallest one in the world.

1. What is one thing you can learn about the ancient Egyptian society from studying this obelisk?

   _____

   _____

   _____

2. What was the main purpose of Egyptian obelisks? How is their purpose similar to that of a pyramid?

   _____

   _____

   _____

3. Twenty Egyptian obelisks ended up in other countries. Why would this have happened?

   _____

   _____

   _____

# Egyptian Gods

**Historical-Thinking Skill**

Students will look for evidence of social conditions in Egypt in written codes and stories.

**Activate**

Ask students to tell stories on single sheets of paper without using any words, only drawings. Encourage students to use symbols and other clues in their drawings to help people understand their stories. Have students share their drawings with partners and interpret each other's stories.

**Analyze**

1. Have students look closely at the image on *Examine Egyptian Gods* (page 175). Read the background information on the page together. Have students guess the identity of each god or goddess.

2. In small groups, have students discuss what this scene may depict. Have students describe in detail what they see and how the figures are drawn.

3. Have students complete *Document Analysis—Use Evidence* (page 299) to support their analysis. In the first column, students should write about who is in the scene and what they think is happening. In the second column, students should write the evidence from the image and/or their background knowledge to support their thinking.

4. Use the following questions to guide a discussion:
   - Explain how these figures were drawn, focusing on the positioning of the feet and torso.
   - Who seems to be the most important figure in this drawing? Why?
   - Do you think these headpieces were significant, and in what way? What makes you think that?

5. Allow time for students to complete *Examine Egyptian Gods*. Discuss their work and strengthen their analysis skills using the How To activity.

**How To . . .**

**Analyze Symbolism**—Explain to students that symbolism in art could be actions, people, places, words, or objects used to represent an abstract idea. One key to understanding symbolism in visual arts is having background knowledge of the subject. Symbols can add dimension to the work's meaning. First, have students identify the symbols and use outside resources to research the background knowledge to make connections. Discuss with students how the background information above the image helps them understand the symbols. What other information would help them?

**Extend**

Have students select a modern-day religion to compare and contrast the religion of ancient Egypt. Have students not only analyze surface-level elements but infer deeper connections and meanings to religious elements of both religions.

**Advanced DBAs**

# Examine Egyptian Gods

**Directions:** Read the background information, study the image, and answer the questions.

This papyrus tells a story involving three gods and Queen Nefertari, the wife of Ramses the Great. The three gods are Isis (the goddess of fertility and sister of Osiris), Maat (the winged goddess of truth and harmony whose feathers were used in judging a human heart), and Horus (the sun god with a hawk's head who leads a good person to the throne of Osiris to worship him prior to entering heaven). The background tells the story in hieroglyphics. Religion was the center of all activity in Egypt, and the goal of citizens was eternal life in the fields of Yaru in the underworld. These tombs were of royalty and the wealthy. They were painted with religious scenes to help them in the afterlife.

1. Do you think this story involves the underworld or some other topic? Explain your answer with specific details.

   _____

   _____

   _____

2. Why did the Egyptians paint scenes in their tombs?

   Ⓐ The pharaoh enjoyed artwork and wanted it in every tomb.

   Ⓑ They wanted to help the dead in the afterlife.

   Ⓒ It was a way to communicate with the dead in the afterlife.

   Ⓓ It was a way to communicate with future generations.

3. What parts of Egyptian society focused on preparing for death?

   _____

   _____

   _____

# Ancient Egypt Document-Based Question

## Historical Context

The Egyptian empire began in 3100 BC under Menes. He declared a supreme monarchy and claimed to have divine lineage. His successors continued to exert a divine hold over the people. He began the tradition of building elaborate tombs for their burial. This pyramid-building phase, which was known as the Old Kingdom, was a time of peace and isolation. Religion became a focal point. Priests and the pharaoh had daily ceremonies to please the many gods. All society focused on preparing for the afterlife. During the Middle Kingdom, trading ships sailed throughout the Mediterranean. Elaborate engineering projects were constructed. During the New Kingdom, armies used horses and chariots to lead their soldiers into battles, defend their country, and conquer new regions. In 323 BC, the Greeks took over Egypt, and the Ptolemaic Empire began.

## Essay Tasks

**Directions:** Using the documents and your knowledge of ancient Egypt, complete **one** of the following essay tasks. Before you begin your essay, complete the *DBQ Essay Planner* (pages 302–305) to plan your writing.

### Essay Task ❶

In a well-organized essay, explain how Egyptian society was focused on and devoted to participating in religious practices and providing for the comfort of their pharaohs, both in life and in death.

In your essay, remember to:

- Identify three religious practices.

- Provide evidence that will convince the reader that the religious practices you selected reveal the devotion of the Egyptian society to the pharaoh.

- Include a topic sentence, introduction, body, and conclusion.

- Give details to support your ideas.

- Use information found in the documents to support your argument.

### Essay Task ❷

In a well-organized essay, explain the three most important contributions of ancient Egyptian society to modern society.

In your essay, remember to:

- Identify the three contributions.

- Provide evidence to support that the contributions made an impact on modern society.

- Include a topic sentence, introduction, body, and conclusion.

- Give details to support your ideas.

- Use information found in the documents to support your argument.

- As a bonus, include evidence from an outside source or a counterargument in your chosen essay.

★ As a bonus, include evidence from an outside source in your essay.

Ancient Egypt

# Teacher Resources

## Background Information

### The Great Pyramid of Giza Lesson

Egyptian pyramid building occurred during the Old Kingdom (2700–2200 BC). Archaeologists believe that the Great Pyramid was built as a tomb for the Pharaoh Khufu (called Cheops by the Greeks). It took 20 years to build and was finished by about 2560 BC. The tomb was robbed long ago, so there is no physical evidence of the king's body or his belongings. The tomb was the tallest man-made structure in the world for more than 3,800 years until the Lincoln Cathedral was constructed. Today, the pyramid is about 452 feet (138 meters) high, but scientists believe the structure was once about 481 feet (146 meters) tall.

Most people think that the pyramids were constructed by slave labor. However, most of the work actually required skilled craftsmen, and archaeological evidence shows that there was a workers' cemetery and a camping area in the Great Pyramid complex. Mark Lehner, an Egyptologist, theorizes that the laborers were organized into two work gangs of 100,000 men each. They were then divided into five units of 20,000 men each. There were possibly other divisions of laborers based on the skills of the workers. It is also believed that these workers camped near the tomb site and were paid for their work.

The Great Pyramid has both ascending and descending ramps (passages), three chambers, and a grand gallery (two stories high). The three chambers consist of an unfinished chamber of unknown purpose, a queen's chamber that never held a queen's body, and the king's chamber. There are two slim shafts coming from the king's chamber that were once thought to be for ventilation. Today, we know that the shafts align with astrological sites.

### Herodotus Lesson

The Greek scholar Herodotus was a traveling historian whose goal was to write the histories and customs of a wide range of cultures and countries. It is believed that he was born in 484 BC. He is often called the "father of history" since he is the first known author to write a collection of books devoted to history. He was interested in Egyptian culture and wrote about the priests, their unique religious practices, their monuments, temples, language, and the role of the Nile River in their lives. This detailed record has been invaluable to Egyptologists as a firsthand account of daily life in Egypt, even though there is doubt as to the accuracy of some of the stories.

The Egyptian temples were the homes of the gods. The main halls of temples contained decorated columns and were available to the public, but only priests could enter the inner sanctums where the shrines were located. Priests mainly focused on the care and feeding of the gods and the performance of other rituals, such as funerals. Herodotus described how the priests prepared themselves with elaborate bathing prior to entering the temples. The priests would chant the awakening hymn for the god. The head priest would then break the seal and enter the god's chamber to wake them with a repeated prayer so the soul could once again enter the god. The image or statue of the god was removed from its shrine, cleaned and dressed, and offered food and drink. Then, it was placed back in the shrine. This ceremony was repeated three times daily.

# Teacher Resources *(cont.)*

## Hieroglyphic Writing Lesson

Egyptians had different forms of writing. Hieratic writing was a type of shorthand or cursive that was used for business transactions and messages. It was written on papyrus or linen. In about 650 BC, another form of writing called *demotic* was introduced. It was used for administrative purposes.

Hieroglyphic writing was used for religious writings and for inscriptions on monuments. This form was very difficult to learn, and young scribes were chosen early in life to study the process. Most writings on monuments, temples, and tombs were to honor pharaohs, gods, or war heroes.

Hieroglyphs started in ancient times as pictographs and then evolved into a combination of pictures or images and sounds for syllables in words. The snake symbol means the letter *r*, and bread is the symbol for the *t* sound.

Writing these images on stone was difficult and involved chiseling words with bronze blades because steel was not available. A stonemason in this case also had to have a scribe's training to combine both tasks.

The Egyptians invented a form of paper called *papyrus* that was made from reeds growing along the Nile River. The reeds were cut into bundles. The green outer fiber was peeled off, and the pith inside was cut into very thin slices. These slices were then pounded into a smooth writing surface. Scribes wrote on this papyrus with brushes dipped in ink.

## Obelisks Lesson

Hatshepsut, the daughter of Thutmose I, declared herself pharaoh after her half-brother (who was also her husband) died. She ruled from 1479 to 1458 BC, and she was considered an innovative leader who restored trade and launched hundreds of grand construction projects throughout Egypt. She commissioned two obelisks to be built at the entrance to the Temple of Karnak. One is still standing, and it is considered the tallest standing obelisk in the world.

Obelisks were found in pairs at the entrances to temples and also served as monuments to great leaders. They were four-sided tapered pillars with pyramid-shaped tops. Amazingly, they were carved from single pieces of granite. The pyramid tops were symbolic of the ancient tombs and pointed to the sun god. The sides were usually inscribed with hieroglyphic writings, some of which were long stories about pharaohs or the accomplishments of military leaders. This giant stone pillar is 97 feet (30 meters) high. Each side is 8 feet (2 meters) wide at the base, and the pillar weighs approximately 320 tons (290 metric tons).

The obelisk was cut from a quarry and then dragged to a site where it was hand-etched and polished. Then, it was shipped by barge to its location. Scientists are not sure how this huge, heavy obelisk was raised and secured in place. The only simple machines they had were levers, inclined planes, and wheels. The etchings were done with sharp stones or bronze tools since there was no steel at this time.

Egypt was conquered by the Greeks, and later the Romans, who took some of these obelisks back to their home countries as trophies.

Advanced DBAs

# Teacher Resources (cont.)

## Egyptian Gods Lesson

The underworld was extremely important to the Egyptians. *The Book of the Dead* described it as a peaceful land called the fields of Yaru. When someone died, they were judged in the court of Osiris, an important Egyptian god. To enter the underworld, the deceased had to answer questions correctly to open a series of doors. Once in the court chamber, the deceased person's heart was weighed against one of the feathers from Maat, the winged goddess of truth. If their heart was not too heavy with sin, they could pass into paradise. If their heart was too heavy, the beast named Ammut immediately ate it, and the person wandered forever without a soul.

Egyptians believed the body's spirit entered at birth and stayed after death in the physical body. Without a physical body, the soul had no place to dwell and became restless forever. So, finding a way to preserve the physical bodies of kings and wealthy citizens became an important task. Egyptians invented a 70-day embalming process. However, poor people could only afford small clay figurines to substitute for preserved bodies.

## Answer Key

### Examine the Great Pyramid of Giza (page 167)
1. The tomb is the only structure of the classical Seven Wonders of the World still standing. It contains three chambers, it is about 452 feet high, and its base is a square with slightly slanted sides that add strength.
2. Kings ordered the pyramids and tombs to be built in such elaborate styles because the Egyptians believed in the afterlife. The kings needed to take items with them for use in the next world and to feel important in the afterlife.
3. Answers may include that the pyramids had to be built in such a way to withstand extreme weather. They had to be built without modern tools as well, using materials available.

### Examine Herodotus (page 169)
1. Students may include that bathing and clean clothes seem to be most important.
2. Students' opinions should be detailed and include supporting reasons.
3. Students should consider the fact that Herodotus wrote *Histories* long after the events actually happened. However, Herodotus is known as a dedicated historian.

### Examine Hieroglyphic Writing (page 171)
1. Answers will vary but may include lizards, insects, bowls, canes, birds, water, etc.
2. Hieroglyphic writing was hard to learn. The pharaohs wanted inscriptions on their tombs and monuments to honor their great deeds, so they needed well-educated scribes to complete the task. Stonemasons were kept busy building obelisks, temples, and monuments.
3. B

### Examine Obelisks (page 173)
1. Students should write things they learned about ancient Egyptian society from studying the obelisk.
2. Obelisks honored famous people or events and were often located at the entrances of temples or pyramids. Like the pyramids, obelisks were sometimes built to honor the dead.
3. Egypt was conquered by the Greeks (and later, the Romans) who wanted to take these obelisks back to their countries as trophies. Obelisks were very popular, and other countries wanted to own them as well.

### Examine Egyptian Gods (page 175)
1. Answers may include that this story involves the underworld because one can see Maat (the winged goddess of truth), the leading of the dead person to judgment, and the weighing of the heart.
2. B
3. Many parts of Egyptian society were focused on preparing for the next life: building tombs, building temples for worship, and learning skills to preserve dead bodies.

### Ancient Egypt Document-Based Question (page 176)
Refer to pages 306–307 for the DBQ Rubrics.

**Advanced DBAs**

116869—Document-Based Assessment Activities

© Shell Education

# Advanced Document-Based Assessments

## Unit 14: The Renaissance

**Lessons**

**Teacher Resources**

# Da Vinci's Notes

**Historical-Thinking Skill**

Students will compare da Vinci's sketches and assess his contribution to modern world inventions.

**Activate**

Have students sketch inventions, no matter how unlikely they are to become reality. Have students share their invention ideas with the class.

**Analyze**

1. Display the sketches of Leonardo da Vinci's inventions. Ask students how likely these sketches would have been to become a reality during the Renaissance. Remind students that many inventions seemed unrealistic until they were actually created.

2. Have students look at the different sketches on *Examine Da Vinci's Notes* (page 183) and complete *Document Analysis—Make Connections* (page 296) to support their analysis by comparing and contrasting the two sketches.

3. Use the following questions to guide a discussion:
   - How do these inventions appear to function?
   - Why is this considered to be groundbreaking for the fifteenth century?
   - Do you think this invention would work?

4. Allow time for students to complete *Examine Da Vinci's Notes*. Discuss their work and strengthen their analysis skills using the How To activity.

**How To . . .**

**Examine Sketches, Diagrams, or Drawings**—Tell students that the words *sketch*, *diagram*, and *drawing* are sometimes used to mean the same thing. They are all handmade pictorial representations of something. There are four main types: floor plan sketches, elevation drawings, exploded-view drawings, and perspective drawings. Floor plan sketches provide a top-down view, and they are drawn on a horizontal plane. Elevation drawings are on a vertical plane. Exploded-view drawings combine the horizontal and vertical views. Perspective drawings are 3-D drawings. Understanding the different types can help provide insight to the purpose and perspective of drawings, sketches, or diagrams. Have students determine which types of drawings are on *Examine Da Vinci's Notes*.

**Extend**

Have students research and identify the contributions of Copernicus, Galileo, Francis Bacon, Newton, and Sir Robert Boyle during the Renaissance and determine which invention was the most significant. Ask them to support their claims with evidence.

**Advanced DBAs**

# Examine Da Vinci's Notes

**Directions:** Read the information, study the sketches, and answer the questions.

The image on the left is Leonardo da Vinci's 1485 sketches of a giant crossbow. At that time in history, a crossbow of this size did not exist. During this time, da Vinci worked on crossbow projects for some military engineers. Along with the Chinese, da Vinci explored the concept of flight as shown in the helicopter sketch on the right. In the 1860s, the word *helicopter* was coined by Gustave de Ponton d'Amécourt. *Helico* means spiral and *petron* means wings.

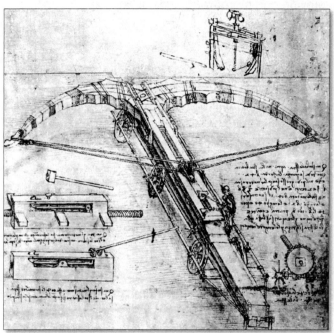 

1. Describe at least two things you notice in these sketches.

   _____

   _____

   _____

2. Why are these sketches considered amazing for the time period?

   Ⓐ They used modern architectural design elements.

   Ⓑ They were shared with other artists and designers to inspire them.

   Ⓒ The ideas were not only sketched but built within a few years.

   Ⓓ The ideas were new at the time and have been experimented with in the modern world.

3. How did da Vinci contribute to modern inventions?

   _____

   _____

   _____

**The Renaissance**

# Renaissance Churches

**Historical-Thinking Skill**

Students will make connections between social and cultural changes that took place during the Renaissance in different places.

**Activate**

Display the following Italian words that are used regularly in the English language, and ask students to define them: *bravo, diva, duo, finale, ghetto, motto, presto, scenario, solo, tempo, trio.* Then, provide one more word, *duomo*, and explain that it means *cathedral* in Italian.

**Analyze**

1. Have students look at both pictures on *Examine Renaissance Churches* (page 185). Then, place students into two groups, and assign each group one of the cathedral pictures to focus on to complete *Document Analysis—Set the Scene* (page 297). On the backs of their sheets, ask students to make lists of observations and information they know about their churches. Allow time for additional research.

2. Then, pair students with partners from opposite groups, and ask them to share their observations. Guide the class in a discussion about how the churches were influenced by the artists, engineers, and time periods in which they were built.

3. Use the following questions to guide a discussion:
   - What is the difference between a basilica and a cathedral, or duomo?
   - How long do you think it took to build each church?
   - Why are churches like these considered great pieces of architecture?
   - In your opinion, which is more beautiful? Why?

4. Allow time for students to complete *Examine Renaissance Churches*. Discuss their work and strengthen their analysis skills using the How To activity.

**How To . . .**

**Compare Images**—Tell students that an easy way to compare images is to take notes directly on the paper. They can look for similarities, circle them, and write thoughts or questions. Challenge them to find as many similarities in the photos as they can. Then, ask students to think of ways they could annotate the images to highlight differences.

**Extend**

Have students use Venn diagrams to compare and contrast Islamic architecture from the same era as when St. Peter's Basilica and Duomo di Milano were built.

*(vertical sidebar)* **Advanced DBAs**

Name: _____ Date: _____

# Examine Renaissance Churches

**Directions:** Read the background information, study the images, and answer the questions.

The building of St. Peter's Basilica in Vatican City began in 1506 and was completed in 1615. It is one of four major basilicas all located in Rome. The Duomo di Milano is located in Milan, Italy. Construction on this building began in 1386, and it took five centuries to complete. It is the second largest cathedral in the world.

St. Peter's Basilica

Duomo di Milano

1. What are some key architectural elements of St. Peter's Basilica?

   _____

   _____

   _____

2. What are some key architectural elements of Duomo di Milano?

   _____

   _____

   _____

3. Why were such large cathedrals and basilicas important to the Catholic Church?

   Ⓐ to inspire awe and interest in Christianity

   Ⓑ to provide jobs for builders and architects

   Ⓒ to make each location a center for worship

   Ⓓ to best use the excess resources of the churches

# Medieval and Renaissance Art

**Historical-Thinking Skill**

Students will analyze significant individuals and ideologies that emerged during the Renaissance.

**Activate**

List the following art characteristics on the board: iconography; Christian subject matter; elaborate patterns; decoration and bright colors; the use of precious metals, gems, and other luxurious materials; a revival of classical Greek/Roman art forms and styles; humanism or the nobility of man; painting techniques that maximize depth; and realism of people's faces. Have students predict if each characteristic describes medieval art or renaissance art. Write *M* or *R* next to each one depending on what students think. (The first five listed are medieval, and the last four are Renaissance.)

**Analyze**

1. Have students look at both pictures on *Examine Medieval and Renaissance Art* (page 187). If possible, project the color versions provided in the Digital Resources. Ask them to complete *Document Analysis—Make Connections* (page 296) to support their analysis by comparing and contrasting the two art pieces.

2. Have students research modern-day churches. What type of art can be found in churches today? How is the artwork similar to and different from paintings in the past? Does the modern artwork serve the same purpose as the past artwork? What is that purpose?

3. Use the following questions to guide a discussion:
   - Who is the central person in the medieval painting?
   - Why do you think the others in the painting are so much smaller?
   - What is the main event in the Renaissance painting?
   - How does Christ compare in both paintings?

4. Allow time for students to complete *Examine Medieval and Renaissance Art*. Discuss their work and strengthen their analysis skills using the How To activity.

**How To . . .**

**Annotate Paintings**—Tell students that annotating paintings can be a great way to begin their analysis and to keep records of their thinking. One tip for analyzing art is to look for specific things, circle them, and make notes. Have students look for the five characteristics typical of medieval art and the four characteristics typical of Renaissance art in the correlating paintings. Ask students to write notes or questions to record their thinking.

**Extend**

Have students select different painters from the Renaissance. Ask them to research to identify the artists' greatest works of art and create a Renaissance art gallery in your classroom. Then, have students do a gallery walk around the room, and have students act as docents to explain the different pieces of art.

**Advanced DBAs**

# Examine Medieval and Renaissance Art

**Directions:** Read the background information, study the paintings, and answer the questions on a separate sheet of paper.

*La Maestà* is an altarpiece finished around 1311 by Duccio di Buoninsegna. It was originally placed in Siena Cathedral. *Giving of the Keys to St. Peter* is a painting by Pietro Perugino. It was finished in 1482 and is located in the Sistine Chapel in Rome.

*La Maestà*

Section of *Giving of the Keys to St. Peter*

The Renaissance

1. What characteristics can you identify and describe in the medieval painting?

2. What characteristics can you identify and describe in the Renaissance painting?

3. What are some similarities among the two paintings?

# Brunelleschi's Dome

## Historical-Thinking Skill

Students will assess how art, literature, and architecture reflect features of different cultures and religions.

**Activate**

Hold up a raw egg, and tell students that the person who can make the egg stand upright on its own will receive a prize. Let students try to make it stand upright. When everyone has had a chance to try, take the egg and crack it against the top of the desk so that the bottom is flat, making it stand upright. Tell students that the experiment you just did is a story from history. The person who won the contest was chosen to build the dome portrayed in the sketch.

**Analyze**

1. Have students look at the images on *Examine Brunelleschi's Dome* (page 189). Ask them to complete *Document Analysis—Think Across Time* (page 300) to support their analysis. Have students think of other major architectural feats across different cultures to include on their time lines.

2. Use the following questions to guide a discussion:
   - How long do you think it took to build this dome?
   - What do you notice about its construction?
   - Why is architecture considered art?

3. Allow time for students to complete *Examine Brunelleschi's Dome*. Discuss their work and strengthen their analysis skills using the How To activity.

**How To . . .**

**Read Architectural Blueprints**—Tell students that architects need blueprints in the same way writers need outlines. Being able to analyze a blueprint will allow them to understand the purpose and design of a building. Tell students that when analyzing a blueprint, they should first read the title. Titles can give insight to the purpose of the design and the audience. Have them look for different types of lines and shading and discuss what they might mean. Finally, have them try to determine the view(s) and establish the scale of the structure in their minds.

**Extend**

Have students research and create presentations of the modern architectural creations of Frank Lloyd Wright. The American architect designed more than 1,000 structures based on a philosophy he called *organic architecture*. Wright believed in designing structures that were in harmony with humanity and the environment.

**Advanced DBAs**

Name: _____ Date:_____

# Examine Brunelleschi's Dome

**Directions:** Read the background information, study the images, and answer the questions.

Filippo Brunelleschi was a talented architect. He is remembered most for his domed ceilings, which were found in many of his designs. The image to the right is a blueprint he created for one of his designs. The photo below is of one of his domes that is part of the Cathedral of Santa Maria del Fiore.

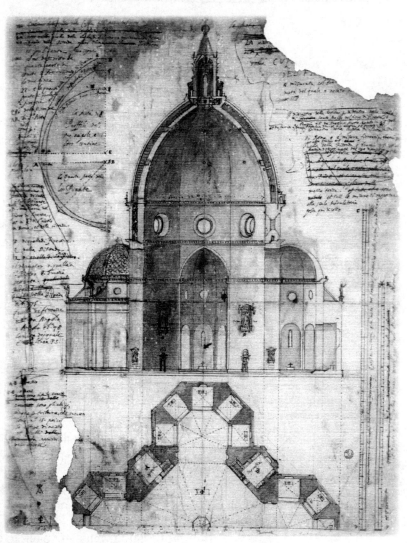

**1.** Why was this dome an innovative idea at that time?

_____

_____

_____

_____

**2.** How has this design influenced building and architecture today?

_____

_____

_____

_____

# Commerce in Venice

**Historical-Thinking Skill**

Students will use the historical context to better understand the rise of Venice as a powerful city.

**Activate**

Ask students to think about how the company Amazon® has changed commerce and trade in today's society. Have students stand and choose a side of the room. One side will argue that Amazon has made society better. The other side will argue that it has made society worse. Once students have chosen their sides, allow for debate.

**Analyze**

1. Have students look at the picture of Venice on *Examine Commerce in Venice* (page 191) and complete *Document Analysis—Set the Scene* (page 297) to support their analysis and think about the historical context of Venice during the Renaissance.

2. Display a map of Europe (from the Renaissance era if possible). Have students identify places and products that Venetians would have had as potential trade partners.

3. Use the following questions to guide a discussion:

   · What are the people doing in the picture?

   · Why would this be an ideal place for a businessman?

   · Why is this a good place to live?

   · Are there disadvantages to living here? Explain.

4. Allow time for students to complete *Examine Commerce in Venice*. Discuss their work and strengthen their analysis skills using the How To activity.

**How To . . .**

**Interpret Photographs**—Explain to students that people can interpret photographs in different ways. Every photograph can trigger emotions, and different people will react to the same photograph in different ways. However, using a photograph to understand history requires more than an emotional interpretation. Have students begin with the historical context. Ask them to imagine being in the location during the Renaissance. What do they observe around them?

**Extend**

Compare and contrast Venice during the Renaissance with modern-day Venice. What is still the same, and what has changed for Venetians? Are Venice and its people better off today, or were they better off during the age of the Renaissance? Have students support their answers with evidence.

**Advanced DBAs**

# Examine Commerce in Venice

**Directions:** Read the background information, study the image, and answer the questions.

This is a modern photo of Venice, Italy. This stone bridge spans across the Grand Canal. The bridge was designed and built in the late sixteenth century by Antonia da Ponte and his nephew. It is at the entrance to the Rialto, which was the commercial hub of Venice.

1. How would living in this city be different from living in your city? Describe at least two differences.

   _____

   _____

   _____

2. In what ways did the geography of Venice help to make it one of the leading city-states of the Renaissance?

   (A) It was surrounded by high mountains, and it was easy to protect.

   (B) It was connected by five rivers so trade could go deep into Europe.

   (C) It had great weather, and the port could stay open year-round.

   (D) It was on the water, and ships could drop off cargo easily.

3. Describe at least two advantages and disadvantages of a city like Venice.

   _____

   _____

   _____

   _____

© Shell Education

# The Renaissance Document-Based Question

## Historical Context

The Renaissance was a time of rapid change. It was a time of cultural rebirth. People abandoned the community, hierarchy, and authority of the Middle Ages in favor of individualism and realism. The growth of commerce and individual wealth led to support for the arts and literature. The spirit of humanism, which encouraged individualism and rediscovery of the classics (the pagan world of the ancient Greeks and Romans), led to a golden age in painting, sculpture, and architecture.

## Essay Tasks

**Directions:** Using the documents and your knowledge of the Renaissance, complete **one** of the following essay tasks. Before you begin your essay, complete the *DBQ Essay Planner* (pages 302–305) to plan your writing.

### Essay Task 1

In a well-organized essay, explain the extent in which the Renaissance served as a bridge from classical times to modern times.

In your essay, remember to:

- Write a clear and concise thesis statement.

- Provide evidence that will convince the reader that the Renaissance was a bridge to modern times.

- Include a topic sentence, introduction, body, and conclusion.

- Give details to support your ideas.

- Use information found in the documents to support your argument.

### Essay Task 2

In a well-organized essay, identify at least two new contributions or innovations of science and mathematics to the visual arts, and explain in detail how Renaissance artists used these techniques.

In your essay, remember to:

- Write a clear and concise thesis statement.

- Provide evidence to support that the innovations of science and mathematics can be found in the artwork of the Renaissance.

- Include a topic sentence, introduction, body, and conclusion.

- Give details to support your ideas.

- Use information found in the documents to support your argument.

★ As a bonus, include evidence from an outside source or a counterargument in your chosen essay.

The Renaissance

# Teacher Resources

## Background Information

### Da Vinci's Notes Lesson

Leonardo da Vinci was born in 1452 in Italy. Da Vinci is widely known as an outstanding genius in almost every field of study. He had many ideas, and he organized his notes in notebooks. His notes consisted of both words and images, and his drawings enabled him to make sense out of the ideas he saw in his head. He was interested in science and how things worked. Da Vinci studied gravity, stability, and maneuverability. He applied what he learned to his sketches of innovative flying machines. Da Vinci designed his own versions of several mechanical devices that would eventually enable flight, including parachutes, gliders, and helicopters. After studying the flight of birds, he drew detailed plans for a human-powered ornithopter. This machine had a bird-like wing flapping device that he felt would enable people to fly just like birds and bats. Although this apparatus did not work, da Vinci was convinced that a flying design would have to be modeled after the flight of birds. Besides flying machines, he also worked on mechanical devices such as bicycles, weapons, and the transmission of energy.

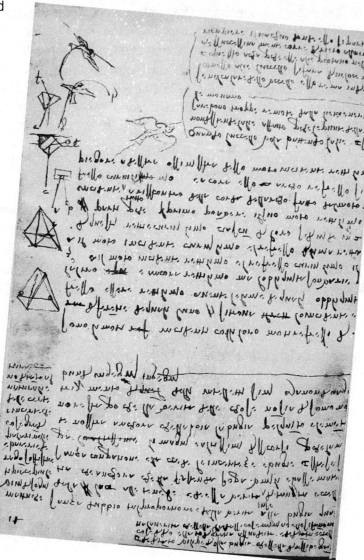

Advanced DBAs

# Teacher Resources (cont.)

## Renaissance Churches Lesson

St. Peter's Basilica is one of the world's largest churches. After the original church was determined beyond repair, Pope Julius II began the rebuilding in 1506. It took 120 years to complete. Many famous architects of the Renaissance and Baroque periods contributed to its design and construction. The architects included such masters as Donato Bramante, Raphael, Michelangelo, Carlo Maderno, Gian Lorenzo Bernini, and many others. The basilica was built in the form of a Latin cross with a dome in the center, which was designed by Michelangelo.

The Duomo di Milano is located in Milan, Italy. Construction on this building began in 1386, and it took five centuries to complete. It is the second-largest cathedral in the world. It has more of a French than Italian influence with a late Gothic architecture style. It is 515 feet (157 meters) long and can hold about 40,000 people at one time. The roofline has open pinnacles with spires and statues that look over the city of Milan. It was built using brick and then covered with marble. Nicolas de Bonaventure was the architect appointed by the church and fundraising began. During the first few years, the engineers worked to improve their methods and instruments. It was halfway completed by 1402, but the lack of funding kept the project from moving forward until after 1480. In the early 1500s, an octagonal cupola was added along with a spire called "Amadeo's Little Spire." Much of the façade began in the seventeenth century.

## Medieval and Renaissance Art Lesson

Medieval art had an order that presented pictures from highest to lowest. The largest figures in a painting were considered the most important. When moving away from the central point of the painting, the figures of less importance become smaller and smaller, depending on how they relate to the subject. Medieval paintings were often two-dimensional. This style highlighted the main theme, which was usually the glory of the subject, the most important part of the artwork. Religious events were often shown in the paintings, and they could tell God's story in that one single frame. If ordinary people were in the painting, they were often small because they were not as important.

In contrast, one of the most important achievements of Renaissance artists was their ability to apply the illusion of depth to their canvases, making them appear more three-dimensional. This approach is credited to the artist Masaccio (1401–1428), and it is used in Pietro Perugino's painting, *Giving of the Keys to St. Peter*. The canvas is treated as if it were a window that one could see through. This "open-window" idea represented a major change in art. Religious themes were still important. After all, the great popes of the period were patrons of the arts, and art was an excellent way to enhance the glory of the church and spread faith. But, Renaissance artists also began to portray the human figure in exact detail, and they made paintings and sculptures that showed male and female bodies.

Advanced DBAs

# Teacher Resources *(cont.)*

## Brunelleschi's Dome Lesson

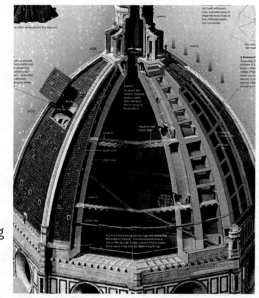

Filippo Brunelleschi was talented in many areas, but he is most widely known for his achievements in architecture. He is remembered most for his domed ceilings, which were found in many of his designs. Before Brunelleschi's time, domes were made by piling one brick on top of another in circles that got smaller and smaller. Brunelleschi figured out how to make domes much lighter. His idea was to use pendentives and bays. By using pendentives, the triangular sections that anchored the dome to its square base, the bay could be filled in with much lighter materials. The difficulty in building domes was not in the architectural design but rather in the engineering and construction.

In 1296, the building of the Santa Maria del Fiore began in Florence, Italy. In 1415, there was a contest to see who would build the dome. The council finally chose Filippo Brunelleschi to build the dome. Brunelleschi knew that the problem lay in the scaffolding. No one knew how to build scaffolding tall enough to construct a dome of this size. Whenever someone tried to extend scaffolding that was tall enough to reach the top of the building, it would topple over. It was built with two layers, an inner dome and an outer shell to protect it from weather. Brunelleschi built the dome without scaffolding in a way that allowed the dome to support itself as it was being built. He laid large wooden planks across the diameter of the dome. He stood on these bases as he built the dome. He placed the bricks in a herringbone pattern. When he had built around the dome reaching as far as he could, he simply took these wooden bases, inserted them at the new top, and began adding to the dome again. The process was repeated until the dome was finished.

## Commerce in Venice Lesson

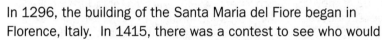

To the Renaissance world, Venice was *La Serenissima Repubblica*, the Most Serene Republic. The marble and stone city located on a lagoon in the Adriatic Sea was looked upon by some statesmen with awe and admiration, while others looked at it with hate and envy. Venice came about after the fall of the Roman Empire. It endured as the longest surviving republic in history while other cities succumbed to factional and civil strife, tyranny, and foreign invasions. The monopoly of eastern trade that Venice enjoyed was kept secure by the power of its galleys and fleets, and it did little to endear them to those who sought to share in the eastern treasures.

The Rialto was the commercial hub of Venice. The headquarters of the merchants, their town dwellings, business stalls, and warehouses were located in this section. The Venetian Republic carefully supervised all the commercial business that took place. Any foreign ships coming into Venice for goods were compelled to expel two-thirds of their cargo at the port. The foreigners were taxed on what they imported, and they were also taxed on goods they purchased as exports. All sorts of luxury goods flowed into Venice, including spices, gold, silver, glass, jewels, damask, cotton, timber, furs, dyes, silks, oil, and grain. Cheap raw materials, such as hides, cloth, tin, copper, steel, and other metals, flowed in the opposite direction. Venetians traded their own goods, such as lace, wool clothing, and Venetian glass.

© Shell Education

Advanced DBAs

# Teacher Resources *(cont.)*

## Answer Key

**Examine da Vinci's Notes** (page 183)

1. Students should notice such things as the intricacy of the mechanical details in the images (cogs, wheels, screws, pulleys).

2. D

3. He sketched out a way for people to fly long before anyone even thought it was possible.

**Examine Renaissance Churches** (page 185)

1. Answers should include a large dome and a large façade.

2. Answers should include spires, white façade, taller building, and statues.

3. A

**Examine Medieval and Renaissance Art** (page 187)

1. Students may identify and describe some of the following characteristics: flat, two-dimensional, smaller subjects; large Madonna and Christ; shallow, or without depth; bright colors.

2. Students may identify and describe some of the following characteristics: open window effect, three-dimensional, all subjects are the same size, or the people look real.

3. Christ is a central character in both paintings.

**Examine Brunelleschi's Dome** (page 189)

1. Brunelleschi's domes were innovative because he figured out a way to make the ceilings lighter. This meant they could be bigger.

2. It has influenced architecture today because domes can be seen all over the world. Architects use what they've learned from the past and then add better designs to their new buildings.

**Examine Commerce in Venice** (page 191)

1. Answers may include that this city has no yards, people travel in boats, and there is plenty of water around.

2. D

3. Advantages: easy to transport cargo, easy to travel by ship, more visitors which would increase the industry there, or have the latest trends and fashions; Disadvantages: flooding, disease from the many visitors, or difficulty getting around the city without canoes or small boats.

**The Renaissance Document-Based Question** (page 192)

Refer to pages 306–307 for the DBQ Rubrics.

# Advanced Document-Based Assessments

## Unit 15: Constitution and New Government

**Lessons**

**Teacher Resources**

# The Articles of Confederation

## Historical-Thinking Skill

Students will examine influences on the ideas established by the Constitution.

**Activate**

Write the following question on the board, and ask students to think about it for a minute: *Does society need rules and laws?* Guide a brief discussion or friendly debate about this question, and encourage students to support their thoughts with reasons and evidence.

**Analyze**

1. Have students read Alexander Hamilton's notes on *Examine the Articles of Confederation* (page 199). Ask students to complete *Document Analysis—Set the Scene* (page 297) to support their analysis and understanding of the historical context in which these words were written.

2. Place students into small groups (about three students in each group). Divide the text into equal parts, and give a different part to each group. Tell students to rewrite the text in their own words. Then, have each group read its rewritten text aloud.

3. Use the following questions to guide a discussion:
   - What was the purpose of these notes?
   - What was going on in the country at this time?
   - How do the place and date for these notes influence your understanding of them?
   - Into what categories might these problems be classified?
   - How might these grievances be summarized?

4. Allow time for students to complete *Examine the Articles of Confederation*. Discuss their work and strengthen their analysis skills using the How To activity.

**How To . . .**

**Use Vocabulary to Unlock a Source**—Explain to students that vocabulary from different time periods can be difficult to understand. When analyzing a document, they should identify key pieces of vocabulary that they do not recognize or understand. Then, they can use a thesaurus to find synonyms for difficult terms. Ask students to try this with Alexander Hamilton's notes.

**Extend**

Have students read the actual Articles of Confederation. Make a counterargument that the Articles were a good framework for government. Ask students to support this argument in short essays or a class discussion.

**Advanced DBAs**

# Examine the Articles of Confederation

**Directions:** Read Alexander Hamilton's notes for a speech proposing a new plan of government. These notes were written in June 1787. Then, answer the questions.

> *Objections to the present confederation*
> *Entrusts the great interests of the nation to hands incapable of managing them—All matters in which foreigners are concerned—The care of the public peace: Debts Power of treaty without power of execution Common defense without power to raise troops, have a fleet—raise money Power to contract debts without the power to pay—*
> *—These great interests of the state must be well managed or the public prosperity must be the victim— Legislates upon communities. Where the legislatures are to act they will deliberate No sanction—* { *To ask money not to collect it and by an unjust measure*

1. Choose one problem with the Articles of Confederation from Hamilton's notes. Explain why it was a problem for the United States. How was this issue addressed in the Constitution?

   _____

   _____

   _____

2. Hamilton fought in the Continental army during the American Revolution. He also served as an assistant to General George Washington. How might these experiences have shaped his views about a new national government?

   _____

   _____

   _____

3. Which of the following statements about the Articles of Confederation is true?

   (A) The weaknesses of the Articles made the country strong in the world view.

   (B) The Articles were made weak on purpose because they did not want another king.

   (C) The Articles would have worked better if there were no states.

   (D) The Articles demonstrated a great working relationship between the states.

**Constitution and New Government**

# Congressional Representation

**Historical-Thinking Skill**
Students will examine the ideas that led to the Great Compromise of 1787.

**Activate**

Give students two minutes to write lists of things they know about Congress. Then, put students into small groups to compare their lists and see who was able to write the most things about Congress that were accurate.

**Analyze**

1. Have students look at the map and read the information on *Examine Congressional Representation* (page 201). Ask them to complete *Document Analysis—Make Connections* (page 296) to support their analysis by comparing and contrasting the three plans. Tell students they can circle or highlight similarities or use arrows to make connections among the plans.

2. Have students make predictions of which states on the map would support which plan. Remind students that representation is not about the geographic size of the state but rather the population.

3. Use the following questions to guide a discussion:

   • Which branch of government is described here?

   • How is representation determined in the Senate? How is it determined in the House of Representatives?

   • In what ways is this map different from a modern map of the United States?

   • Why were these plans named for states?

   • Compare and contrast these ideas to those in the Articles of Confederation.

4. Allow time for students to complete *Examine Congressional Representation*. Discuss their work and strengthen their analysis skills using the How To activity.

**How To . . .**

**Read a Map**—Explain to students that maps do more than teach geography. They can show change over time as well as information about the people who made them and the time periods in which they lived. First, students should examine and identify the different parts of maps, such as titles, labels, and symbols. The time period of a map can give the reader an idea about its purpose and reason for creation. Have students circle the parts of the map on page 201 that give them information and help them understand the time/place in which it was created or is referring.

**Extend**

Ask students to create lists of pros and cons of the Great Compromise. Then, have students discuss the following question: If the vote on the representation plans were to happen today, which states and how many would vote for each plan? Have students create modern maps of the vote for the big state or small state plan.

Name: _____ Date: _____

# Examine Congressional Representation

**Directions:** This is a map of the United States under the Articles of Confederation. In boxes are the representation plans proposed at the Constitutional Convention. Study the map, read the plans, and answer the questions.

**Virginia Plan**—all congressional representation based on the population of states; supported by the large states

**New Jersey Plan**—all states should have equal congressional representation regardless of population; supported by the small states

**Great Compromise (the Connecticut Plan)**—two houses of Congress; Senate has equal representation with two senators for each state; House of Representatives varies, based on population

1. Which states supported the Virginia Plan?

   _____

   _____

2. Give at least one reason why some states did not support the Virginia Plan.

   _____

   _____

   _____

3. Why is the issue of congressional representation important?

   _____

   _____

   _____

# Article II of the Constitution

**Historical-Thinking Skill**

Students will assess the relevance of the ideas established by the Constitution.

### Activate

Show students the results of the electoral college map of the 2000 presidential election (visit **constitutioncenter.org** for an interactive version). Ask them to analyze the map and draw conclusions based on the information from the map.

### Analyze

1. Have students read the excerpt on *Examine Article II of the Constitution* (page 203). Ask them to complete *Document Analysis—Consider the Source* (page 298) to support their analysis.

2. Display all the parts of Article II of the Constitution. Have students work in small groups to place the excerpt in the larger context of Article II. What were the top priorities of Article II? Have groups come to a consensus and present their ideas to the class.

3. Use the following questions to guide a discussion:

   · What is the subject of this document?

   · What is the purpose of this document?

   · Who wrote this document? How does that influence its contents?

   · When and where was this document written?

   · What does this excerpt not tell you?

4. Allow time for students to complete *Examine Article II of the Constitution*. Discuss their work and strengthen their analysis skills using the How To activity.

**How To . . .**

**Summarize to Understand**—Explain to students that summarizing a difficult or unfamiliar text into their own words can help them gain a better understanding of the document. Have them first read the excerpt of Article II closely. They may need to read the document more than one time. Next, have them make lists or outlines that include the main idea and any supporting details in their own words. Then, have them write the summaries using their lists, and limit their summaries to just two or three sentences.

### Extend

Have the class break into groups and examine all seven articles of the Constitution. Have them summarize their articles and create posters with illustrations and summaries. Then, have students complete a gallery walk, taking notes about all the posters.

**Advanced DBAs**

# Examine Article II of the Constitution

**Directions:** Read the excerpt from Article II of the U.S. Constitution, and answer the questions.

"The executive power shall be vested in a President of the United States of America. He shall hold his office during the term of four years, and, together with the Vice President, chosen for the same term, be elected, as follows: Each state shall appoint, in such manner as the Legislature thereof may direct, a number of electors, equal to the whole number of Senators and Representatives to which the State may be entitled in the Congress: but no Senator or Representative, or person holding an office of trust or profit under the United States, shall be appointed an elector."

—*Excerpt of Article II, U.S. Constitution*

---

**Opposing Viewpoints**

Manner of election—direct election vs. state legislatures elect

Length of term in office—short-term (1 year) vs. long-term (7 years, life)

Number of terms—set term limits vs. no term limits

---

**1.** Describe one way in which the two sides compromised on this issue.

_____

_____

_____

**2.** How many electors does each state get?

(A) total number of senators

(B) total number of representatives

(C) total number of senators and representatives

(D) total number of people in the state

**3.** The Electoral College was created during this compromise. Does the Electoral College work well today? Why or why not?

_____

_____

_____

Constitution and New Government

# The Three-Fifths Compromise

## Historical-Thinking Skill

Students will make distinctions between the contradictory ideas established by the Constitution.

### Activate

Ask students to define the difference between *equality* and *equity*. Then, ask them which concept they think is more important and have them explain their reasoning in small groups.

### Analyze

1. Have students read the background information and look at the image on *Examine the Three-Fifths Compromise* (page 205). Ask them to complete *Document Analysis—Use Evidence* (page 299) to support their analysis. Guide students as necessary to make claims and draw conclusions from the document on their analysis sheets.

2. Have students create propaganda posters explaining to the public why this compromise was such a contradiction to the Constitution itself.

3. Use the following questions to guide a discussion:
   - What type of document is this?
   - What is the subject of this document?
   - Who is the audience for this document?
   - What are the connections between this document and the U.S. Constitution?
   - What are the most important things about this document?

4. Allow time for students to complete *Examine the Three-Fifths Compromise*. Discuss their work and strengthen their analysis skills using the How To activity.

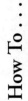

**How To . . .**

**Read Difficult Text**—Explain to students that during the time this document was written, the letter *s* was sometimes written to look more like an *f* or a long *s*. Ask students to find examples of this in the document. Then, ask students to look for any other things about the writing or language that is different.

### Extend

Explain to students that there have been many changes to the census over the years. Explain that recently, a question of citizenship was going to be added to the census. Ask them to make arguments either for or against adding a citizenship question to the census.

**Advanced DBAs**

Name: _____ Date:_____

# Examine the Three-Fifths Compromise

**Directions:** Read the background information about the states in the table. Then, study the census population count from 1800, and answer the questions.

| Southern States | Northern States |
|---|---|
| • large percentage of the population were enslaved people<br>• favored counting enslaved people as part of a state's population<br>• opposed counting enslaved people for taxation | • small percentage of the population were enslaved people<br>• opposed counting enslaved people as part of a state's population<br>• favored counting enslaved people for taxation |

1. How many total enslaved people lived in the states in October 1800?

   _____

2. Why did the Southern states want to count enslaved people as part of the population?

   _____

   _____

   _____

3. Which of the following statements about the Three-Fifths Compromise is accurate?

   (A) Southern states wanted enslaved people counted for taxation.

   (B) Southern states wanted enslaved people counted as part of their population.

   (C) Northern states wanted enslaved people counted as part of their population.

   (D) Northern states did not want enslaved people counted for taxation.

# Federalists vs. Anti-Federalists

**Historical-Thinking Skill!**

Students will evaluate the differing views of the federalists and anti-federalists.

**Activate**

Guide students to set up a debate, either as a whole class or with partners. Guide students to choose appropriate debate topics of interest to them. If students are with partners, assign them a side to argue for. Give students time to plan their arguments and then hold a short debate, allowing both sides to share their arguments. Ask students to give one another feedback on the quality of their arguments. Briefly discuss the importance of debate throughout the history of the United States.

**Analyze**

1. Have students study the chart on *Examine Federalists vs. Anti-Federalists* (page 207). Ask students to complete *Document Analysis—Make Connections* (page 296) to support their analysis. Explain that they should compare and contrast the statements and beliefs of John Jay and Patrick Henry.

2. Post four sheets of chart paper around the room with the following titles: *Federalist Large State*, *Federalist Small State*, *Anti-Federalist Large State*, and *Anti-Federalist Small State*. Place students into four groups, and have each group go to a sheet of chart paper. Have the groups write arguments to support the view written on the chart paper. Rotate each group through all four posters.

3. Debrief each poster at the end of the final rotation.

4. Use the following questions to guide a discussion:
   - For what purpose was it written?
   - What is the author's point of view?
   - What risks did the person take in writing this document?
   - How and why are these documents different?

5. Allow time for students to complete *Examine Federalists vs. Anti-Federalists*. Discuss their work and strengthen their analysis skills using the How To activity.

**How To . . .**

**Summarize to Understand**—Explain to students that summarizing a difficult or unfamiliar text into their own words can help them gain a better understanding of the document. Have them first read the words of John Jay and Patrick Henry closely. They should read the quotations more than one time. Next, have them make lists or outlines that include the main idea and any supporting details in their own words. Then, have them write the summaries using their lists, and limit their summaries to just two or three sentences.

**Extend**

Challenge students to read and then summarize Federalist #10 from the *Federalist Papers*.

**Advanced DBAs**

© Shell Education

# Examine Federalists vs. Anti-Federalists

**Directions:** Read the background summary about the opposing views at the top of the chart. Then, read the words of John Jay and Patrick Henry, and answer the questions.

| Federalists | Anti-Federalists |
|---|---|
| • favored a stronger central government | • favored a weaker federal government |
| • urged states to ratify the Constitution | • urged states not to ratify the Constitution as it was |
| • felt that no Bill of Rights was needed | • insisted that a Bill of Rights was needed |

"Complaints are also made that the proposed Constitution is not accompanied by a bill of rights; and yet they who make these complaints know, and are content, that no bill of rights accompanied the Constitution of this state (New York). In days and countries where monarchs and their subjects were frequently disputing about prerogative and privileges, the latter then found it necessary, as it were, to run out the line between them, and oblige the former to admit, by solemn acts, called bills of rights, that certain enumerated rights belonged to the people, and were not comprehended in the royal prerogative. But, thank God, we have no such disputes; we have no monarchs to contend with, or demand admissions from."

—John Jay, 1788

"It is on a supposition that your American governors shall be honest that all the good qualities of this government are founded; but its defective and imperfect construction puts it in their power to perpetrate the worst of mischiefs should they be bad men; and, sir, would not all the world, blame our distracted folly in resting our rights upon the contingency of our rulers being good or bad? Show me that age and country where the rights and liberties of the people were placed on the sole chance of their rulers being good men without a consequent loss of liberty! I say that the loss of that dearest privilege has ever followed, with absolute certainty, every such mad attempt."

—Patrick Henry, 1788

**1.** In what ways did the anti-federalists try to preserve what they thought the nation had fought for in 1776?

_____

_____

_____

**2.** What was one argument Jay made against the need for a bill of rights?

Ⓐ The governors are sure to be honest and trustworthy.

Ⓑ A strong central government is dangerous.

Ⓒ The state of New York has a bill of rights.

Ⓓ They have no monarch to fight against.

**Constitution and New Government**

# Approving the Constitution

## Historical-Thinking Skill

Students will study the voting record of the Constitution to learn how different states voted.

**Activate**

Have students define the terms *affirmative* and *negative*. Divide the class into 10 groups, and have each group read a different section of the Bill of Rights. Have each group summarize their section for the class.

**Analyze**

1. Have students look at the document on *Examine Approving the Constitution* (page 209) and complete *Document Analysis—Use Evidence* (page 299) to support their analysis. Guide students as needed to make claims and draw conclusions from the document and their background knowledge.

2. Have students create scripts for ten-second video ads supporting or opposing the Constitution and the Bill of Rights.

3. Have students share their ads, and have the class vote on approval.

4. Use the following questions to guide a discussion:
   - What was the purpose of the document?
   - What are some conclusions that can be drawn based on this information?
   - What questions do you have about the document?

5. Allow time for students to complete *Examine Approving the Constitution*. Discuss their work and strengthen their analysis skills using the How To activity.

**How To . . .**

**Find Additional Sources**—Explain to students that when they are given a primary source, no matter how detailed, it is limiting in the information it can provide. A great strategy to increase knowledge is to find additional sources that will add to their knowledge and corroborate information learned from the original primary source. Ask students to practice this skill by researching to find other primary sources related to the approval of the Constitution. Then, have students compare the information from the two sources.

**Extend**

The right to privacy is embedded into several different amendments, but it is never explicitly mentioned. Ask students to write a modern-day amendment that will deal with people's right to privacy.

**Advanced DBAs**

# Examine Approving the Constitution

**Directions:** This is a record of voting on the amendments to the U.S. Constitution. Three-fourths of the states has to approve an amendment for it to take effect. Examine the record, and answer the questions.

| Arti-cles. | Affirmative. | | | | | | Negative | | | | | | | |
|---|---|---|---|---|---|---|---|---|---|---|---|---|---|---|
| I. | N.H. | R.I. | N.Y.N.J.P. | M. V. N.C. S.C. | | | | | | | | D | | |
| II. | | | D. M. V. N.C. S.C. | | | N.H | R.I. | N.Y. N.J. P. | | | | | | |
| III. | N.H. | R.I. | N.Y. N.J. P. D. M. V. N.C. S.C. | | | | | | | | | | | |
| IV. | N.H | R.I. | N.Y. N.J. P. D. M. V. N.C. S.C. | | | | | | | | | | | |
| V. | N.H. | R.I. | N.Y N.J. P. D. M. V. N.C. S.C. | | | | | | | | | | | |
| VI. | N.H. | R.I. | N.Y N.J. P. D. M. V. N.C. S.C. | | | | | | | | | | | |
| VII. | N.H. | R.I. | N.Y N.J. P. D. M. V. N.C. S.C. | | | | | | | | | | | |
| VIII. | N.H. | R.I. | N.Y N.J. P. D. M. V. N.C. S.C. | | | | | | | | | | | |
| IX. | N.H. | R.I. | N.Y N.J. P. D. M. V. N.C. S.C. | | | | | | | | | | | |
| X. | N.H. | R.I. | N.Y N.J. P. D. M. V. N.C. S.C. | | | | | | | | | | | |
| XI. | N.H. | R.I. | N.Y N.J. P. D. M. V. N.C. S.C. | | | | | | | | | | | |
| XII. | N.H. | R.I. | N.Y N.J. P. D. M. V. N.C. S.C. | | | | | | | | | | | |

1. How many proposed amendments were sent for approval by the states?

   (A) 9

   (B) 10

   (C) 11

   (D) 12

2. Which states are absent on this voting record? Pick one missing state and give a reason why it might not be listed on the document.

   _____

   _____

   _____

3. Did the second proposed amendment pass? How do you know?

   _____

   _____

   _____

   _____

Constitution and New Government

Name: _____ Date: _____

# Constitution and New Government Document-Based Question

## Historical Context

The members of the Constitutional Convention of 1787 made compromises to address issues facing the new nation. These issues included representation in Congress, how to choose a president, and issues surrounding slavery. The Constitution remains a flexible, guiding document that continues to affect the nation today.

### Essay Tasks

**Directions:** Using the documents and your knowledge of the Constitution, complete **one** of the following essay tasks. Before you begin your essay, complete the *DBQ Essay Planner* (pages 302–305) to plan your writing.

#### Essay Task ❶

Choose three conflicts that arose during the creation of the Constitution of the United States. Explain how each conflict was resolved.

- whether to amend the Articles of Confederation or create a new document
- how to elect a president
- the Great Compromise
- the Three-Fifths Compromise
- whether to include a Bill of Rights

In your essay, remember to:

- Explain the three conflicts.
- Provide evidence that the resolutions were either good solutions or they created new problems for the future.
- Include a topic sentence, introduction, body, and conclusion.
- Give details to support your ideas.
- Use information found in the documents to support your argument.

★ As a bonus, include evidence from an outside source or a counterargument in your chosen essay.

#### Essay Task ❷

Make an argument about how the Constitution could have been made even stronger.

In your essay, remember to:

- Identify the issue or issues that needed to be stronger.
- Provide evidence that will convince the reader that the suggested changes would make the Constitution even stronger.
- Include a topic sentence, introduction, body, and conclusion.
- Give details to support your ideas.
- Use information found in the documents to support your argument.

Constitution and New Government

# Teacher Resources

## Background Information

### The Articles of Confederation Lesson

The Second Continental Congress declared independence from Great Britain in 1776. Congress then created a committee to write the Articles of Confederation, which united the states into a loose union governed by a national Congress. However, Congress had minimal powers that were restricted by states fiercely guarding their individual powers. Additionally, the Articles of Confederation were written in a way that made it difficult for Congress to enforce.

During the 1780s, Alexander Hamilton pushed for a convention to amend the Articles several times, writing his own series of articles called *The Continentalist*. He played a prominent role at the Annapolis Convention of 1786. There, several states met to discuss trade problems because Congress did not have the authority to regulate commerce.

The revolt in 1786 by Massachusetts farmers, also known as Shays's Rebellion, made it apparent to many of the nation's leaders that the nation had reached a crisis because of the inability of Congress to act. There was no national court system, so state disputes (and there were many) went unresolved. Foreign nations did not know if they were dealing with one nation or 13 separate countries when it came to tariffs and trade. Most importantly, Congress did not have the power to tax and, as a result, was neither able to pay for its debts nor fund the military for defense. Finally, the Articles of Confederation did not specify whose powers were supreme, the state's powers or the nation's powers. In the summer of 1787, the states sent representatives to Philadelphia to revise the Articles. In the end, they produced an entirely new document—the U.S. Constitution.

### Congressional Representation Lesson

Arriving in Philadelphia in May 1787, James Madison had prepared an alternative government plan to the Articles of Confederation. His plan, the Virginia Plan, was proposed to the convention and immediately caused a stir. Many representatives realized that they were no longer there to revise the Articles of Confederation. This plan was entirely new, and it created a stronger national government with three separate branches. The national government would now have more power than ever before.

The Virginia Plan distributed power in the two-house national legislature by granting states with higher populations more representation. But smaller states objected to the Virginia Plan because many of their state powers had been reduced, and since they had smaller populations, they would lose even more power. Most delegates agreed that Congress needed additional power, such as the power to tax and regulate trade. The New Jersey plan, presented by William Paterson from the same state, kept most of the organization of powers for the states as the Articles of Confederation dictated. Its main component was a one-house legislature with equal representation for the states.

Instead, the delegates approved the Great Compromise, which created a bicameral legislature. This meant there was one house with proportional representation, giving larger states more power, and there was one house with equal representation and equal powers. It was decided that population would determine representation and how much each state should be taxed. Additionally, to distinguish between

Advanced DBAs

# Teacher Resources (cont.)

the national and state powers, the powers of Congress were enumerated in Article I, Section 8. The powers of the states were denied, such as no longer allowing individual states to conduct their own affairs with foreign countries as explained in Article I, Section 10.

## Article II of the Constitution Lesson

One of the great debates at the Constitutional Convention after the legislative branch was agreed upon, revolved around the creation of the executive branch. This was especially important because under the separation of powers principle, this branch could limit the power of the legislative branch.

While designing the office of the presidency, the greatest concern was to avoid the creation of a monarchy with unlimited powers, especially after what the states had experienced as colonies under George III. In the 69th Federalist paper, Alexander Hamilton contrasted the new office of the presidency with that of the king of Great Britain, pointing out how the new president would be elected for a specific term and could be impeached if necessary. The president did not have the power to make laws but only to suggest, sign, or veto them.

The Virginia Plan originally proposed that the president be chosen through the national legislature, and this idea was debated at the Philadelphia Convention. Many representatives preferred the idea that local electors would choose the president. James Madison objected to the proposal that state legislatures choose the president because they might use this power to pressure the president to agree to their terms. As a result, the idea for the Electoral College was created. The rationale for the Electoral College was that since the electors only met for the purpose of electing the president and were then dismissed, they would be less likely to become corrupted.

## The Three-Fifths Compromise Lesson

James Madison's original Virginia Plan included proportional representation in both houses of Congress. However, as part of the Great Compromise, only one of the two houses of Congress would be based on population. Yet, counting a state's population to determine its number of representatives presented another dilemma for the members of the Philadelphia Convention. Would enslaved people be included in the population count? If they were, some states would have an advantage over the states who had taken steps to eradicate slavery. Thus, slavery also entered the debate, though most of the delegates tried to avoid discussing it.

In 1783, Congress proposed an amendment to the Articles of Confederation that determined taxation by a state's population. This amendment included a three-fifths ratio, meaning that three out of every five enslaved people counted as one vote. However, the amendment failed to pass. The three-fifths federal ratio was resurrected in the summer of 1787, and after much debate, it became the solution to the proportional representation issue in Congress. However, it was not without controversy. Because of the inflated numbers, the compromise gave slave states a slight advantage in the House of Representatives and also in presidential elections through the Electoral College. At the time though, many people believed slavery was a dying institution, and the proportional representation issue would not be a permanent problem. Some historians argue that the compromise created a slave-power conspiracy. The three-fifths compromise remains the source of much debate in the history of slavery in the United States.

Advanced DBAs

# Teacher Resources <small>(cont.)</small>

## Federalists vs. Anti-Federalists Lesson

The campaign to persuade the states to approve the new Constitution began almost as soon as the ink dried. The federalists immediately began their robust propaganda campaign, which included numerous newspaper articles. The anti-federalists did their best to react, but they started late, and their lack of organization gave their opponents a clear advantage. For many anti-federalists, the consolidated national government under the Constitution seemed to be a break from the principles they had fought for in the Revolution. For them, the federalists supported a government remarkably similar to the monarchy that they had once defeated.

John Jay, future governor of New York and Chief Justice of the Supreme Court, reacted to the request that the new Constitution outline a bill of rights to protect individual liberties from the possible tyranny of this new, more imposing government. He argued that the anti-federalist complaint made little sense because New York's constitution had no bill of rights, either. Besides, he added, there was no need for protection of rights from a tyrannical monarch because there was no longer a monarch and the president would not become one.

Patrick Henry, famous for his "Give me liberty or give me death!" speech of 1775, refused to attend the Constitutional Convention because he was suspicious of the planned activities. He regretted that the states had lost so much power in the new Constitution. He worried that the new Constitution gave too much power to leaders who might not be as honest as necessary. The federalists argued that if citizens had the power to remove leaders who showed poor judgment from office, their rights and liberties would remain secure.

## Approving the Constitution Lesson

This document is a voting record kept by Thomas Jefferson. It shows the ratification of the amendments to the U.S. Constitution that eventually became the Bill of Rights. The anti-federalists had agreed to ratify the Constitution but only on the condition that a bill of rights be added later. James Madison, elected to the first United States Congress representing Virginia, pushed 17 proposed amendments through the House of Representatives. Only 12 passed through the Senate and were sent to the states for approval. However, by the time three-fourths of the states had approved them, as required, only ten amendments remained.

Upon further examination, the document indicates that 10 states approved the first article. However, there were now a total of 14 states because Vermont had joined the Union on March 4, 1791. This meant that 11 states were necessary to approve the amendments. Just to the left of the initials for New York is a small letter *v* for the new state of Vermont. The states of Massachusetts, Connecticut, and Georgia show no voting record because they either had not ratified the amendments or did not notify President Washington that they had done so. Thomas Jefferson, as secretary of state, delivered the official notice of the amendments' ratification to the states. The Bill of Rights was officially ratified on December 15, 1791. The first proposed amendment deals with limiting the congressional district size and the second proposed amendment specifies that any change in the congressional representatives' compensation could not take effect until after an election. These two original amendments did not pass. The third proposed amendment then became the first amendment regarding freedom of speech.

Advanced DBAs

# Teacher Resources (cont.)

## Answer Key

### Examine The Articles of Confederation (page 199)

1. Students should choose one problem from the Articles of Confederation, such as the care of public peace or matters dealing with foreigners, and write about how the issue was addressed in the Constitution.

2. Answers may include that Hamilton had experience serving under a capable general. He saw firsthand that a leader needs power to do his job successfully, and he related his experience to the issue of the president's power.

3. B

### Examine Congressional Representation (page 201)

1. States with the largest populations, including Virginia, North Carolina, South Carolina, Massachusetts, New York, and Pennsylvania, would have supported the Virginia Plan.

2. Smaller states probably felt that they would lose more power under the Virginia Plan because of the small populations of their states.

3. The more representation a state has in Congress, the more power it has.

### Examine Article II of the Constitution (page 203)

1. Answers may include that they compromised on the length of term in office. The president would serve a four-year term.

2. C

3. Students should explain whether the Electoral College works well today, in their opinions.

### Examine the Three-Fifths Compromise (page 205)

1. There were 894,345 enslaved people living in the states in October 1800.

2. Answers may include that if enslaved people were counted, Southern states would have more representation in the House of Representatives.

3. B

### Examine Federalists vs. Anti-Federalists (page 207)

1. The anti-federalists wanted to secure the liberties of the people, and they thought this would best be accomplished through local and state governments. They saw the creation of the federal government as a return to the strong, centralized power of the British. This is why the compromise of demanding a bill of rights was so important. If they were to agree to a federal constitution, then it must contain a bill of rights that stated what the central government could not do and what powers the states would still retain.

2. D

### Examine Approving the Constitution (page 209)

1. D

2. Answers will vary and may include that Massachusetts, Connecticut, and Georgia had no record of voting because they had not ratified the amendments or did not notify President Washington they had done so.

3. Article II did not pass because only half of the states approved it, and it needed three-fourths to pass.

### Constitution and New Government Document-Based Question (page 210)

Refer to pages 306–307 for the DBQ Rubrics.

# Advanced Document-Based Assessments

## Unit 16: Industrial Revolution

**Lessons**

**Teacher Resources**

# Child Labor

**Historical-Thinking Skill**
Students will evaluate the evolution of child labor in America.

1500
1600
1700

**Activate**

Discuss with students the difference between a job and a career. List students' ideas on the board. Then, create a four corners activity about job/career priorities. The four corners should be: safety, pay, happiness, and benefits (health, dental, vacation, etc.). Have students choose the corner they believe is the most important when finding a job or choosing a career. Then, have students defend their choices.

**Analyze**

1. Have students study the picture on *Examine Child Labor* (page 217). Ask students if they see any obvious OSHA (Occupational Safety and Health Administration) violations in this photograph. Ask why they think this situation was allowed to happen.

2. Discuss with students the lax standards for child labor that existed in the United States until 1938, when the Federal Wage and Hour Law was finally passed to protect young people in the workplace.

3. Have students complete *Document Analysis—Think Across Time* (page 300) to support their analysis. Guide them as needed to include causes and effects of child labor on their time lines.

4. Use the following questions to guide a discussion:
   - Who appears to be in more danger?
   - What are the ages of the two boys?
   - What type of work is being done?
   - Was this illegal at this time in history? Why or why not?

5. Allow time for students to complete *Examine Child Labor*. Discuss their work and strengthen their analysis skills using the How To activity.

**How To . . .**

**Identify Time Periods**—Explain to students that it is possible to still learn the time period of a primary source, especially a photograph, even if the date is not provided. Using context clues, such as clothing and setting, can be one strategy. Identifying the author or creator of the primary source is another. Explain that they can also identify additional events that can be connected with the primary source. Have students look at the photograph and circle anything that could serve as a clue as to what time period the picture is from.

**Extend**

Have students find additional photographs from Hine. Then, have students create websites opposing child labor using Hine's photographs and adding their own written arguments.

**Advanced DBAs**

Name: _____ Date: _____

# Examine Child Labor

**Directions:** Read the background information, examine the image, and answer the questions.

This photo was taken by Lewis Hine, who traveled throughout the United States from 1908–1912 photographing children in a variety of labor situations. His goal was to expose the dangerous conditions that children faced while working in factories and mines. He wrote a caption for each photo. This photo, taken in 1909, had the following caption: *Bibb Mill No. 1, Macon, Ga. Many youngsters here.* Some boys and girls were so small they had to climb up on the spinning frames to mend the broken threads and put back the empty bobbins.

1. All the following were possible reasons it took so long to pass an effective child labor law EXCEPT:

   Ⓐ Child labor was cheap, and companies made a higher profit using it.

   Ⓑ Migrant workers and other families needed their children to work to help the family survive.

   Ⓒ Children had always worked on family farms, so hard work was expected of them.

   Ⓓ Children could work faster before and after school, so there was no reason to change.

2. There is an old saying that "a picture is worth a thousand words." How does this statement apply to this photo by Hine?

   _____

   _____

   _____

3. Based on this image, describe what a week might have been like for one of these boys.

   _____

   _____

   _____

# Haymarket Square

**Historical-Thinking Skill**

Students will compare and contrast the different points of view over labor unions.

**Activate**

Show students different news clips about teacher strikes that occurred across the country in the late 2010s. Ask students to react to the concept of teacher strikes. Were they effective? If so, why? Who, if anyone, was hurt by the strikes? Is striking necessary in the teaching profession? In other professions?

**Analyze**

1. Have students look at the poster on *Examine Haymarket Square* (page 219). Ask students to complete *Document Analysis—Set the Scene* (page 297) to support their analysis and place the poster in a historical context.

2. Read the background information about the Haymarket Riot (page 229) if students are not familiar with it. Then, have students discuss with partners who was to blame for the riot.

3. Take a vote to see where the class stands in regards to blame for the riot. Ask students to defend their decisions.

4. Use the following questions to guide a discussion:
   · Would a meeting like this lead to violence?
   · Why would an eight-hour workday be an early goal of unions?
   · Why did workers feel the need to form unions?
   · Why did factory owners dislike unions?

5. Allow time for students to complete *Examine Haymarket Square*. Discuss their work and strengthen their analysis skills using the How To activity.

**How To . . .**

**Analyze Posters**—Tell students that there are some specific strategies they can use when analyzing posters. Have them determine if the poster tries to persuade more through words or visuals. Explain to students that this can give them a clue to know who the intended audience is for the poster. Then, have students put the poster into its historical time period. Have them write one-sentence summaries of the poster to help explain its purpose.

**Extend**

Have students select an industry or profession that they feel should be unionized. Then, have students create new posters to recruit workers from that industry or profession to unionize.

**Advanced DBAs**

# Examine Haymarket Square

**Directions:** This poster was published in Chicago, Illinois, in 1886. Examine the poster, and answer the questions.

1. Labor unions wanted all the following EXCEPT:

   (A) better pay          (C) safer working conditions

   (B) eight-hour workday   (D) weekend work hours

2. Why would labor unions advertise in public with a poster like this?

   _____

   _____

   _____

3. Why would this poster be in two languages?

   _____

   _____

   _____

# Changes in Communications

**Advanced DBAs**

## Historical-Thinking Skill

Students will evaluate the development of business and technology in the late nineteenth century.

**Activate**

Tell students that the cell phone was invented in 1973 by a researcher for Motorola named Martin Cooper. The first iPhone® was released on June 29, 2007. Place students into small groups, and have them create lists of everything that would not exist today if cell phones were not invented.

**Analyze**

1. Have students read the background information and look at both pictures on *Examine Changes in Communications* (page 221). Discuss how each device revolutionized communication. Ask students to imagine what life was like before these two inventions.

2. Have students work with partners and complete *Document Analysis—Make Connections* (page 296) to support their analysis. Ask students to determine the best way to set up the chart to show the cause-and-effect relationships of these new technologies.

3. Use the following questions to guide a discussion:
   - What are the basic parts of this telephone?
   - In what ways are the original telephone and a cell phone alike and different?
   - How is text messaging similar to the telegraph?
   - What do you think the next major change in telecommunication might be?

4. Allow time for students to complete *Examine Changes in Communications*. Discuss their work and strengthen their analysis skills using the How To activity.

**How To . . .**

**Find Additional Sources**—Explain to students that when they are given a primary source, no matter how detailed, it is limiting in the information it can provide. A great strategy to increase knowledge is to find additional sources that will add to their knowledge and corroborate information learned from the original primary source. Ask students to practice this skill by researching to find another primary source related to these inventions. Then, have them compare the information from the two sources.

**Extend**

Ask students to predict the next great communication inventions. Then, challenge them to create 30-second advertisements explaining their new inventions and how they will revolutionize communication.

Name: _____ Date: _____

# Examine Changes in Communications

**Directions:** Read the background information, examine the images, and answer the questions.

The image on the left shows a telegraph transmitter set. A form of this type of communication was used from the 1840s through the 1980s. In 1836, Samuel F. B. Morse developed a telegraph machine that could send messages using dots and dashes, which was later called the Morse code. Wires for transmitting messages via telegraphy were soon installed across the nation.

The image on the right shows the first telephone invented by Alexander Graham Bell. Bell's mother and wife were both deaf. This influenced him to study sound. He experimented with hearing devices and ways to improve the telegraph. He wanted voice messages rather than dots and dashes to be sent. His partnership with James Watson resulted in Bell being awarded the first U.S. patent for the invention.

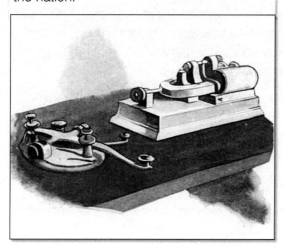

1. How did the invention of the telegraph system improve military and railroad communications during the Civil War and later?

   _____

   _____

2. What type of training do you think is needed to operate this telegraph system?

   (A) training in Morse code and how to tap at a good pace

   (B) training in basic alphabet phonics

   (C) training in the military applications of Morse code

   (D) training in the transcribing of one message to another message

3. How did communication change from 1865 to 1925 for Americans?

   _____

   _____

   _____

# Thomas Edison

## Historical-Thinking Skill

Students will compare and contrast the development of business in the late nineteenth century.

**Activate**

Ask students to tell partners about times when they failed at something more than once before they got it right. Have students share what lessons they learned with the class. Then, share Thomas Edison's quotes, "I have not failed. I've just found 10,000 ways that won't work." and "Never get discouraged if you fail. Learn from it. Keep trying." Discuss the quotes as a class.

**Analyze**

1. Have students look at the picture on *Examine Thomas Edison* (page 223). Ask students to analyze the photo, paying special attention to the contents of the laboratory. Discuss what students observe. Have them share what they already know or think they know about Thomas Edison. Be sure to correct any misconceptions students may have about Edison.

2. Have students complete *Document Analysis—Use Evidence* (page 299) to support their analysis.

3. Use the following questions to guide a discussion:

   · Why would Edison be called a wizard?

   · What impact did his inventions have on today's technology?

   · How is this laboratory similar to or different from today's laboratory technology?

   · The photo shows Edison standing alone; however, he is credited with pulling together a team of inventors and then using mass production and teamwork to accomplish a unique invention process. How was this first industrial research lab an innovative idea?

4. Allow time for students to complete *Examine Thomas Edison*. Discuss their work and strengthen their analysis skills using the How To activity.

**How To . . .**

**Summarize to Understand**—Explain to students that summarizing a primary source into their own words can help them gain a better understanding of the primary source. To summarize, they should first examine the photograph closely. Tell them they will need to look at the photograph very closely and more than once. Next, they should make lists or outlines in their own words with the main idea and any supporting details found in the photograph. Then, have them write summaries in two or three sentences.

**Extend**

Have students research other inspirational quotes from Thomas Edison. Have them select their favorite quotes and create posters, flyers, or other artwork to represent the quotes. Then, display them around the classroom for continued inspiration.

**Advanced DBAs**

# Examine Thomas Edison

**Directions:** Read the background information, examine the image, and answer the questions.

This photo was taken of Thomas Edison (1847–1931) in his laboratory at Menlo Park, New Jersey. Menlo Park was a community of scientists working on a variety of projects, mostly using electricity. Inventions by Edison and others in his group netted more than 1,000 patents. He was the founder of Edison Electric, which later became General Electric. Edison is considered by many to be the greatest American inventor and is most remembered for inventing the practical light bulb, an electrical system for street lighting, the phonograph, and motion pictures.

1. Choose one of Edison's inventions, and explain how it changed society.

   _____

   _____

   _____

2. Why was the Menlo Park community important to the success of Edison's inventions?

   Ⓐ It was near the major banks of the time, and they invested in the area.

   Ⓑ The competition to be the best inventor drove innovation.

   Ⓒ The scientists and inventors collaborated in well-equipped laboratories.

   Ⓓ There was already electricity powering the laboratories.

3. In your opinion, what three factors led to Edison's success as an inventor? Explain your choices.

   _____

   _____

   _____

Industrial Revolution

# Time Line of Inventions

## Historical-Thinking Skill

Students will study the progression of inventions during the Industrial Revolution.

**Activate**

Take the list of inventions from *Examine a Time Line of Inventions* (page 225), and make two sets of note cards. One note card should have the year and the inventor. The other note card should have the invention. Make as many sets as necessary for your class. Shuffle the cards together, and in small groups, see if students can match the correct inventor to the invention. Then, share the time line of inventions, and have students check their matches.

**Analyze**

1. Ask students to study the chart on *Examine a Time Line of Inventions*. Then, have them circle the inventions they know and put squares around the inventions they do not know. Ask them to write notes about any of the people or inventions they recognize.

2. Ask students to complete *Document Analysis—Think Across Time* (page 300) to support their analysis. Ask them to include a few of the inventions they find most important on their time lines. Have them include a few recent inventions that were influenced by these inventions of the past.

3. Use the following questions to guide a discussion:
   · Why do so many of the inventions rely on steam?
   · Which inventions benefited the textile industry (making of thread, cloth, etc.)?
   · Which inventions directly affected transportation?
   · Which inventions directly affected communication?

4. Allow time for students to complete *Examine a Time Line of Inventions*. Discuss their work and strengthen their analysis skills using the How To activity.

**How To . . .**

**Analyze Time Lines**—Explain that time lines are powerful because they help people understand the larger scope of events while also seeing important details. Tell students that when they analyze time lines, they should first identify the span of history the time line covers. Second, have them determine how the periods of time have been divided, such as 1-year, 5-year, or 20-year. Third, have them examine the events to determine any connections. Ask students to look at the time line of inventions again and mark the time differences between each invention and any other observations.

**Extend**

Have students choose a second topic, such as world events, U.S. political events, or women's history. Have each student re-create the time line of inventions on the top half of a sheet of paper. Then, on the bottom half of the time line, have students list events from their second topic. Discuss any relationships they notice.

**Advanced DBAs**

Name: _____ Date: _____

# Examine a Time Line of Inventions

**Directions:** Read the background information and the time line of inventions. Then, answer the questions on a separate sheet of paper.

This time line lists several of the major inventors and their inventions from 1733 through 1903. This time frame is known as the Industrial Revolution. Inventions such as new forms of power and energy, factories, the discovery of new chemicals, improved communications, and improved transportation systems changed the way people lived, worked, played, invested, and dreamed of the future. Cottage industries and family farms dwindled, and cities and factory systems took their places.

## Time Line of Inventions

**1733** Thomas Newcomen invents the steam engine.

**1733** John Kay invents the flying shuttle.

**1764** James Hargreaves invents the spinning jenny.

**1769** Richard Arkwright patents the water frame.

**1769** James Watt is credited with having created the first efficient steam engine.

**1779** Samuel Crompton perfects the spinning mule.

**1785** Edmund Cartwright patents a power loom.

**1793** Eli Whitney patents the cotton gin.

**1807** Robert Fulton begins steamboat service on the Hudson River.

**1830** George Stephenson begins rail service between Liverpool and Manchester.

**1836** Samuel F. B. Morse invents the telegraph.

**1840** Samuel Cunard begins transatlantic steamship service.

**1856** Henry Bessemer develops the Bessemer converter.

**1858** Cyrus Field completes the first successful transatlantic cable.

**1859** George Bissell and Edwin L. Drake drill the first commercial oil well in Pennsylvania.

**1866** The Siemens brothers improve steel-making by developing the open-hearth furnace.

**1876** Alexander Graham Bell invents the telephone.

**1879** Thomas Edison invents the incandescent light bulb.

**1892** Rudolf Diesel patents the diesel engine.

**1899** Guglielmo Marconi invents the wireless telegraph.

**1903** The Wright Brothers make the first successful airplane flight.

**Industrial Revolution**

1. Why are so many of the earlier inventions focused on spinning and weaving?

   (A) The jobs were easy and well paid.

   (B) There was so much land to grow cotton in England.

   (C) England's textile industry had been based on a home cottage industry.

   (D) England had many rivers to send the finished product to other countries.

2. In what ways did steam engines change society?

3. Describe the progress of communication from the telegraph to the telephone.

# Transportation

**Historical-Thinking Skill**

Students will examine how transportation influenced economic conditions in various regions of the country.

**Activate**

Show students a map of the United States, and identify the cities of Boston and Los Angeles. Using the map scale, ask students to estimate the distance in miles between the two cities. Ask students if they think there are more miles of railroads or highways in America. Have them estimate the total amount of miles of each. **Note:** There are approximately 150,000 miles (241,402 kilometers) of railroad track and 164,000 miles (263,932 km) of highways in the United States.

**Analyze**

1. Have students study the images on *Examine Transportation* (page 227). Ask students which invention came first. Briefly explain the background of each invention. Ask students which invention they think had a greater social impact.

2. Have students complete *Document Analysis—Make Connections* (page 296) to support their analysis by comparing the two transportation vehicles.

3. Use the following questions to guide a discussion:

   · What are the benefits and the limitations of this 1903 automobile?

   · What energy source provided the power for these locomotives?

   · What would be the attraction of this new automobile? Where and when would it be used?

4. Allow time for students to complete *Examine Transportation*. Discuss their work and strengthen their analysis skills using the How To activity.

**How To . . .**

**Identify Time Periods**—Tell students that it is possible to still know the time period of a primary source even if the date is not provided. Using context clues, such as materials and setting, can be one strategy. Identifying the author or creator of the primary source is also helpful. Ask students to look at the photos on *Examine Transportation* and circle any clues of the time period from which these photos were taken.

**Extend**

Have students find photos of modern trains and cars. Then, have them compare and contrast the changes between trains and cars of the past to the present.

Advanced DBAs

© Shell Education

# Examine Transportation

**Directions:** Read the background information, study the photos, and answer the questions.

The photo on the left is of a two-steam engine locomotive, and the other is of a 1903 Ford automobile. The steam locomotive here dates to the 1870s after the building of the transcontinental railway that linked the East and West by rail. The photo on the right is Henry Ford's first successful automobile. He sold more than 600 custom assembled models in eight months.

 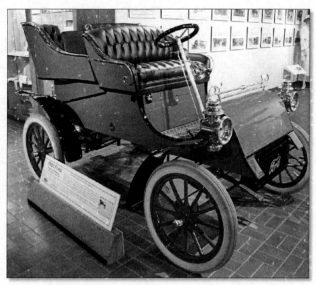

1. How did steam locomotives change travel for the average person in the 1860s?

   (A) They allowed people to move alongside their property.

   (B) They made travel faster, and people began to travel for pleasure.

   (C) They made it possible to move to big cities.

   (D) They created many jobs for people building the railroad.

2. By 1925, a Model T Ford cost only $260. This was about one-fifth of an average worker's yearly salary at that time. How did this price for a car change the lives of average Americans?

   _____

   _____

   _____

3. Assume that you live in 1905 and have some money to invest in a railroad or automobile company. Which would you choose and why? Explain your answer based on what you would have known during that time period.

   _____

   _____

   _____

Industrial Revolution

# Industrial Revolution Document-Based Question

## Historical Context

The Industrial Revolution began in England. It was a response to finding new ways to improve the country's textile industry and keep up with the worldwide demand for textile products. The steam engine changed everything. It allowed a factory system to be established and to spin and weave in record time. After the Revolutionary War, Americans also jumped on the inventing bandwagon. The free-enterprise system spurred inventors to test their creativity and build their fortunes. Their inventions changed America from an agricultural society into an industrial culture in one century.

## Essay Tasks

**Directions:** Using the documents and your knowledge of the Industrial Revolution, complete **one** of the following essay tasks. Before you begin your essay, complete the *DBQ Essay Planner* (pages 302–305) to plan your writing.

### Essay Task ❶

In a well-organized essay, explain how the Industrial Revolution promoted positive changes in the lifestyles of American citizens while at the same time creating new problems and challenges.

In the essay, remember to:

- Incorporate specific details that prove an understanding and knowledge of this topic.
- Demonstrate an understanding of the key issues through accurate analysis of at least three of the primary source documents.
- Include a topic sentence, introduction, body, and conclusion.
- Give details to support your ideas.
- Use information found in the documents to support your argument.

### Essay Task ❷

In a well-organized essay, identify the three inventions that had the single largest influence on changing America's society.

In the essay, remember to:

- Identify the three inventions and the changes they brought to America.
- Provide evidence that reveals how society was changed by these inventions.
- Include a topic sentence, introduction, body, and conclusion.
- Give details to support your ideas.
- Use information found in the documents to support your argument.

★ As a bonus, include evidence from an outside source or a counterargument in your chosen essay.

Industrial Revolution

# Teacher Resources

## Background Information

### Child Labor Lesson

As the Industrial Revolution progressed from the 1700s to the early 1900s, child labor became a serious issue throughout Europe and America. Factories hired children at low wages and for long hours as more families left the farms to work in crowded cities. Owners of cotton mills organized a system of orphanages where children lived in ghetto-like housing and worked 13–16 hours daily. Other children sought factory and migrant jobs to help their families meet living expenses.

Concerned citizens united to end child labor, but they achieved only small victories. In 1904, the National Child Labor Committee was formed. Around this time, most states had "officially" raised the minimum age for factory work to 14 years and 16 for mining, but the laws were seldom enforced.

To prove how bad conditions were for children, the Child Labor Committee hired Lewis Hine to photograph the working conditions for children throughout the United States. Hine took more than 500 photographs of child workers from 1908 to 1912. He included a written caption with each photo that commented on the dangerous or unhealthy situations he observed. Hine traveled to 24 states and photographed children working as newsboys, coal miners, mill workers, migrant farmers, dockworkers, sorters of shellfish, and cannery workers. The photos were printed in magazines and books and used as evidence by the Child Labor Committee to promote the passage of child labor laws.

Finally, after many failed attempts to protect children, a strict Fair Labor Standards Act was passed in 1938 to protect young people in the workplace.

### Haymarket Square Lesson

Labor unions did not begin in America. They were first formed as a reaction to the terrible conditions in Europe's factories and mines. The first well-organized national union in America was the Knights of Labor, formed in Philadelphia four years after the Civil War ended. Within 15 years, the union had more than 700,000 members. Union leaders began to argue, and eventually the organization lost power and effectiveness. The next union, the American Federation of Labor (AFL), was headed by Samuel Gompers. By 1904, this union boasted a membership of 1.7 million, and it was considered the most important union in the country. Factory owners did not like unions interfering in their factories, and many owners threatened to fire the people who joined them.

The U.S. government leaders at this time did not support union activity. Unions fought back by holding strikes. Sometimes, these strikes became violent. On May 4, 1886, labor supporters organized a rally at Haymarket Square in Chicago. The protest turned into a riot after someone in the crowd threw a bomb at police. At least eight people died as a result of the bomb.

The Haymarket Riot was viewed as a setback for organized labor in America. After the Haymarket Riot and the trial and executions that followed, many people were skeptical of labor unions. The country was divided. Some Americans became anti-labor. Others believed the men from the Haymarket Riot had been wrongly convicted and viewed them as heroes to the labor movement. For a while, the unions lost influence, but slowly, the pendulum swung in their favor. As new unions developed, politicians took notice and sought their support in elections.

Advanced DBAs

# Teacher Resources *(cont.)*

## Changes in Communications Lesson

As an artist of considerable talent, Samuel Morse helped found the National Academy of Design and taught art at New York University. He enjoyed tinkering and became interested in chemical and electrical experiments. His tinkering paid off in 1835 when he developed a prototype of a telegraph machine to send messages by a unique tapping system. What made his invention so special was the tapping code he designed to relay messages. It was a series of "dots and dashes" (short and long taps) sent through electronic impulses that became known throughout the world as Morse code. In 1843, the U.S. government realized the importance of this invention and allocated $30,000 to construct a telegraph line from Washington, DC, to Baltimore. Soon, telegraph lines were being built everywhere. The device became a common means for the railroads to communicate. Most railway stations had installed a telegraph system by the Civil War. Stringing up telegraph wires was an important part of military operations for both Union and Confederate forces. Citizens also benefited from the invention. They could go to their local station and pay for important messages to be sent to friends and family who lived far away. The high cost prohibited casual communication.

A family interest in helping the hearing impaired inspired Alexander Graham Bell to study sound. He became especially interested in experimenting with methods to expand Morse's telegraph invention into a device that could send voice messages rather than just dots and dashes. He then linked up with James Watson, a brilliant electrical designer and machinist. Together, they gained the financial support needed to experiment with different methods of transmission—acid water and electromagnetism. In 1876, they chose to submit a patent for the telephone just hours ahead of their competitor, Elisha Gray. They then decided to focus on improving their electromagnetic telephone. On August 3, 1876, Bell was ready to send a long-distance transmission four miles away. In front of many witnesses, he sent a message that came through clearly, proving the invention could be used over long distances. The Bell Company was created in 1877. Nine years later, 150,000 people owned telephones.

## Thomas Edison Lesson

Thomas Edison (1847–1931) was not the inventor of the first light bulb, but he was the inventor of the first practical electrical light bulb that could be mass produced. Edison was one of the most prolific inventors in the world and, singly or jointly, held patents for 1,093 inventions in the United States alone. He was a pioneer in mass telecommunications with such inventions as the phonograph, improved telegraphic equipment, the carbon transmitter, the incandescent light bulb, the electric distribution system to bring electricity to homes and businesses, the megaphone, and motion pictures.

Around the age of 12, he wrote and typeset his own newspaper called the *World Herald*, which he sold to 300 customers. Eventually, Edison worked for Western Union. Working the night shift allowed him to read and conduct experiments. A failed experiment one evening led him to be demoted, so he quit. An older telegrapher and inventor named Franklin Pope became his mentor, giving Edison a place to live and conduct his experiments. His first significant inventions were all related to improving the telegraph systems for Western Union's rivals.

Eventually, Edison bought property in Menlo Park, New Jersey, and he built a home and laboratory on the 34-acre (13.8-hectare) site. This would be the site of many inventions that would change the world. This was the first industrial research laboratory—a safe sanctuary in which his scientific team could create, dream, and invent. It was in this laboratory that Edison invented a practical incandescent light bulb and a way to transmit electricity. On New Year's Eve, 1879, the first use of practical incandescent street lighting was demonstrated at Menlo Park.

Advanced DBAs

# Teacher Resources (cont.)

## Time Line of Inventions Lesson

The Industrial Revolution had its roots in Great Britain. Great Britain's industry focused on the making of textiles, which were sold to markets all over the world. During colonial times, the cotton grown in America was shipped back to England to be made into cloth. Colonists were not allowed to start their own textile industries. The British textile industry was a wide network of smaller cottage industries in which people worked at spinning wheels and hand looms in their homes or in small shops. By the mid-1700s, the textile industry had increased so much that English spinners and weavers could not keep up with the demand. One weaver, James Hargreaves, invented the spinning jenny around 1765. It used several spindles instead of one. His fellow weavers, afraid their shops would be closed due to the new invention, scorned Hargreaves. In the mid-1700s, British inventors revolutionized the industry with water-powered spinning and weaving machinery.

Other inventors worked on using steam to power machinery. When the cotton gin was invented after the Revolutionary War, the Southern cotton industry got a tremendous boost. After 1800, the United States became a major hub for inventors. Robert Fulton invented the first successful commercial steamboat, and river traffic changed dramatically. More than 33 years later, Samuel Cunard began a transatlantic steamship service. Improved methods of coal and steel production led to a wave of factories being built. Workers left their farms, and along with immigrants, flooded into the cities to take factory jobs. Communication changed dramatically with the telegraph, transatlantic cable, and the telephone. Electricity that was used for lighting and power resulted in even more changes in factory production and home life. When the Wright brothers flew their first successful airplane in 1903, the age of flight began and launched new possibilities for fighting in wars, personal traveling, and the transportation of goods.

## Transportation Lesson

The first railroads were horse-drawn carts on wooden tracks in Europe. In the mid-1700s, iron rails replaced wooden tracks, and the carts had grooved wheels that fit better over those tracks. The invention of the steam engine for trains is credited to three English inventors: Richard Trevithick, who designed the first steam tramway (no tracks) locomotive in 1804; George Stephenson, who invented the first steam railway locomotive in 1813; and Julius Griffiths, who patented the first passenger road locomotive in 1821. American inventor John Stevens was granted the first U.S. railway charter in 1815. Peter Cooper is credited for building the first steam locomotive to be operated on a common carrier railroad. George Pullman invented the sleeping car that enabled passengers to sleep comfortably on long trips. In 1853, Congress allocated $150,000 to survey the best route for a transcontinental railroad to the Pacific. The Union Pacific Railroad and the Central Pacific Railroad joined their eastern and western tracks together at Promontory Summit, Utah, in 1869.

Contrary to popular belief, Henry Ford did not invent the motorcar. His true claim to fame was designing a practical and marketable car that the average American could afford. His attempts to build that car involved many trial models. In 1903, several partners financed his new automobile design and his company, the Ford Motor Company. The new car was called the Model A, which became a success. Within eight months, 658 cars had been sold. Ford continued to improve the car and its method of production. In a four-year period, he designed Models B, C, F, K, N, R, and S. When Ford found a new material—vanadium steel—he knew he could make a new car design that would be stronger, lighter in weight, and more reliable. This new car was the Model T, and it sold for $850 in 1908. Ford also introduced and refined his idea of assembly line production. By 1925, he had decreased the cost of a Model T Ford to less than $300. Ford had successfully made an affordable car.

Advanced DBAs

# Teacher Resources *(cont.)*

## Answer Key

### Examine Child Labor (page 217)

1. D
2. Answers may include that these photos told the truth about the horrible conditions children faced in the workplace. Some people did not understand how bad things were until they saw these pictures.
3. Students should describe what a week might have been like for one of the boys in the photograph, including long work hours.

### Examine Haymarket Square (page 219)

1. D
2. Answers may include that the labor unions were not a secret, and they needed to recruit as many workers as possible.
3. The poster was probably in two languages because there was a large population of German workers in the area, and they wanted to invite everyone to join.

### Examine Changes in Communications (page 221)

1. Answers may include that the invention of the telegraph system improved military and railroad communications during the Civil War by allowing generals to get information about troop movement, which helped trains know what problems might be ahead on the tracks.
2. A
3. Answers may include that communication changed because people could send telegraph messages, and there were telephones and radios in many homes.

### Examine Thomas Edison (page 223)

1. Students should explain how Edison's inventions changed society.
2. C
3. Answers may include his intelligence, his determination to keep trying new ideas, his ability to involve others in his work, his inquiring mind, or the support of family and friends.

### Examine a Time Line of Inventions (page 225)

1. C
2. Answers may include that steam engines changed society by providing a source of transportation and a source of power so that factories could be built and operated to make products that were once made at home. People moved to big cities to get jobs in the factories, so family farms and cottage businesses decreased. Also, fathers went to work away from the homes and children worked in factories too.
3. Answers may include that the telegraph station was located in a public place, but phones would be installed in individual homes; the telegraph took a trained operator to send and receive, but the phone could be used by anyone.

### Examine Transportation (page 227)

1. B
2. Answers may include that the lower price for cars allowed the average American to own an automobile, and this luxury was no longer just available to the rich; families could go on vacations by car and visit family members who lived far away; people no longer needed to own and feed horses to pull their carriages; people did not have to completely rely on public transportation.
3. Students should clearly explain their investment choices.

### Industrial Revolution Document-Based Question (page 228)

Refer to pages 306–307 for the DBQ Rubrics.

Advanced DBAs

# Advanced Document-Based Assessments

## Unit 17: World War I

**Lessons**

**Teacher Resources**

# Trench Warfare

## Historical-Thinking Skill

Students will discover the conditions for soldiers in the trenches during World War I.

**Activate**

Have students arrange desks in two rows facing one another. Then, have students kneel behind the two rows. Ask students to try and look over their desks at the other row without having the other students see them. As students sit in their rows, discuss how they are feeling. How uncomfortable are they? Can they see anything across the rows with certainty? Briefly discuss their experiences.

**Analyze**

1. Have students look at the pictures on *Examine Trench Warfare* (page 235). Have students work in pairs to explain what is happening in each photograph. If possible, provide a magnifying glass for each pair of students. Ask students to tell what they see in the foreground and in the background. Discuss their observations.

2. Have students use both pictures and complete *Document Analysis—Use Evidence* (page 299) to support their analysis. Tell students to use the observations they made about the images to make claims and draw conclusions about the soldiers and the conditions of trench warfare.

3. Use the following questions to guide a discussion:
   - What is the purpose of the tangled wire in the first picture?
   - What is the difference in the poses of the soldiers in these pictures?
   - How is the weapon in the second picture the same and different from other weapons?
   - How are the soldiers dressed?

4. Allow time for students to complete *Examine Trench Warfare*. Discuss their work and strengthen their analysis skills using the How To activity.

**How To . . .**

**Evaluate Photographs as Evidence**—Explain to students that photographs can be great sources of evidence. However, it is important to consider how and why photographs were taken. Ask students to think about official documents that include their photographs. What do they actually prove? How reliable is an Instagram™ or Facebook™ feed at providing evidence of people's lives? How is a posed picture different from a candid one? Have students look at the images of trench warfare and discuss what evidence the images provide.

**Extend**

Have students write letters home to their families as if they were soldiers in the trenches of World War I. Have them write their letters in first person, and describe in detail the conditions of the trench and the emotions they experienced.

**Advanced DBAs**

# Examine Trench Warfare

**Directions:** Read the background information, study the images, and answer the questions.

The left image shows French soldiers crawling through a trench fortified with barbed wire. The picture on the right shows an Indian soldier serving with the British Army. He is keeping watch on German trenches by using a periscope. Miles of trenches stretched across Western Europe during World War I. Both sides used these fortifications for fighting, shelter, and for transporting men between units.

**1.** What were the trenches used for during World War I?

_____

_____

_____

**2.** Why were barbed wire and the periscope important inventions for this type of warfare?

_____

_____

_____

**3.** What did the land between the trenches become known as?

    (A) Scorched Earth Zone

    (B) Demilitarized Zone

    (C) No Man's Land

    (D) Land Between the Trenches

**World War I**

# Poisonous Gas

### Historical-Thinking Skill

Students will examine the morality of chemical weapons used during World War I.

**Advanced DBAs**

**Activate**

Tell students you will read a series of statements. If they agree with the statement, they should stand, pause a moment to see who is standing, and sit back down. Repeat this process until you complete the statements. Then, discuss the results a class. Statement 1: War is sometimes necessary. Statement 2: Only volunteers should have to fight in a war. Statement 3: There should be rules during a war. Statement 4: There should be rules against using chemical weapons during wartime.

**Analyze**

1. Have students look at the images on *Examine Poisonous Gas* (page 237). Ask them to complete *Document Analysis—Consider the Source* (page 298) to support their analysis.

2. Explain the use of poisonous gases during the war and the methods that were used to protect the soldiers from the harmful effects of those gases.

3. Ask students to debate the morality of using chemical weapons during war.

4. Use the following questions to guide a discussion:
   · Who or what is the target of the cartoon?
   · What symbolism do you see?
   · Which poisonous gas was the deadliest? Why?

5. Allow time for students to complete *Examine Poisonous Gas*. Discuss their work and strengthen their analysis skills using the How To activity.

**How To . . .**

**Identify Time Periods**—Tell students that it is possible to know the time period of a primary source even if the date is not provided. Using context clues, such as setting and clothing, can be one strategy. Identifying the author or creator of the primary source can also give clues. Have students annotate the image of the soldiers with masks by circling and commenting on anything in the photo that give clues of the time period.

**Extend**

Have students research the Chemical Weapons Convention (CWC) treaty from the United Nations. Have students evaluate and find evidence that this multilateral treaty banning chemical weapons and requiring their destruction within a specified period of time is either a success or a failure.

# Examine Poisonous Gas

**Directions:** Read the background information, study the images, and answer the questions.

This political cartoon was drawn by McKee Barclay and published between 1914 and 1918. The cartoon is a reaction to the use of poisonous gas as a weapon in World War I. The skeleton in the trench wears a helmet resembling that of Mars, the Roman god of war. The photo on the bottom right shows real soldiers wearing masks.

**1.** Why were gas masks necessary during World War I?

_____

_____

_____

**2.** How does Barclay feel about the use of gas as a weapon? Explain your answer.

_____

_____

_____

_____

World War I

# The *Lusitania*

**Historical-Thinking Skill**

Students will examine events that led to the United States joining the war.

**Activate**

Project or have students visit the U.S. Department of State travel advisory website (**travelmaps.state.gov/TSGMap**). Explain how to read the map, and have students explore the site. Ask students what they notice or find interesting about the travel restrictions. Ask students to consider why a travel ban would be placed on a particular country or location. Then, ask if this warning would keep them from traveling to those places.

**Analyze**

1. Have students read the background information, look at the image, and read the warning on *Examine the Lusitania* (page 239). Have students compare this warning with the map they just examined. Ask them if this warning would keep them from traveling.

2. Ask students to complete *Document Analysis—Set the Scene* (page 297) to support their analysis.

3. Use the following questions to guide a discussion:

   · What breach of warfare did the Germans commit by sinking this ship?

   · Why were U-boats an effective new invention of this war?

   · At what group of people was this warning targeted?

   · What was the German motive for issuing this warning?

   · Did the captain act irresponsibly in saying the trip was safe?

4. Allow time for students to complete *Examine the Lusitania*. Discuss their work and strengthen their analysis skills using the How To activity.

**How To . . .**

**Identify Bias**—Explain that bias is when something shows a preference or prejudice that is for or against a person or idea. The purpose of identifying bias in any material is to learn the point of view of the creator. Tell students that as they read, see, or listen to materials, they should keep the following questions in mind to help identify bias: *What facts has the creator left out? What other information is needed to understand the entire story? What words or images create a positive or negative point of view?* Ask students if they can identify any biases in the image or warning.

**Extend**

Have students create newspapers that incorporate different stories from World War I. There should be headline stories, including photographs or images, as well as additional stories about people, places, and events from the war.

**Advanced DBAs**

© Shell Education

# Examine the *Lusitania*

**Directions:** Read the background information, study the image, and answer the questions.

The advertisement for this voyage included a warning from the German Embassy in Washington. However, the *Lusitania*'s captain successfully reduced fears by telling tourists that his ship was too fast for U-boat attacks. So the ship departed from New York on May 1, 1915. This drawing depicts the sinking of the *Lusitania* on May 7, 1915. It was torpedoed by a German submarine. The picture was featured in *Punch* magazine.

### NOTICE!

TRAVELERS intending to embark on the Atlantic voyage are reminded that a state of war exists between Germany and her allies and Great Britain and her allies; that the zone of war includes the waters adjacent to the British Isles; that, in accordance with formal notice given by the Imperial German Government, vessels flying the flag of Great Britain, or any of her allies, are liable to destruction in those waters and that travelers sailing in the war zone on the ships of Great Britain or her allies do so at their own risk.

IMPERIAL GERMAN EMBASSY,

Washington, D.C.  April 22, 1915

**1.** Did the warning in the advertisement give the German navy the right to sink a ship containing passengers, including women and children? Explain your answer.

_____

_____

_____

**2.** Why did the sinking of the *Lusitania* make Americans want to declare war against Germany?

  (A) The *Lusitania* had more weapons for the Allied forces than a normal ship.

  (B) American citizens were killed in the attack.

  (C) This was a sneak attack on a passenger ship rather than a military or cargo ship.

  (D) both B and C

**3.** How was this incident similar to and different from the *Titanic*?

_____

_____

_____

World War I

# Communications

**Historical-Thinking Skill**
Students will evaluate the technology that influenced World War I.

### Activate

Ask students to define the word *technology* on a sticky note. Then, have them write examples of technology on four more sticky notes. Have students take their four sticky notes with examples of technology and trade them with other students until they have four different examples. Have each student return to their seat and see if their definition of technology works for each example they received. As a class, discuss the different examples and why technology can be defined in different ways.

### Analyze

1. Have students look at the photograph on *Examine Communications* (page 241). Have students describe what each of the 12 men are doing in this picture.

2. Have students focus on the two items in this picture that represent new technologies used in this war (motorcycle and radio communications). Discuss how these inventions were significant.

3. Have students complete *Document Analysis—Make Connections* (page 296) to support their analysis. Ask students to compare the communication during World War I to communication used in modern warfare on their sheets.

4. Use the following questions to guide a discussion:

   • What type of radio system is this, and how was it transported?

   • Why is one soldier on a motorcycle?

   • How could this radio system benefit this U.S. unit?

   • What is the difference between a radio system and a telephone system?

5. Allow time for students to complete *Examine Communications*. Discuss their work and strengthen their analysis skills using the How To activity.

**How To . . .**

**Find Additional Sources**—Explain to students that when they are given a primary source, no matter how detailed, it is limiting in the information it can provide. A great strategy is to find additional primary sources that can add to their knowledge or corroborate what they learned from the original primary source. Ask students to research and find additional primary or secondary sources related to communications during World War I.

### Extend

Have students make charts ranking five new inventions that were developed during World War I. Have them list the inventions, the year each one was developed, their purposes, and the effects they had on the war. Then, have students explain their rankings.

**Advanced DBAs**

# Examine Communications

**Directions:** Read the background information, examine the image, and answer the questions.

This is a photo of a United States Army Signal Corps operating a field radio station. It was taken in France in July 1918. World War I communication stations used different methods. They used carrier pigeons, radio "wireless" operators in the fields, messengers running in relays through the trenches, and soldiers on motorcycles to deliver messages. The wireless station in the photo was hard to carry and to set up. Radio technology also advanced during the war. This helped operators pick up enemy signals.

1. What is happening in this image? Provide details about what you think the roles of certain key individuals are.

   _____

   _____

   _____

2. How did communications improve during World War I?

   _____

   _____

   _____

3. All the following were important uses of messages sent by wireless operators during the war EXCEPT:

   (A) warning the enemy about a poisonous gas attack

   (B) getting messages to troops quickly

   (C) relaying information about battle command posts

   (D) keeping track of supplies needed and delivered

World War I

# Role of Airplanes

## Historical-Thinking Skill

Students will examine the impact of airplanes during World War I.

**Activate**

Show students a clip from YouTube™ of the training exercise from the film *Top Gun* without sound. Allow them to focus on the flying and the abilities of the planes. Have students share their reactions and describe what happened.

**Analyze**

1. Have students look at the photo on *Examine the Role of Airplanes* (page 243). Explain to students that the airplane became the glamour weapon in World War I. Have students describe the pilot's uniform and the plane in the picture. Pilots were frequently called *flying aces* once they had a certain number of kills. Ask students to discuss why that was the case.

2. Direct students to the Eight Rules of Air Conduct next to the photograph. Discuss for whom these rules were written. Have students compare these rules to the scene they just watched. Did they observe these rules being followed?

3. Ask students to complete *Document Analysis—Set the Scene* (page 297) to support their analysis.

4. Use the following questions to guide a discussion:
   - How is this pilot's uniform similar to and different from the uniforms that fighter pilots wear today?
   - What were some difficulties pilots in these planes might have faced?
   - What was the role of these planes during World War I?
   - Who took this pilot's picture and why?
   - What is your opinion of the Eight Rules of Air Conduct?

5. Allow time for students to complete *Examine the Role of Airplanes*. Discuss their work and strengthen their analysis skills using the How To activity.

**How To . . .**

**Annotate Written Documents**—Explain to students that one way to better understand a written document is to annotate it, or make notes and markings that show their thinking. Tell students that one way to do this is to highlight the most important parts of a text. Ask students to reread each of the rules of air conduct. As they read, they should each highlight a maximum of three words per rule that best summarizes each rule.

**Extend**

Have students research American pilots during World War I. Have students select one pilot and create presentations that discuss the pilot's life prior to the war, how they became a pilot, and what happened to them after the war.

**Advanced DBAs**

Name: _____ Date: _____

# Examine the Role of Airplanes

**Directions:** Read the background information, examine the photograph, and answer the questions.

This photograph shows a World War I American pilot in front of his plane. The United States entered the war in April 1917. The war ended in November 1918. American pilots were latecomers to the "dogfight" style of air warfare already in progress in France and Germany. But American pilots were fast learners. Next to the photo are the German Ace's Eight Rules of Air Conduct.

**German Ace's Eight Rules of Air Conduct**
by Oswald Boelcke, Germany's Leading Flying Ace

1. Always try to secure advantages before attacking. If possible, keep the sun behind you.
2. Always carry through with an attack when you have started it.
3. Fire only at close range and only when the opponent is properly in your sights.
4. Always keep your eye on your opponent, and never let yourself be deceived by ruses.
5. In any attack, it is essential to assail your opponent from behind.
6. If your opponent dives on you, do not try to evade his attack but fly to meet it.
7. When over enemy lines, never forget your own line of retreat.
8. For squadrons: it is better to attack in groups of four or six; avoid two aircraft ATTACKING THE SAME OPPONENT.

**1.** What role did pilots play in World War I?

_____

_____

_____

**2.** Which rule gave advice about battling more than one plane?

(A) #2          (C) #6

(B) #4          (D) #8

**3.** Why were pilots on both sides admired and made into celebrities?

_____

_____

_____

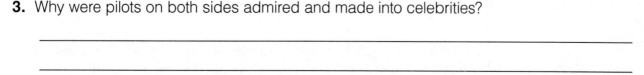

World War I

# Writing Home

## Historical-Thinking Skill

Students will examine a letter from Harry S. Truman to his wife to learn about the details of the war.

**Activate**

Ask students to volunteer to share if they have family or friends in the military. Ask them how often they are able to communicate with them. Ask students how important they think it is for people in the military to be able to communicate with loved ones back home and explain why.

**Analyze**

1. Have students read the background information and the letter from Truman on *Examine Writing Home* (page 245).

2. This letter, sent to Bess Wallace by Harry S. Truman, gives insight into how one soldier felt about the battlefield. Distribute red, blue, and yellow markers, crayons, or colored pencils to students. Have them read the letter individually, and ask them to respond by underlining the words that match each of the following categories: things said to reassure Bess of Truman's safety (red), things Truman felt safe telling Bess about the battles (blue), and things Truman mentioned that he lost (yellow).

3. Ask students to complete *Document Analysis—Use Evidence* (page 299) to support their analysis.

4. Use the following questions to guide a discussion:
   - What is the tone of this letter?
   - What information does this letter provide about a soldier's life during World War I?
   - How is the letter communication system working during the war?
   - Why will this experience be useful to Truman in the future?

5. Allow time for students to complete *Examine Writing Home*. Discuss their work and strengthen their analysis skills using the How To activity.

**How To . . .**

**Use Vocabulary to Unlock a Source**—Explain to students that vocabulary in historical documents, such as letters, can sometimes be difficult to understand. One strategy is to use a thesaurus (book or computer) to find the vocabulary term and look up its synonyms. Then, they can go back to the document and replace the difficult vocabulary with synonyms that they do know. Ask students to practice this skill with Truman's letter.

**Extend**

Have students begin a supply drive to send care packages to current soldiers stationed abroad. Research which items are in high demand and where different soldiers are currently stationed around the world. Have students include personal letters in their care packages.

**Advanced DBAs**

# Examine Writing Home

**Directions:** Read the background information and the letter. Then, answer the questions.

Captain Harry S. Truman (who would one day be president) wrote to his fiancée, Bess Wallace, back home. The letter is dated October 20, 1918. Truman was a captain in the infantry in France. In this letter, he described a series of battles he fought in. Letters during World War I were slow coming and going, but for the most part, they eventually got through via cargo ships and trains.

Dear Bess:

This is certainly a banner day. I received four letters from you. You were still without any letters from me except one. I wrote you at the first place we were in action. That was a very tame affair compared with what we have been through since as I told you in my last letters. I am awfully sorry I could not write to you in all that last time but it was simply an impossibility. For one thing I had nothing to write with and another I could not have written a sane coherent letter if I had tried. It was the most terrific experience of my life and I hope I don't have to go through with it many more times although we are going to bust Heine if it takes us all and I don't think there is a man in the organization who wouldn't give his life to do it. Please don't worry about us or about me I should say because I am egotistical enough to think that I am your principle worry. I am very comfortably situated now in a finely furnished dugout with stoves and everything. If I am lucky we may remain a good long time. I think they are trying to let us rest up from our hard work of last month. We marched half across France and were at it every night. I lost nearly all my horses just from marching so far without getting enough rest. We are recuperating now and I hope that before long everyone will be as good as new. [...] None of our officers were hurt except one whom you never met. He was gassed slightly. [...] I haven't taken any unnecessary chances but I had to go back after my guns. No good battery commander would send anyone else after guns he'd left in position under the same circumstances I left those two. I don't claim to be a good B.C. but I have to act like one anyway. [...] I am so pleased that I was lucky enough to get in on the drive that bade the Boche squeal for peace that I sometimes have to pinch myself to see if I am dreaming or not. It really doesn't seem possible that a common old farmer boy could take a battery in and shoot it on such a drive and I sometimes think I just dreamed it. You may be sure that we will make up for lost time when I do get home. I think of you and dream of you all the time. [...] Keep on writing because your letters brighten the days. I'll never cease loving you.

Yours always, Harry

World War I

**1.** Why does Truman mention horses?

_____

_____

**2.** In what ways does Truman try to assure his fiancée that he is safe?

_____

_____

_____

_____

# World War I Document-Based Question

## Historical Context

The Industrial Revolution and the age of steel led to many changes. Many cities were growing. Technology was making companies richer. Thousands of people who moved from farms to the cities could not find shelter or jobs. A new nationalism arose as European countries vied for new territories. France, Britain, and Germany all increased the strength of their military. They added new weapons and built stronger ships. When World War I finally began, artillery and infantry units performed the same duties as before. But new technologies soon took center stage in all aspects of the war. New ways to communicate and new ways to kill made this war the first modern war.

## Essay Tasks

**Directions:** Using the documents and your knowledge of World War I, complete **one** of the following essay tasks. Before you begin your essay, complete the *DBQ Essay Planner* (pages 302–305) to plan your writing.

### Essay Task ❶

During World War I, soldiers rode horseback in artillery units, supplies were delivered by wagons pulled by horses, and some messages arrived by carrier pigeons. In a well-organized essay, explain why World War I was considered the first modern war.

In your essay, remember to:

- Identify what advancements made World War I different from past wars.
- Include a topic sentence, introduction, body, and conclusion.
- Give details to support your ideas.
- Use information found in the documents to support your argument.

### Essay Task ❷

In a well-organized essay, evaluate the ways and extent to which the world changed because of World War I.

In your essay, remember to:

- Identify how soldiers and people back home were affected by the war.
- Provide evidence that will convince the reader that society did in fact change.
- Include a topic sentence, introduction, body, and conclusion.
- Give details to support your ideas.
- Use information found in the documents to support your argument.

★ As a bonus, include evidence from an outside source or a counterargument in your chosen essay.

# Teacher Resources

## Background Information

### Trench Warfare Lesson

World War I was the first war to use the advanced technologies that developed in the latter years of the Industrial Revolution. Electricity, the telegraph, the telephone, automobiles, steel manufacturing, barbed wire, advanced ammunition, chemical industries, and airplanes were all sources for improving daily lives, but they could also be easily converted into new military innovations. In this war, soldiers faced new types of offensive strikes instead of the typical cannon and rifle fire. Weapons such as Vickers or Maxim machine guns, howitzers, the incendiary bomb, gas shells, shrapnel shells, shrapnel bombs, grenades, high-explosive shells, and high-explosive bombs were used to attack the enemy. Setting up camps with tents was not a safe practice anymore. By 1915, miles of trenches had been dug from the coast of Belgium to Switzerland.

Trenches were used as fighting zones, shelters from attacks, places to launch counterattacks, places to live, and even as network "road systems" to move soldiers from one location to another. The typical trench system consisted of two or more trenches running parallel to each other. The trenches were about 10 feet (3 meters) deep and were reinforced with boards or cut branches and sandbags. Some trenches were fortified with a new invention from the American West: barbed wire. The trenches were miserable places to live. The men fought off rats and lived in dirty clothing infested with lice. When snow and rain filled the trenches, the mud sometimes became like quicksand. Innovative systems of firing rifles also became necessary. A soldier could not rise up to fire his gun safely, so a periscope was invented. There were even periscope rifles. The area between the trenches of the two opponents was called No Man's Land.

### Poisonous Gas Lesson

One of the worst inventions of World War I was poison gas. The gases included simple tear gas, severe mustard gas that burned victims, and lethal gases of chlorine and phosgene. Counter measures were needed to protect soldiers from the gases, and thus, the gas mask was invented. Several types of masks were designed. One was a PH-type anti-gas helmet that contained a chemical agent to counter the deadly phosgene gas. Another type was a small box respirator that had a close-fitting rubberized mask with eye goggles. The apparatus contained a filter that changed dangerous air to be safe. However, these devices were not effective against mustard gas, which could penetrate the skin even through uniforms. It burned victims' skin and lungs, leading to blindness and suffocation. Some veterans of World War I were crippled for life after being gassed. By April 1915, the Germans had acquired 150 tons (136 metric tons) of chlorine gas. They shot more than 6,000 cylinders against the French army. The Allied governments rapidly protested that the firing of chlorine gas was a violation of international law, even though they were considering retaliating with chemical warfare. However, the Germans ignored the accusations, continued to use poisonous gas, and expanded their research to develop more lethal varieties. As a defensive measure, the French started to produce and use the gases. Eventually, the French developed a deadlier variety of gas, a chlorine and phosgene mixture. The British and Americans also manufactured and used poisonous gases as a weapon.

© Shell Education

Advanced DBAs

# Teacher Resources *(cont.)*

## The *Lusitania* Lesson

U-boats were assigned the role of enforcing naval blockades to cut off enemy trade routes, mainly between Great Britain and the United States. These German submarines targeted merchant convoys and sunk these ships before they could reach their destinations. The *Lusitania* was a luxury liner owned by the Cunard Steamship Company in Great Britain. It had been sailing for nine years when it was torpedoed by a German U-boat submarine on May 7, 1915. The huge ship sunk in just 18 minutes, killing 1,198 of the people on board, including 100 children. When it was reported that 128 citizens of the United States had died, Americans were furious about this act of war against civilians.

The German torpedo hit under the ship's bridge and a heavier explosion followed. The order was quickly issued to abandon ship, but panic ensued when the ship tilted to the side, making it impossible to lower the lifeboats into the water. On the other side of the ship, the lifeboats were hung on the ship's bolts, which made them hard to lower. Of the *Lusitania's* 48 lifeboats, only 6 made it safely into the water with passengers.

President Wilson issued a stern statement to the German government affirming the right of Americans to travel on merchant ships. He called for Germans to abandon submarine warfare against commercial ships, condemning the attack as illegal and cruel. He also denied that the luxury liner carried any munition. The German government promised to stop targeting merchant and passenger vessels with surprise attacks. But the memories of the *Lusitania* remained and festered. Two years later, America declared war on Germany.

## Communications Lesson

Communication is essential during a war so that orders can be given and requests for supplies can be sent and received. In the early days of World War I, messengers ran in relays to get messages to the right location on time. Even carrier pigeons were trained for message duty. In the later stages of the war, messengers could quickly reach a radio—or wireless telegraph station—via motorcycle. At the beginning of the war, military leaders in Britain realized that the wireless telegraph had great strategic importance. Technicians soon designed a new counteroffensive wireless communication system in which signals could be intercepted. Enemy transmitters could also be located.

Eventually, British units used trench wireless sets to pinpoint enemy troop positions and detect the flight patterns of hostile aircraft. Wireless signals then alerted the British navy to the movements of the German fleet. However, wireless communications still encountered problems because of the large number of messages, and each wireless station had to wait its turn to relay messages back to the main direction station. These portable wireless stations were also awkward to carry, requiring four men to transport and set up all the gear. Telegraph systems were installed in France that included 100,000 miles (160,934 kilometers) of wire strung across France to handle a load of more than 40,000 telegrams a day. This network was useful in managing the movement of millions of soldiers. Telephone technology was also improving, and U.S. military leaders tapped into its benefits. The army recruited teams of technicians to build and operate the telephone system of the American Expeditionary Forces in France. They also recruited hundreds of American operators, known as "Hello Girls," who could speak French to serve as civilian telephone operators on the switchboards in France. Thus, American military could communicate throughout France.

Advanced DBAs

# Teacher Resources (cont.)

## Role of Airplanes Lesson

World War I was the first war since the Wright Brothers invented the airplane. Both the Allies and the Axis powers used the new biplanes with open cockpits for conducting photographic reconnaissance, spotting artillery fire and enemy ships, and shooting down enemy planes that were trying to perform the same missions. Many planes carried a pilot and their partner, who was either a gunner, a photographer, or a wireless operator who would relay reconnaissance messages. Eventually, a special synchronized machine gun system was developed to allow a gun to fire through the propeller blades.

During the war, plane construction rapidly increased in Britain, France, Germany, and the United States. Manfred Baron von Richthofen, nicknamed the "Red Baron," downed 80 Allied planes before he was shot down in April 1918. He was idolized and admired by both sides in the war. To achieve ace status, a pilot usually had to destroy five or more enemy aircraft, although the number varied with the country. Planes and pilots were lost in these battles due to plane malfunctions and being shot down by the enemy. These flying aces set the stage for the Air Force to have a strategic role in the next war.

Ironically, each pilot had a certain respect for his foe, the enemy pilot, and certain codes of conduct prevailed in these air battles. Hollywood decided to profit from these air battles, and dogfights were reenacted in propaganda and movies. Besides the biplanes flown by these pilot aces, the German forces also used giant gas-filled balloons called Zeppelins for long-range bombing. These balloons could rise as high as 22,000 feet (6,706 meters) in the air away from Allied ground fire. The balloon could carry about 2,000 pounds (907 kg) of bombs.

## Writing Home Lesson

Harry S. Truman dreamed of attending West Point and having a career as an army officer, but he failed the eye exam. So, he held a number of jobs, went to night school, and eventually began working on his family farm. While visiting his friends at the local National Guard unit, he checked out the eye chart on the wall and memorized its contents. When he went to the recruiting office to register for the Guard, he passed the eye exam without his glasses because he had memorized the chart. Americans were called to serve in Europe in 1917, and Truman's National Guard unit was ordered to France. In preparation for battle, Truman was assigned to Camp Donovan. There, he learned how to dig trenches and ride a horse in a battle setting. Upon arrival in France, Truman attended officers' school and then artillery school. At age 33, Truman was put in command of Battery "D" of the 129th Field Artillery, a Kansas City unit. Battery "D" was considered to be a rowdy group, and Captain Truman said he felt he would have to work hard to gain their acceptance and approval. He won the confidence and the support of its members and organized them into an outstanding unit. They later presented their captain with a loving cup (a shared drinking container made of silver) as a token of their respect. When his regiment boarded a train headed to the battle zone, his unit took the following cargo: guns, caissons (chests for carrying ammunition), horses, field kitchens, harnesses, hay, feed, battery records, and extra supplies to care for the battalion. Battery "D" fought in several major battles and continued its frontline activities until armistice on November 11, 1918.

© Shell Education

Advanced DBAs

# Teacher Resources *(cont.)*

## Answer Key

### Examine Trench Warfare (page 235)

1. Answers may include that they were used as fighting zones, shelter from attacks, places to live, and as a type of road system to move from one site to another.
2. Barbed wire could slow down or stop enemy troops from advancing into the trenches, and the periscope helped soldiers see out of the trench without having to stick their heads up, thereby exposing themselves to enemy fire.
3. C

### Examine Poisonous Gas (page 237)

1. Answers may include that these masks were used to protect soldiers from harmful or even lethal gases that were used as weapons during the war. Students may mention the types of gases used, the different types of masks needed to protect the soldiers, and what the gases could do to soldiers who were not protected.
2. Answers may include that Barclay wants to show the dangers of poisonous gases. He sees it as a cowardly weapon, showing the god of war hiding in trenches while blowing death onto the enemies.

### Examine the *Lusitania* (page 239)

1. Answers may include information that Germany notified and warned travelers about the dangers, but those warnings did not justify targeting ships that were mainly passenger vessels.
2. D
3. Similarities may include that there was a large number of deaths, including women and children; there were problems getting everyone into the rescue boats; and both the captains showed poor judgment. Differences may include the type of disaster (the *Titanic* hit an iceberg, and there was poor judgment on the part of the ship owners and captain; the *Lusitania* was bombed by a U-boat, and there was poor judgment of the captain to take passengers into a war zone).

### Examine Communications (page 241)

1. Answers may include that the rider on the motorcycle is delivering a message or taking a message; the radio station is being used for communications; there is a box communication system; the roles of the men in the picture could be to carry equipment and protect the communication team.
2. Answers may include the use of telegraphy; radio communications; messages delivered via motorized vehicles, such as motorcycles and truck convoys; telephones and "Hello Girls;" carrier pigeons; or relay runners through trenches.
3. A

### Examine the Role of Airplanes (page 243)

1. Answers may include spying on enemy troops; fighting enemy planes in dogfights; delivering important messages; bombing targets by flying at low levels; serving as flying ace heroes to bolster the morale for the war.
2. D
3. The fighter pilots were admired for their daring and skill at flying these new planes that had just recently been invented. They became heroes for their gladiator-like status, patriotism, and death-defying battle stunts. They were rewarded for the number of kills they had in the war; a certain number of kills gave them ace status.

### Examine Writing Home (page 245)

1. His unit used horses to ride to battle sites and to pull cannons and supply wagons.
2. Truman writes such things as, "Please don't worry about us or about me [...] I am very comfortably situated now in a finely furnished dugout with stoves and everything. If I am lucky we may remain a good long time. [...] None of our officers were hurt except one whom you never met."

### World War I Document-Based Question (page 246)

Refer to pages 306–307 for the DBQ Rubrics.

# Advanced Document-Based Assessments

## Unit 18: World War II

**Lessons**

**Teacher Resources**

# Women at Work

**Historical-Thinking Skill**

Students will analyze how World War II influenced the home front in the United States.

**Activate**

Ask the class to define the word *stereotype*. Draw a T-chart on the board or chart paper. On sticky notes, have students write stereotypes about men and women. Then, have them place their sticky notes on the T-chart. Review the list with the class and discuss the effects of stereotypes.

**Analyze**

1. Have students study the two images on *Examine Women at Work* (page 253). Have students talk with partners about the clothing, hair, and physical appearance of the two women.

2. Ask students to complete *Document Analysis—Use Evidence* (page 299) to support their analysis. Guide students as necessary to make claims and draw conclusions from the images about women at work during World War II. Remind them to list the evidence to support their claims and conclusions.

3. Use the following questions to guide a discussion:
   - How did women gain respect in the workforce during the war?
   - How is the real woman riveter dressed in the picture?
   - Why was this poster so popular during and after the war?

4. Allow time for students to complete *Examine Women at Work*. Discuss their work and strengthen their analysis skills using the How To activity.

**How To . . .**

**Evaluate Propaganda**—Explain to students that propaganda is defined as information that is used to promote a particular political issue or point of view. Analysis of propaganda can be challenging because propaganda is typically biased and uses stereotypes behind its messaging. Key elements for evaluating it include identifying the purpose, the context, the target audience, and the media techniques used in its creation. The true evaluation of propaganda is to measure the success of the entire campaign in achieving its purpose. Ask students to discuss in small groups the propaganda of the poster.

**Extend**

Ask students to think about political, social, or economic issues (or choose one as a class). Have each student select one issue and create a digital or physical propaganda poster. Have students share their posters.

© Shell Education

Name: _____ Date:_____

# Examine Women at Work

**Directions:** Read the background information, study the images, and answer the questions.

These two images are of women riveters during World War II. One is a propaganda poster, and the other is a political cartoon published in 1943. Riveting was a skilled job in the aircraft industry. The "Rosie the Riveter" poster was a very popular advertising tool. It encouraged women to join the workforce and support the war effort.

Letting the Genie Out of the Bottle

**1.** Why were women needed at this time in the workforce?

    (A) They had special skills men did not.

    (B) Women were finally guaranteed equal rights.

    (C) Most of the men were fighting overseas.

    (D) They traded positions with their husbands who stayed home.

**2.** What is the political cartoon implying?

_____

_____

_____

**3.** What were some issues women faced during war times?

_____

_____

_____

© Shell Education

World War II

# Contributions of Minorities

## Historical-Thinking Skill

Students will consider the context of World War II to understand its contributions by and effects on minority groups in the United States.

**Activate**

Ask students to stand up and choose a side. Students should go to one side of the class if they think discrimination occurs less today than it did in the past, and they should go to the other side of the class if they think discrimination occurs more today than it did in the past. Once they have decided, ask students to share their opinions.

**Analyze**

1. Have students read the background information and look at the picture on *Examine Contributions of Minorities* (page 255). Ask them to complete *Document Analysis—Consider the Source* (page 298) to support their analysis.

2. Discuss with students why it is important to consider that this is a staged picture. Ask them to think of reasons why someone would want to take a photo like this.

3. Ask students to evaluate the authenticity of the photo and the message in regards to dealing with discrimination. Have students share their answers, and discuss them as a class. Explain that while different races did work together in these plants in teams, the conditions were not always ideal for minorities in the workforce during the war.

4. Use the following questions to guide a discussion:
   - What was the purpose of this photo?
   - How was this workplace different from the military?
   - What three races are represented in this photo?

5. Allow time for students to complete *Examine Contributions of Minorities*. Discuss their work and strengthen their analysis skills using the How To activity.

**How To . . .**

**Identify Bias**—Explain that a bias is when something shows a preference or prejudice for or against a person or idea. The purpose of identifying bias in any material is to learn the point of view of the creator. Explain that as students read, see, or listen to materials, they should keep the following questions in mind to help them identify bias: *What facts has the photographer not shown? What other information is needed to understand the entire story? What words or images create a positive or negative point of view?* Ask students whether they can identify bias in the image.

**Extend**

Have students compare and contrast the contributions of American Indians and Mexican Americans during World War II. Have students create presentations of their findings.

**Advanced DBAs**

© Shell Education

Name: _____ Date:_____

# Examine Contributions of Minorities

**Directions:** Read the background information, examine the image, and answer the questions.

This is a staged picture showing three male workers, each of a different race. They are workers at an aircraft plant. In 1941, President Franklin Roosevelt signed into law Executive Order 8802 that banned discrimination in defense industries and government, but not in the military. Until that time, it was difficult for African Americans and Asian Americans to get jobs in both the government and private industries.

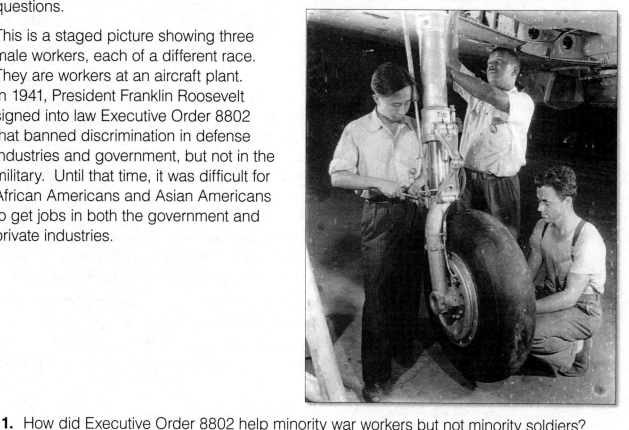

1. How did Executive Order 8802 help minority war workers but not minority soldiers?

_____

_____

_____

2. Why were Japanese Americans treated differently from other minorities?

_____

_____

_____

_____

3. In what ways did life improve for minorities during the war? What hurdles remained to be overcome?

_____

_____

_____

_____

© Shell Education

# 442nd Regiment

## Historical-Thinking Skill

Students will analyze how World War II affected different minority groups in the United States.

**Activate**

Ask students to list the five things they would take from their home if that was all they could keep. Tell them they have one minute to decide and everything else they own will have to be left behind (try to create a slight, brief sense of controlled urgency and panic.) Collect the papers after one minute, regardless of whether students are finished. Then, ask students to discuss how they felt and how they decided what to take.

**Analyze**

1. Read the background information to students if they are not familiar with the 442nd Regiment (page 268). Draw connections to their experience in the opening activity, and ask students to share their reactions to the background information.

2. Ask students if they would have still joined the army for a country that took their freedom away. Discuss the idea as a class.

3. Have students look at the photograph on *Examine the 442nd Regiment* (page 257). Ask them to complete *Document Analysis—Set the Scene* (page 297) to support their analysis.

4. Use the following questions to guide a discussion:

   · How do you know which war this is from?

   · How do you know which country these soldiers represent?

   · Would you have rather stayed in the internment camps or fought as part of the 442nd Regiment?

5. Allow time for students to complete *Examine the 442nd Regiment*. Discuss their work and strengthen their analysis skills using the How To activity.

**How To . . .**

**Find Additional Sources**—Explain to students that when they are given a primary source, no matter how detailed, it is limiting in the information it can provide. A great strategy is to find additional primary sources that can add to their knowledge or corroborate what they learned from the original primary source. Ask students to research and find additional primary or secondary sources related to the 442nd Regiment.

**Extend**

On August 10, 1988, President Ronald Reagan signed the Civil Liberties Act of 1988. The act provided financial reparations of $20,000 for each surviving detainee of the internment camps, totaling $1.2 billion. Have students write op-ed articles that either support or refute the act.

**Advanced DBAs**

# Examine the 442nd Regiment

**Directions:** Read the background information, examine the image, and answer the questions.

The U.S. Army 442nd Regimental Combat Team was comprised almost entirely of second-generation Japanese Americans. The regiment was only allowed to fight in Europe. It is the most-decorated unit in the history of American warfare. In the photograph, members of the 442nd hike up a muddy road in France in 1944.

1. All the following is true of the 442nd Regiment EXCEPT:

   (A) It was made of men who escaped the internment camps.

   (B) It was comprised almost entirely of second-generation Japanese Americans.

   (C) They were only allowed to fight in Europe.

   (D) It was the most decorated unit in the history of American warfare.

2. Why would the government only allow the 442nd Regiment to fight in Europe?

   _____

   _____

   _____

3. Why would it have been difficult for the men of the 442nd Regiment to fight for their country?

   _____

   _____

   _____

World War II

# Reusing and Recycling

**Historical-Thinking Skill**

Students will evaluate World War II recycling on the home front and compare it to recycling today.

**Activate**

Display the modern image of "reduce, reuse, and recycle" without displaying the words. Ask students to identify the image. Once they have correctly identified the image, ask students to share their thoughts about what should be reduced, reused, and recycled. Write their responses on the board.

**Analyze**

1. Explain that the modern environmental saying "reduce, reuse, and recycle" is not new. During the Great Depression and World War II, America already had that philosophy, although it was not about the environment—it was for survival.

2. Have students look at both pictures on *Examine Reusing and Recycling* (page 259) and complete *Document Analysis—Make Connections* (page 296) to support their analysis. For step 2 on their sheets, ask them to compare and contrast reusing and recycling during World War II to reusing and recycling today.

3. Use the following questions to guide a discussion:

   · Why would silk and nylon stockings be needed for the war?

   · What does the girl's clothing tell you about her?

   · In the brigade photo, what kinds of items are the children collecting? What do these items have in common?

   · What types of items do people donate to the armed forces today?

4. Allow time for students to complete *Examine Reusing and Recycling*. Discuss their work and strengthen their analysis skills using the How To activity.

**How To . . .**

**Identify Time Periods**—Tell students that it is possible to learn the time period of a primary source even if the date is not provided. Using context clues, such as the setting and people's clothing, can be one strategy. Identifying the author or creator of the primary source can also give clues. Have students annotate the images by circling and writing comments or questions on things in the photos that serve as clues of the time period.

**Extend**

Have students create recycling campaigns at school. Their campaigns should include lists of materials needed and to which organization the collected materials will be donated.

Name: _____ Date: _____

# Examine Reusing and Recycling

**Directions:** Read the background information, examine the images, and answer the questions.

The photo on the left is of a young woman leaving her silk or nylon stockings in a store's recycling bin. The photo on the right is a group of children on a recycling brigade to collect scrap metal. Children frequently collected old tires, tin, other metals, and clean paper for recycling to show their patriotism and support of the war effort.

**1.** Why was recycling so important during this war?

_____

_____

_____

**2.** What were the nylon stockings and metals used for?

_____

_____

_____

**3.** How were children's lives different in these war years compared to children's lives today?

_____

_____

_____

© Shell Education

World War II

# Food Supplies and Rationing

**Historical-Thinking Skill**

Students will examine evidence of the effects of World War II on the American economy.

**Activate**

Have students work in groups to make grocery shopping lists of 20 items. Explain that their lists should include the amounts of the products they intend to purchase as well. Once their lists are complete, tell them they must completely eliminate 10 items. Then, tell them to cut the 10 items down to 5. Discuss their final decisions and the rationale each group used to make their decisions.

**Analyze**

1. Discuss the idea of rationing with students. Rationing is a difficult concept for many of today's students and adults to understand. We often stop at fast food restaurants, throw away large amounts of food, and expect exotic and out-of-season foods from around the world to be available for our consumption all year. Making this comparison between habits then and now is essential for students to understand rationing.

2. Have students read the background information and look at the images on *Examine Food Supplies and Rationing* (page 261). Ask them to complete *Document Analysis—Use Evidence* (page 299) to support their analysis.

3. Use the following questions to guide a discussion:
   - Two pounds (0.9 kilograms) per person per month seems like a lot of sugar. What was sugar used for?
   - Why was rationing necessary during World War II?
   - Being frugal and growing food was patriotic during World War II. How do people show patriotism today?

4. Allow time for students to complete *Examine Food Supplies and Rationing*. Discuss their work and strengthen their analysis skills using the How To activity.

**How To . . .**

**Evaluate Propaganda**—Tell students that there are some specific strategies they can use when analyzing propaganda images. They can determine if the image tries to persuade through words or visuals. This can be a clue as to the intended audience. Students can also pay attention to the size and location of the words and images. This can help determine what is most important or what the viewer is supposed to notice. Ask students to look for these things in the images, write their observations, and compare the two images.

**Extend**

Have students identify the top 10 rationed products during World War II. Have each student create an original rationing propaganda poster about one of the products other than sugar or meat.

**Advanced DBAs**

Name: _____ Date:_____

# Examine Food Supplies and Rationing

**Directions:** Read the background information, examine the images, and answer the questions.

These propaganda images were used to encourage and remind people to ration and grow food during World War II. Individuals, including children, were issued ration booklets that controlled how many of certain items they could buy. Today, it is estimated that most Americans consume one-third of a pound of sugar each day in processed foods and drinks. This poster allows 2 pounds (0.9 kilograms) per month.

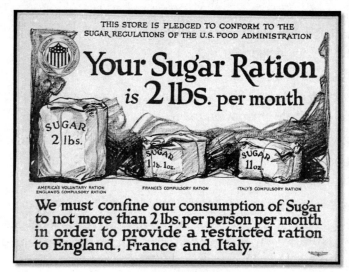

1. How does sugar consumption in America today compare with the rationed amount of sugar in World War II?

_____

_____

_____

2. Why was rationing necessary during World War II?

_____

_____

_____

3. Explain the symbolism in the political cartoon on the right.

_____

_____

_____

# D-Day

**Historical-Thinking Skill**

Students will examine a map of military action during World War II.

**Activate**

Project a map of the world from 1945. Select as many different battles of World War II as you have students, and write the battle names on sticky notes. Be sure to include battles both from the Pacific and Europe. Provide each student with a sticky note that has a battle name on it. Allow them time to research and place their sticky notes representing each battle on the map. (**Note:** Do not include D-Day.)

**Analyze**

1. Have students look at the map on *Examine D-Day* (page 263). Make a connection to the world map activity and identify Normandy on the map.

2. Have students create a KWL chart for D-Day. Then, read the background information to the class. If possible, project the full version of the map from the Digital Resources and zoom in to read the text.

3. Ask students to complete *Document Analysis—Make Connections* (page 296) to support their analysis. For step 2, have students decide what type of connections they will make (e.g., compare the map to a map of another famous battle or record the causes and effects of D-Day).

4. Use the following questions to guide a discussion:
   - Is this an official map of the D-Day invasion? How do you know?
   - Is this an accurate map of the D-Day invasion? How do you know?
   - What is more helpful, the drawings or the writings on this map?
   - Do you think there were other maps like this created by soldiers? Why or why not?

5. Allow time for students to complete *Examine D-Day*. Discuss their work and strengthen their analysis skills using the How To activity.

**How To . . .**

**Read a Map**—Explain to students that maps do more than teach geography. They can show change over time as well as information about the people who made them and the time periods in which they lived. First, students should examine and identify the different parts of maps, such as titles, labels, and symbols. The author, or source, of a map can give the reader an idea about its purpose and reason for creation. Tell students that map legends help explain the symbols used on the map. Have students circle the parts of the D-Day map that give them information and help them understand the time and place in which it was created.

**Extend**

Have students research the island-hopping strategy in the Pacific during World War II. Then, have students create maps of the island hopping in the Pacific from the perspective of the U.S. Marines who actually fought those battles. Ask them to include legends and keys for their maps.

**Advanced DBAs**

Name: _____ Date: _____

# Examine D-Day

**Directions:** Read the background information, study the map, and answer the questions.

The 743rd Tank Battalion was from Fort Lewis, Washington. They were one of the three tank battalions to cross and land on the beaches of Normandy. The map shows the D-Day Normandy invasion and the first 48 days of action with the 743rd Tank Battalion in France.

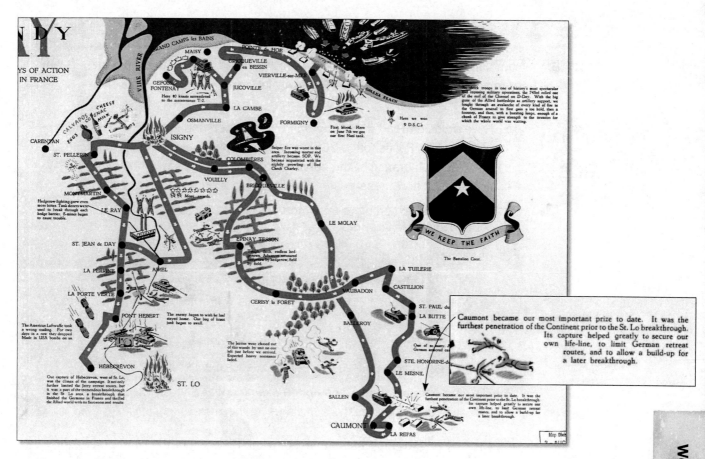

1. What was significant about the Battle of Caumont?

   _____

   _____

   _____

   _____

2. How do you know this map was created by members of the 743rd Tank Battalion?

   _____

   _____

   _____

# War Bonds

**Activate**

Ask students to individually create mind maps of how we measure the economy. Have students share with partners and add to their mind maps. Discuss the commonalities that each student had on their mind map. Have them identify any examples that are connected to the government.

**Analyze**

1. Have students read the background information and look at the poster on *Examine War Bonds* (page 265). Have students analyze the poster, focusing on what each branch of the service is doing. Discuss why bonds were needed and how these posters helped raise money for the troops.

2. Ask students to complete *Document Analysis—Consider the Source* (page 298) to support their analysis.

3. Use the following questions to guide a discussion:
   - What is the purpose of this poster? Is it effective?
   - Why were bonds sold to citizens for this war but are not sold for wars today?
   - What group is being attacked and by whom?
   - Why is it called an invasion bond instead of a war bond?

4. Allow time for students to complete *Examine War Bonds*. Discuss their work and strengthen their analysis skills using the How To activity.

**How To . . .**

**Evaluate Propaganda**—Review the meaning of the word *propaganda* with students. Explain that key elements to evaluating it include identifying the purpose, context, target audience, and media techniques used in its creation. The true evaluation of propaganda is to measure the success of the entire campaign in achieving its purpose. Ask students to discuss in small groups the propaganda of the poster. What techniques were used?

**Extend**

Ask students to write economic impact reports on World War II. Explain to students that an economic impact report looks at the effect of an event on the economy during a specific time period. Students should focus on changes in business, wages, jobs, or the cost of goods and services. Challenge them to include charts or graphs to support their reports.

**Advanced DBAs**

Name: _____ Date:_____

# Examine War Bonds

**Directions:** Read the background information, study the image, and answer the questions.

This war bond poster features an invasion on a beach. It is an artist's painting of a battle setting including all branches of the service. Bonds were issued in denominations from $25 to $10,000. The average wage during this time period was $200 per month.

**BUY THAT INVASION BOND!**

1. How much money did an average worker make per year? If they bought one $25 bond a month, how much would they save? What percent of their income would they be saving?

   _____

   _____

   _____

2. How did the war bond poster appeal to emotions of the American people?

   (A) It was relatively inexpensive for most Americans.

   (B) It showed soldiers in danger and fighting for their country.

   (C) It included references to the home front.

   (D) It made people sad and fearful for an invasion of America.

3. Why was the war bond campaign a successful idea?

   _____

   _____

# World War II Document-Based Question

## Historical Context

While American soldiers fought bravely abroad, Americans at home worked hard to support them. They worked long hours to help provide food, weapons, ammunition, airplanes, ships, and moral support for troops. The home front effort showed that citizens were willing and able to sacrifice for the cause. They put patriotism above their personal comfort. Most citizens had a family member involved in the war, and they were dedicated to supporting their loved ones.

## Essay Tasks

**Directions:** Using the documents and your knowledge of World War II, complete **one** of the following essay tasks. Before you begin your essay, complete the *DBQ Essay Planner* (pages 302–305) to plan your writing.

### Essay Task ❶

Tom Brokaw called the citizens who lived during WWII "the greatest generation." Many people who lived through this period of history called this era "the best of times and the worst of times," such as in the beginning quote in *A Tale of Two Cities* by Charles Dickens. Choose one of these two quotes, and explain how the home front response of Americans during World War II fits that quote.

In your essay, remember to:

- Identify only one quote to explain the home front.

- Provide evidence from the documents that will convince the reader of your point of view.

- Include a topic sentence, introduction, body, and conclusion.

- Give details to support your ideas.

- Use information found in the documents to support your argument.

### Essay Task ❷

Propaganda played a big role during World War II on the home front. In a well-organized essay, evaluate the success of propaganda in achieving its goals for the U.S. government.

In your essay, remember to:

- Write a strong thesis that establishes your argument.

- Provide evidence from the documents that will support your thesis.

- Include a topic sentence, introduction, body, and conclusion.

- Give details to support your ideas.

- Use information found in the documents to support your argument.

★ As a bonus, include evidence from an outside source or a counterargument in your chosen essay.

# Teacher Resources

## Background Information

### Women at Work Lesson

More than 12 million American men served in World War II from 1941 to 1945. Industries needed millions of new workers to meet their production quotas for the war. The first women to train for wartime manufacturing jobs were single women who already worked in similar jobs. But the need was too great, and even more women were recruited from all walks of life through the War Advertising Council. The "Rosie the Riveter" poster was one theme of the campaign. Around seven million women answered the call and went to work in war-related jobs.

At this time, the tradition was that mothers should stay at home with their children. Even though child care was provided at the job sites, only a small number of young, married women joined the workforce, and most of these mothers left their children in the care of family members. Women at home cared for their children, tended their victory gardens, volunteered in war support programs, sewed, canned fresh produce, and waited in lines to buy food.

Male supervisors found their female employees to be reliable, accurate, fast learners, patient, and skilled in precision work. Safety standards in the airline industry, shipyards, and other factories radically changed women's uniforms on the job from skirts and dresses to shirts and pants. Women also worked as scientists, machinists, truck drivers, and in logging camps, railroad yards, munitions factories, and large-scale farms. Some women even flew the planes that were built at aviation plants to war zone destinations in Europe.

Life was not easy for these women. Although the pay was more than they could make in other jobs, it was still less than what men made for the same amount of work. The war work schedule for most factories was six days a week with eight hours of work daily. The shifts were around the clock. Some working mothers chose the midnight shift so that they could still shop using their ration stamps, clean their homes, and care for their children during the day.

### Contributions of Minorities Lesson

Fearing a major protest march on Washington, President Roosevelt met with leaders of an African American labor union who were requesting an end to racial discrimination in employment in the government and private industries. These leaders also wanted to end discrimination in the military services. Roosevelt agreed to sign into law Executive Order 8802. It banned discrimination in defense industries and the government, but not in the military. The order to desegregate the armed forces did not come until after the war in 1948. In 1942, African Americans began a campaign called the Double V Campaign. It stood for victory in the war against Germany and Japan and for victory against discrimination at home. African Americans moved into cities to fill jobs in war plants, but they soon found that they had very few decent places to live and shop. Some race riots occurred in several areas of the country. African Americans gradually began to get better paying jobs at factories and government positions. More than one million African American men and women served in the armed forces during World War II. The Tuskegee Airmen, an African American flying squadron, gained fame and admiration for their piloting and fighting skills.

Advanced DBAs

# Teacher Resources (cont.)

## 442nd Regiment Lesson

The Japanese faced discrimination in the workplace, could not vote or own land in white communities, and were banned from some public places. They lived in isolated communities mostly in California or along the West Coast. Many of them had lived in the United States all their lives, but they could not become citizens because of immigration laws passed in the 1920s. Pearl Harbor increased hatred against the Japanese, and white citizens pressured the government to put them in camps where they could be watched so they could not aid the enemy. Roosevelt issued Executive Order 9066, and 120,000 Japanese were sent to internment, or detainment, camps in several states. Over half of the Japanese were American citizens. The camps had barbed wire, armed guards, and public toilets and baths. Conditions were deplorable. The camps began to close between 1942 and 1945. Ironically, in 1943, native-born Japanese Americans could join the military and serve in the war, and about 33,000 chose to do so.

Those volunteers joined the 442nd Infantry Regiment that was part of the U.S. Army. The unit was composed almost entirely of Nisei, or second-generation Japanese Americans. Many of the soldiers had family members in internment camps back in the United States. In 1944, after a year of training, the regiment began fighting in the war. They fought mostly in Italy, southern France, and Germany. A total of 18,000 men served overall. The motto of the 442nd Regiment was "Go for Broke." They became the most decorated unit in U.S. military history, earning more than 18,000 awards in less than two years.

## Reusing and Recycling Lesson

No new automobiles, radios, furniture, or appliances were produced during the war years. Few new houses were built. Families and individuals who moved to cities rented small apartments, and owners of large homes took in boarders for extra money and to help with the housing shortage. Civilians were asked to collect scrap metal, rubber tires, and even silk and nylon stockings for the war effort. Cooking fat was also collected. "Use it up—wear it out—make it do, or do without" was the popular slogan. Chicken feed sacks were made of durable cotton cloth in attractive patterns, and women used those sacks to sew clothing and curtains. The War Production Board reminded households to be frugal with electricity, water, telephone usage, and gasoline. Homemakers and butchers were urged to save waste fats to be recycled into glycerin, which was needed for explosives. Silk and nylon stockings were collected and recycled into gunpowder bags and parachutes. While some products were recycled, new products were also being invented. During the 1940s, materials such as nylon, acrylic, neoprene, SBR (styrene butadiene rubber), polyethylene, and many more polymers took the place of the natural material supplies that were depleted. Children did their part for the war effort by organizing clubs dedicated to recycling campaigns. They collected clean paper, scrap metal, and old tires. Since metal was needed for tanks and armaments, bicycles, toy cars, and toy trucks were not made during the war. Instead, wooden toy tanks were popular with the boys. Glass marbles, checkers, and wooden dominoes were popular games. Girls enjoyed paper dolls and a cloth doll called Raggedy Ann.

## Food Supplies and Rationing Lesson

As soon as war was declared, farmers in the United States began working overtime to supply massive amounts of food for people at home, the soldiers abroad, and the nation's Allies. All over the country, victory gardens were planted in backyards, vacant lots, parks, schoolyards, and prison yards. The war meant a major shift in the economy's focus from domestic to wartime production. President Roosevelt knew certain items would be limited. So, Roosevelt set up an Office of Price Administration to stabilize

Advanced DBAs

# Teacher Resources (cont.)

prices during wartime. In 1942, local governing boards staffed by volunteers were established in counties throughout the nation. Rationing rules were set, and the first ration book containing coupons and stamps was issued to every man, woman, and child.

Rationed food items included sugar, coffee (because it was imported), meat, fish, and butter. Meat shortages occurred in the winter of 1942, and stricter meat rationing was needed. Flour, cornmeal, and fresh fruits and vegetables that were in season were not rationed. Coffee was limited to one pound per adult every five weeks. A second ration book was issued in 1943 and included canned goods and dried beans. It used a point system with A–F categories in which each letter and food item counted for a certain number of points. When an item became scarce, the points for that item changed. The government also encouraged people to grow their own food gardens, or victory gardens.

## D-Day Lesson

Operation Overlord was the code name for the Allied invasion of Europe during World War II. The invasion, also known as D-Day, began on June 6, 1944. Twelve nations joined in the invasion lead by British, Canadian, and American troops. The Allied forces landed on five beaches along the Normandy coast of France. The beaches stretched for 50 miles and were heavily fortified by the Nazi army.

Then, the amphibious invasion began at 6:30 in the morning. Thousands of paratroopers were already on the ground behind enemy lines. British and Canadian troops captured the beaches with the code names Gold, Juno, and Sword. American troops had little resistance at Utah Beach but faced heavy resistance at Omaha Beach. There were over 2,000 American casualties at Omaha Beach. Overall, more than 4,000 Allied troops lost their lives, and thousands more were wounded. Still, the invasion was a success, and approximately 156,000 Allied troops had landed on the beaches of Normandy.

This became the turning point in the war in Europe. The Allied forces were now on the offensive, and they were focused on pushing the Nazi army back into Germany. In the weeks that followed D-Day, the Allies fought their way across Normandy, including the 743rd Tank Battalion. This battalion was from Fort Lewis, Washington. They were selected to be one of the three tank battalions to cross and land on D-Day. After D-Day, the battalion pushed through France and Germany. On April 13, 1945, the battalion liberated prisoners from a train that was heading to a concentration camp.

## War Bonds Lesson

Wars are always expensive, and World War II was no exception. However, the wartime economy provided an increase in jobs and productivity by moving the nation out of the Great Depression. The unemployment rate dropped so low that there seemed to be a job for anyone who wanted one, and the total value of goods and services produced more than doubled. War workers were paid good wages. Because there was a scarcity of consumer goods, people did not buy a lot of things. Instead, they saved their money. The U.S. government had a huge war time yearly budget of around $90,000,000. This is low in comparison to today's billions, but it was very high in comparison to the budget just six years before World War I began. The budget then was about $9,000,000! This war cost about $75,000,000 a year, so it was essential to find new ways to boost the government's revenue.

President Roosevelt, a wealthy man himself, believed that taxes should be raised for the wealthy. But Congress was afraid to put the entire burden on the wealthy owners of corporations, who already paid most of the taxes. Instead, Congress devised the Revenue Act so that most Americans would have to pay at least some income tax. In 1939, only four million citizens paid income taxes. By 1945,

Advanced DBAs

# Teacher Resources *(cont.)*

43 million people filed their income taxes. To collect these taxes on a regular basis, payroll deductions were established. The public did not protest and paid taxes as part of their patriotic duty.

However, even more money was needed, and an idea was conceived to sell war bonds. The public was in a saving mode, so why not allow citizens to save their money by purchasing bonds backed by the government that would eventually, after the war, pay them back with interest? The idea was brilliant, and artists from all over the country contributed their designs for posters to publicize the war bonds campaign. Hollywood stars volunteered to tour the nation to drum up support for the bonds. Insurance companies, large companies, and even banks bought bonds.

## Answer Key

### Examine Women at Work (page 253)

1. C
2. It is implying that women won't want to give up their jobs after the war is over. These factory jobs were appealing to young women because they allowed them to make more money, be more independent, serve their country, and help win the war.
3. Women faced issues such as lower pay than men and long hours at work. After an eight-hour work day, they still had to go home and complete their chores without the help of the modern conveniences (dishwashers, washing machines, etc.) that we have today.

### Examine Contributions of Minorities (page 255)

1. Executive Order 8802 protected against discrimination in the work force, allowing different races to work together. However, in the military, there were still separate units for different races.
2. They were treated with more hatred because of the events of Pearl Harbor.
3. Answers may include that life improved for minorities now that they were allowed to work in the government and defense industries and were receiving better wages for their work. However, the military had yet to be desegregated, and many minorities were still banned from public places and faced racial discrimination in their daily lives.

### Examine the 442nd Regiment (page 257)

1. A
2. Answers could include that the U.S. government was afraid that some Japanese Americans still held loyalty to Japan. Therefore, they were only allowed to fight in Europe.
3. Answers could include that it may have been emotionally difficult because they were fighting for freedom and for a country that took their own freedom away.

### Examine Reusing and Recycling (page 259)

1. Recycling was important because it helped people and factories make items the soldiers needed for the war, such as parachutes, ammunition, and metal and rubber items.
2. Stockings were used for parachutes and gunpowder bags; metals were used for a variety of weapons, including tanks and other items.
3. Answers should describe what life was like for children during the 1940s.

### Examine Food Supplies and Rationing (page 261)

1. Today, Americans consume about one-third of a pound of sugar a day. That is a lot more than the ration allowed during World War II.
2. Answers may include that the United States now had to help feed its allies, and it also had to have materials to build military items, such as weapons and parachutes.
3. The vegetables are shown as weapons against the Nazis. This symbolizes that growing food is a way to help win the war.

### Examine D-Day (page 263)

1. The Battle of Caumont was significant because it was the furthest penetration of the European continent prior to the St. Lô breakthrough, and it limited the German retreat routes.
2. The pictures and unofficial slang used clearly shows this was a map created by the 743rd Tank Battalion members.

### Examine War Bonds (page 265)

1. The average worker made $2,400 a year. A worker buying a $25 bond a month would save $300, which is 12.5 percent of his income.
2. B
3. It showed people that investing in the government was a safe and patriotic way to save money.

### World War II Document-Based Question (page 266)

Refer to pages 306–307 for the DBQ Rubrics.

# Advanced Document-Based Assessments

## Unit 19: Civil Rights Movement

**Lessons**

**Teacher Resources**

# Police Report

**Historical-Thinking Skill**

Students will investigate the strategies used by the protesters during the civil rights movement.

1500
1600
1700

**Activate**

Display photographs of Martin Luther King Jr., Rosa Parks, Thurgood Marshall, and Jackie Robinson. Ask students to identify each person and a contribution each of them made to the civil rights movement.

**Analyze**

1. Have students look at the document on *Examine the Police Report* (page 273). Ask them to complete *Document Analysis—Think Across Time* (page 300) to support their analysis. Have students work with partners on their time lines. Ask them to include 10 or more major events of the civil rights movement. Be sure to include the Montgomery bus boycott and events that became before and after it.

2. Use the following questions to guide a discussion:
   - Where did this incident take place?
   - Who were the officers on duty?
   - What do the abbreviations in parentheses (*wm* and *cf*) stand for?
   - What kind of consequences did Rosa Parks's actions have for African Americans?
   - Could anyone have predicted that Rosa Parks's actions would have had such lasting consequences?

3. Allow time for students to complete *Examine the Police Report*. Discuss their work and strengthen their analysis skills using the How To activity.

**How To . . .**

**Identify Bias**—Review with students that a bias is when something shows a preference or prejudice for or against a person or idea. The purpose of identifying bias in any materials is to learn the point of view of the creator. As students read, see, or listen to materials, they should keep the following questions in mind to help them identify bias: *What facts are not mentioned? What words reveal a positive or negative point of view?* Ask students if they can identify language in the police report that suggests bias.

**Extend**

Have students create posters in support of the Montgomery bus boycott. Be sure they include justification for the boycott on their posters.

**Advanced DBAs**

# Examine the Police Report

**Directions:** Read the background information, study the image, and answer the questions.

This is a police report from the city of Montgomery, Alabama. It is signed by the arresting officers F. B. Day and D. W. Mixon. It described the offense committed by Rosa Parks on December 1, 1955.

POLICE DEPARTMENT
CITY OF MONTGOMERY

Date 12-1-55            19___

Complainant    J.F.Blake   (wm)

Address    27 No. Lewis St.                               Phone No.

Offense    Misc.                         Reported By    Same as above

Address                                                  Phone No.

Date and Time Offense Committed    12-1-55    6:06 pm

Place of Occurrence    In Front of Empire Theatre  (On Montgomery Street)

Person or Property Attacked

How Attacked

Person Wanted

Value of Property Stolen_____Value Recovered

Details of Complaint (list, describe and give value of property stolen)

We received a call upon arrival the bus operator said he had a colored female

sitting in the white section of the bus, and would not move back.

We (Day & Mixon) also saw her.

The bus operator signed a warrant for her. Rosa Parks, (cf) 634 Cleveland Court.

Rosa Parks (cf) was charged with chapter 6 section 11 of the Montgomery City Code.

Warrant #14254

THIS OFFENSE IS DECLARED:
UNFOUNDED              ☐
CLEARED BY ARREST      ☐
EXCEPTIONALLY CLEARED  ☐
INACTIVE (NOT CLEARED) ☐

Officers  F. B. Day
          D. W. Mixon

Division  Patrol            Time  7:00 pm
                                  12-1-55

10M—PARAGON PRESS—2850

1. When was the offense committed?

_____

2. What was the offense, and who committed it?

_____

_____

_____

3. This same offense had been committed by others many times before. Why did the case of Parks become so important and well known?

_____

_____

_____

**Civil Rights Movement**

# Protests

## Historical-Thinking Skill

Students will understand how diverse groups united during the civil rights movement.

### Activate

Write the names of some famous protesters on the board. Examples include John Brown, Ghandi, Martin Luther King Jr., and suffragists Alice Paul and Lucy Burns. Do not tell students that these people were all protesters. Have students form small groups and list all the things these people have in common. Then, write the following events on the board: Tiananmen Square, Haymarket Riot of 1886, Protestant Reformation, and March on Washington for Jobs and Freedom. Ask students what all these things have in common. Explain that these were famous protests and the people listed were famous protesters.

### Analyze

1. Have students look at both pictures on *Examine Protests* (page 275). Ask them to complete *Document Analysis—Make Connections* (page 296) to support their analysis. For step 2, ask students to decide what type of connections they will make (e.g., compare/contrast to another protest or record the causes and effects of the protest).

2. Use the following questions to guide a discussion:
   - Have you ever participated in a protest?
   - Which photo looks more like a protest to you?
   - What would you expect to see in a protest photo?
   - Compare and contrast what is going on in the two photos.

3. Allow time for students to complete *Examine Protests*. Discuss their work and strengthen their analysis skills using the How To activity.

**How To . . .**

**Identify a Historical Time Period**—A historical time period or era is a specific time in history that historians have organized because of shared elements within that defined time frame. To help identify historical time periods or eras in photographs, it is helpful to examine the context and details of the photograph. Have students circle elements such as clothing, signs, people, or technology in the photograph. Have them use their background knowledge of history to place the photograph into an era.

### Extend

Have students look up the names of the lunch counter protesters at Woolworth's department store in Greensboro, North Carolina. Discuss what happened in their lives after the protests.

Name: _____ Date: _____

# Examine Protests

**Directions:** Read the background information, study the images, and answer the questions.

In the left image, protesters in Washington, DC, march for equal rights in 1963. In the right photo, from 1960, four college students are sitting at a "whites only" lunch counter at Woolworth's department store in Greensboro, North Carolina.

1. Name at least two things the marchers are demanding.

   _____

   _____

   _____

2. Why was the Woolworth sit-in considered a protest?

   (A) Protesters sat and waited to be served peacefully.

   (B) Protesters took seats of paying customers.

   (C) Protesters blocked entry to local restaurants.

   (D) all the above

3. Based on what you know, which of these protests was more effective?

   _____

   _____

   _____

# Literacy Tests

## Historical-Thinking Skill

Students will evaluate the purpose and the effects of literacy tests administered to potential voters.

**Activate**

Write one or two of the questions from the literacy test from *Examine Literacy Tests* (page 277) on the board. Do not write the answers. Ask students to answer the questions on separate sheets of paper. When time is up, discuss the questions that gave students problems and where they could go to find the answers.

**Analyze**

1. Have students study the literacy test example on *Examine Literacy Tests*. Ask them to complete *Document Analysis—Set the Scene* (page 297) to support their analysis.

2. Have students write letters to the Supreme Court arguing why they think literacy tests were unconstitutional. Tell them to use specific evidence from the test to support their arguments.

3. Use the following questions to guide a discussion:
   - What are the requirements for voting today?
   - Are these requirements fair? Why or why not?
   - Should some type of test be given to people who want to vote? Why or why not?
   - Are any of these questions relevant to a person's ability to vote?
   - Why were these questions given to African Americans?

4. Allow time for students to complete *Examine Literacy Tests*. Discuss their work and strengthen their analysis skills using the How To activity.

**How To . . .**

**Find Additional Sources**—Explain to students that when they are given a primary source, no matter how detailed, it is limiting in the information it can provide. A great strategy is to find additional primary sources that will add to their knowledge or corroborate what they learned from the original primary source. Ask students to research and find additional primary or secondary sources related to these literacy tests (the Library of Congress website can be a good place to start).

**Extend**

Have students look up different Supreme Court cases from the civil rights movement and discuss the decisions—*Brown v. Board of Education of Topeka* (1954); *Heart of Atlanta Motel, Inc. v. United States* (1964); *Loving v. Virginia* (1967).

**Advanced DBAs**

# Examine Literacy Tests

**Directions:** Read the background information, study the text of a literacy test, and answer the questions.

This is just one version of a literacy test administered to African Americans when they appeared to vote on election day. These tests were administered between the 1890s and 1960s. The correct answer to each question is in italics.

---

**Literacy Test**

1. If a person charged with treason denies his guilt, how many persons must testify against him before he can be convicted? *Two*

2. At what time of day on January 20 each four years does the term of the president of the United States end? *12 noon*

3. If the president does not wish to sign a bill, how many days is he allowed in which to return it to Congress for reconsideration? *Ten*

4. If a bill is passed by Congress and the president refuses to sign it and does not send it back to Congress in session within the specified period of time, is the bill defeated or does it become law? *It becomes law unless Congress adjourns before the expiration of 10 days.*

---

1. What do these questions have in common?

   _____

   _____

   _____

2. Who do you think wrote these questions? Support your answer.

   _____

   _____

   _____

3. Why is this literacy test an unfair requirement for allowing people to vote?

   _____

   _____

   _____

# Letter to the President

## Historical-Thinking Skill

Students will measure the significance of specific people's influences on the civil rights movement.

**Activate**

Ask students to write letters to the president asking them to change something or do something they think would make the country better. Have students make their letters clear and concise so there is no question about what they are asking to be changed. Have students share with partners and then share with the class.

**Analyze**

1. Read the background information to the class on *Examine a Letter to the President* (page 279). Then, have a student volunteer read their letter to the president aloud to the class.

2. Have students complete *Document Analysis—Consider the Source* (page 298) to support their analysis.

3. Ask students to evaluate the strength of Jackie Robinson's letter. Have students use evidence to support their evaluation.

4. Use the following questions to guide a discussion:
   - Who was the president in 1958?
   - How persuasive is this letter?
   - How does the writer's background and fame make his letter more compelling?

5. Allow time for students to complete *Examine a Letter to the President*. Discuss their work and strengthen their analysis skills using the How To activity.

**How To . . .**

**Summarize Longer Text**—Tell students that it can be helpful to summarize a text, especially the longer it is, to get a better gist of the main ideas. One way to do this is to stop after different sections and write a few notes. The notes can be a few words or phrases to summarize the text. Explain that this can be especially helpful when looking at multiple documents. The summary notes make it easier to recall the most important ideas. Ask students to practice with Jackie Robinson's letter, stopping after each paragraph to write a few words that summarize each section.

**Extend**

Some athletes today have protested various social issues. Have each student select a modern-day athlete and an issue they protested to evaluate the success or shortcomings of that athlete's efforts.

**Advanced DBAs**

# Examine a Letter to the President

**Directions:** Read the background information and the text of the letter. Then, answer the questions on a separate sheet of paper.

This is a letter written by Jackie Robinson to President Eisenhower in 1958. Robinson was a former baseball player for the Brooklyn Dodgers. He was the first African American allowed to play in major league baseball in 1947. At the time he wrote this letter, he was an executive at the Chock Full o' Nuts coffee company. The letter concerns the actions of the governor of Arkansas.

The President
The White House
Washington, D. C.

My dear Mr. President:

I was sitting in the audience at the Summit Meeting of Negro Leaders yesterday when you said we must have patience. On hearing you say this, I felt like standing up and saying, "Oh no! Not again."

I respectfully remind you sir, that we have been the most patient of all people. When you said we must have self-respect, I wondered how we could have self-respect and remain patient considering the treatment accorded us through the years.

17 million Negroes cannot do as you suggest and wait for the hearts of men to change. We want to enjoy now the rights that we feel we are entitled to as Americans. This we cannot do unless we pursue aggressively goals which all other Americans achieved over 150 years ago.

As the chief executive of our nation, I respectfully suggest that you unwittingly crush the spirit of freedom in Negroes by constantly urging forbearance and give hope to those pro-segregation leaders like Governor Faubus who would take from us even those freedoms we now enjoy. Your own experience with Governor Faubus is proof enough that forbearance and not eventual integration is the goal the pro-segregation leaders seek.

In my view, an unequivocal statement backed up by action such as you demonstrated you could take last fall in deal-

ing with Governor Faubus if it became necessary, would let it be known that America is determined to provide -- in the near future -- for Negroes -- the freedoms we are entitled to under the constitution.

Respectfully yours,

Jackie Robinson

Jackie Robinson

JR:cc

1. Why has Robinson written this letter to the president?

   (A) to let the president know how much progress has been made for civil rights

   (B) to let the president know the people will be patient in waiting for change

   (C) to encourage the president to enforce the civil rights laws

   (D) to encourage the president to tour the South to see for himself the struggles for civil rights

2. What clues does the letter give about Robinson's race?

3. Based on what you know about the civil rights movement, how had African Americans demonstrated their patience?

# Freedom Riders

**Historical-Thinking Skill**

Students will understand how diverse groups united during the civil rights movement.

**Activate**

Show video news clips or provide news articles about the Occupy Wall Street protests from 2011. Using those clips or articles, have students compare and contrast the similarities and differences between this protest and the civil rights movement protests.

**Analyze**

1. Have students read the interview on *Examine Freedom Riders* (page 281). Ask them to complete *Document Analysis—Make Connections* (page 296) to support their analysis. Guide students to compare this type of protest to others, such as the lunch counter sit-in and the peace march. Have students work in small groups to complete the charts on their analysis sheets. Discuss as a class what they have written.

2. Use the following questions to guide a discussion:
   - How would you feel if you were one of the Freedom Riders?
   - How would you feel if you were opposed to them?
   - Do you think the nonviolent approach is best? Why or why not?

3. Allow time for students to complete *Examine Freedom Riders*. Discuss their work and strengthen their analysis skills using the How To activity.

**How To . . .**

**Identify Point of View**—Tell students there are three basic points of view: objective, first person, and third person. Understanding the point of view in a document can help identify bias and allow you to draw your own conclusions. First-person point of view is used when a person tells the story directly from their experiences using the word "I." Third-person point of view is more limited because the person can retell the story from indirect experiences. Objective point of view is used when just the facts are given without interpretation. Have students identify the point of view of this document.

**Extend**

Have students conduct interviews with one another about an event from the civil rights movement. Have one student act as the participant or witness in the event and the other act as the interviewer. Both students should research information to accurately role-play their parts. The interviewer should research the same event to develop relevant questions to ask.

**Advanced DBAs**

# Examine Freedom Riders

**Directions:** Read the background information and quotation. Then, answer the questions.

Robert Singleton participated in the Freedom Rides. In this interview, he discusses his journey to Jackson, Mississippi, to participate in the Freedom Rides.

> **"The journey was an eye-opener. Our journey began at UCLA, we actually knew at the time that we would have to have bail money before we went in. The first Freedom Riders were bailed out and that broke CORE at the bank. We were notified that we couldn't come if we didn't have prospects for raising our bail. We were a group of seventeen all together. We had arranged with professors and others to help us raise our bail money. We were pretty certain we had enough when we left. I thought we would go with the first group, but I found there were even more people who wanted to go, so I went with the second group from UCLA. We flew down to New Orleans, and got an orientation on what to expect and what not to do. When we finally went into Jackson, we went in by train and walked into the white waiting room. We were confronted immediately by the police who told us to move on—they were going to tell us three time—it didn't take very long. We were arrested immediately and put in the paddy wagon. "**
>
> **—Robert Singleton**

**1.** What does this quotation reveal about the organization of the Freedom Rides?

_____

_____

_____

**2.** What risks did Freedom Riders, such as Singleton, take in their actions?

_____

_____

_____

**3.** How was the way Singleton protested similar to the lunch sit-in protests?

- (A) They carried signs.
- (B) They were nonviolent.
- (C) They received little attention.
- (D) They were alone.

**Civil Rights Movement**

# Dr. King

## Historical-Thinking Skill

Students will examine the actions and beliefs of Dr. Martin Luther King Jr.

**Activate**

Ask students to imagine a situation in which they are either peaceful protesters or violent protesters. Which type of protest (peaceful or violent) do they think would get more attention? Help students understand how controversial Martin Luther King Jr.'s methods were at the time, though he is now considered an American hero. Discuss the controversy between King and Malcolm X. Have students read about both men and how their attitudes toward protests differed.

**Analyze**

1. Have students look at the picture and read the quotation on *Examine Dr. King* (page 283). Ask them to complete *Document Analysis—Use Evidence* (page 299) to support their analysis.

2. Ask students if King's quotation is more or less relevant today. Lead the class in an open discussion, and apply as many current events as possible to the discussion to compare and contrast the past with the present.

3. Use the following questions to guide a discussion:

   · Is everyone who goes to jail guilty of a crime?

   · Is the law always right?

   · What would you do if you were sent to prison for peacefully opposing an unjust law?

4. Allow time for students to complete *Examine Dr. King*. Discuss their work and strengthen their analysis skills using the How To activity.

**How To . . .**

**Analyze a Quotation**—Explain to students that a quotation is an excellent source because it is the actual words spoken by a person. However, a quotation taken out of context can be misleading and confusing. It is important to focus on the facts and keep the bigger context of the quotation in mind. Tell students that paraphrasing the quotation can help them understand the meaning of it. Analyzing the writing style may also reveal clues to its purpose. Determining the intended audience and how important the quotation is to its intended audience is also key. Ask students to annotate Dr. King's quotation with comments and questions, keeping all these things in mind.

**Extend**

Provide a copy of King's "I Have a Dream" speech, and ask students to identify quotations that they feel are the most significant. Then, have students paraphrase their quotations and explain why they selected their quotations as the most significant. Have students share their quotations in small groups.

Name: _____ Date: _____

# Examine Dr. King

**Directions:** Read the background information, study the image, and answer the questions.

Martin Luther King Jr. was arrested in Birmingham, Alabama, for a peaceful protest against segregation laws. He wrote a letter from jail to a local clergymen, who urged King and others to obey all laws. This quotation is taken from that letter.

**" An individual who breaks a law that conscience tells him is unjust, and who willingly accepts the penalty of imprisonment in order to arouse the conscience of the community over its injustice, is in reality expressing the highest respect for the law. "**
**—Martin Luther King Jr.**

**1.** What does King say is the purpose of breaking an unjust law?

Ⓐ to help others understand that the law is unfair

Ⓑ to see how far he was willing to go to fight for equal rights

Ⓒ to maintain authority over the citizens without cause

Ⓓ to show the world how strong his leadership can be

**2.** Was King saying that anyone who did not join him in his protests was acting unjustly? Support your answer.

_____

_____

_____

**3.** From King's perspective, how do you think his civil disobedience is an expression of the "highest respect for the law"? Do you agree or disagree? Why?

_____

_____

_____

# Civil Rights Act of 1964

### Historical-Thinking Skill

Students will evaluate the successes of the civil rights movement.

**Activate**

Ask students to define *success* in their own words and then share their definitions with partners. Lead a class discussion about success and how success is judged in social, economic, political, and legal context.

**Analyze**

1. Have students read the excerpt on *Examine the Civil Rights Act of 1964* (page 285). Ask students to complete *Document Analysis—Make Connections* (page 296) to support their analysis. Ask students to compare the goals of the civil rights movement to the actual Civil Rights Act.

2. Divide the class into two sides. Have one side argue that the Civil Rights Act of 1964 was a success. Have the other side argue that it did not accomplish the goals of the civil rights movement. Allow time for students to research, discuss, and prepare for the debate as needed.

3. Use the following questions to guide a discussion:
   - What part of the Civil Rights Act of 1964 made the most difference in society?
   - What part made the least difference in society?
   - Why was it significant that President Johnson supported the act?
   - Did the Civil Rights Act of 1964 accomplish all the goals of the civil rights movement?

4. Allow time for students to complete *Examine the Civil Rights Act of 1964*. Discuss their work and strengthen their analysis skills using the How To activity.

**How To . . .**

**Analyze Laws**—Explain to students that laws enacted by governments are intended to help and protect the people. Not all laws are written well, so sometimes they do not help or protect the people. A law is a primary source and should be analyzed thoroughly rather than just taken as fact. Laws should contain the critical basic components to make them effective and practical. For example, a strongly written law provides a clear purpose, and it should not have any parts that are contradictory. Finally, a law should also have a method of enforcing the law, and it must be constitutional. Have students try to locate these things in the Civil Rights Act.

**Extend**

Have students research and evaluate the decision in the 2013 Supreme Court case of *Shelby County v. Holder*. Have students determine the effect this case had on voting rights, and ask them what conclusions can be drawn to the effects of this case for democracy in the United States.

**Advanced DBAs**

Name: _____ Date: _____

# Examine the Civil Rights Act of 1964

**Directions:** Read the background information and text of the act, study the images, and answer the questions.

President Lyndon Johnson signed the Civil Rights Act of 1964 into law on July 2, 1964. It prohibited discrimination in public places, provided for the integration of schools and other public facilities, and made employment discrimination illegal. It was the most important and relevant civil rights law since Reconstruction. The photo shows Johnson about to address the nation before signing the act. Next to the photo is an excerpt of the beginning of the Civil Rights Act of 1964.

**An Act**

To enforce the constitutional right to vote, to confer jurisdiction upon the district courts of the United States to provide injunctive relief against discrimination in public accommodations, to authorize the Attorney General to institute suits to protect constitutional rights in public facilities and public education, to extend the Commission on Civil Rights, to prevent discrimination in federally assisted programs, to establish a Commission on Equal Employment Opportunity, and for other purposes.

Be it enacted by the Senate and House of Representatives of the United States of America in Congress assembled, That this Act may be cited as the "Civil Rights Act of 1964."

**1.** What did the Civil Rights Act of 1964 do to outlaw discrimination?

_____

_____

_____

**2.** What did the federal government establish to help enforce the law?

Ⓐ Attorney General's Office on Civil Rights

Ⓑ Commission on Equal Employment Opportunity

Ⓒ Commission on Civil Rights

Ⓓ Commission on Equality and Civil Rights

**3.** Why was this such a landmark law in the United States?

_____

_____

_____

Civil Rights Movement

# Civil Rights Movement Document-Based Question

## Historical Context

The Emancipation Proclamation freed enslaved people, but that was just the beginning. There was a very long journey to equality ahead for African Americans. The Constitution was amended, but new laws were passed that violated the Constitution. A new generation of activists arose to fight racial injustice. More than one hundred years would pass before the Constitution guaranteed equal rights to African Americans specifically living in the South.

## Essay Tasks

**Directions:** Using the documents and your knowledge of the civil rights movement, complete **one** of the following essay tasks. Before you begin your essay, complete the *DBQ Essay Planner* (pages 302–305) to plan your writing.

### Essay Task ❶

In a well-organized essay, describe the three most significant events in the civil rights era and their effects on the success of the movement.

In your essay, remember to:

- Identify and describe details of the three events.

- Provide evidence that will convince the reader that the events you selected are the most important.

- Include a topic sentence, introduction, body, and conclusion.

- Give details to support your ideas.

- Use information found in the documents to support your argument.

### Essay Task ❷

In a well-organized essay, explain why a new civil rights movement is necessary in America today. What lessons can we learn from the original civil rights movement to make a greater and more permanent change?

In your essay, remember to:

- Write a clear and strong thesis statement.

- Identify and describe specific lessons to take from the original civil rights movement.

- Provide evidence that will convince the reader that a new civil rights movement will be more successful than the original.

- Include a topic sentence, introduction, body, and conclusion.

- Give details to support your ideas.

- Use information found in the documents to support your argument.

★ As a bonus, include evidence from an outside source or a counterargument in your chosen essay.

# Teacher Resources

## Background Information

### Police Report Lesson

Rosa Parks worked as a seamstress in a department store in Montgomery, Alabama. Every day, she rode the bus between home and work. Most of the bus riders in Montgomery were African American. The bus system was segregated. There was a "colored" (or black) section in the back and a white section in the front of each bus. When the bus was full, a white person could demand to sit in a seat occupied by an African American, even if that seat was in the back of the bus. Parks refused to give up her seat in the front of the bus to a white person who asked for it. Parks was not the first African American to be arrested for refusing to abide by these rules. To protest her arrest, the local NAACP (National Association for the Advancement of Colored People) organized a boycott of the Montgomery bus system for the following Monday. Rosa Parks had been a secretary in the local NAACP, and her participation in the organization caused it to rally around and support her.

Martin Luther King Jr. played a large role in organizing this boycott. He knew that it would take the entire African American community standing together to make a real change happen. The absence of so many African American bus riders was widely noticed. The boycott grew from a single day to an entire year. It hurt the bus companies financially, but they were not willing to give in on this issue. Eventually, the bus system in Montgomery was desegregated because the Supreme Court ruled that bus segregation was against the law.

### Protests Lesson

Starting with Rosa Parks's arrest in 1955, African Americans found many ways to focus attention on the inequalities in American culture. African Americans began to challenge other "whites-only" restrictions in restaurants, parks, and public transportation. By protesting these restrictions, African Americans called attention to the unfairness of these restrictions.

One type of protest is the "sit-in." Laws segregated many lunch counters in drugstores and department stores. African Americans would sit down to eat in a whites-only section, and they were refused service. They would continue to sit until one person was served or arrested. If the person got arrested, someone else would take that person's place until they were served or arrested. Many of the participants were college students. Their actions led to the desegregation of lunch counters throughout the South in the United States.

Another protest method was to organize peaceful marches to publicize demand for change. The largest of these marches was in 1963 in the nation's capital. Nearly one quarter of a million people marched peacefully in the nation's capital on August 28. They carried signs and sang songs while marching from the Capitol building to the Lincoln Memorial. The most striking image of that day is the memory of Martin Luther King Jr. giving his inspirational "I Have a Dream" speech.

**Advanced DBAs**

# Teacher Resources (cont.)

## Literacy Tests Lesson

Enslaved people had been freed, declared citizens, and guaranteed the right to vote. But when African American men actually started casting their votes, the Southerners were less than thrilled. This is because African American men were in the majority in certain states. Despite the changes to the Constitution, Southern states passed laws that effectively denied African Americans their right to vote. One of these new laws was a poll tax. The poll tax prevented many African Americans from voting because they could not afford to pay the poll tax. The administration of the tax was an unfair tactic that blocked many African Americans from the polls.

Another measure that prevented African Americans from voting was the literacy test. The reasoning behind the measure seemed legitimate on the surface: voters should be informed of the issues and candidates on the ballot. However, white people were exempt from the literacy test through a grandfather clause that stated if that person or a family member had voted before 1867, then that person was not required to take the test. Of course, most African Americans had never voted before this date. The tests included questions that were either impossible to answer or dealt with Constitutional minutiae that most white people would also be unable to answer. Some tests required African American voters to recite the entire Constitution from memory.

## Letter to the President Lesson

Jackie Robinson was the first African American baseball player allowed to play major league baseball. He began playing for the Brooklyn Dodgers in 1947. He endured intense racial persecution for breaking this racial barrier. Robinson responded by becoming one of the best players in the league. In 1949, he was named the league's Most Valuable Player. He retired from baseball in 1956 and was elected to baseball's Hall of Fame in 1962. In 1957, he joined the Chock Full o' Nuts Corporation as vice president for personnel. Also in 1957, Governor Faubus in Arkansas ordered the National Guard to prevent nine African American students from entering Central High School in Little Rock. President Eisenhower sent U.S. soldiers to enforce the integration of the city's public high school. In this letter, Mr. Robinson reminds the president of this action and urges him to continue to take action rather than merely urge African Americans to have patience. Mr. Robinson also wrote letters to President John F. Kennedy, President Lyndon B. Johnson, and President Richard Nixon.

## Freedom Riders Lesson

In Tennessee, efforts to desegregate movie theaters and lunch counters had been a success. Students who led those protests set their sights on changing another law that required segregation of interstate travel. This new form of protest involved both African Americans and white people who volunteered to ride together on a chartered bus through the South. The very first of these trips was named the Journey of Reconciliation in 1947. It faced stiff resistance, the participants were imprisoned, and no changes were made to the law. White people who acted in violence against these freedom riders and protestors were not punished. In May of 1961, a new Freedom Ride was organized. It would begin in Washington, DC, and end in New Orleans. In Alabama, buses were attacked, tires were slashed, protesters were beaten, and one bus was firebombed. The Freedom Ride participants were trained to not respond with violence. As a result of the Freedom Ride, the Kennedy administration implemented new measures to protect interstate travelers from segregation laws.

Advanced DBAs

# Teacher Resources *(cont.)*

## Dr. King Lesson

Martin Luther King Jr. was jailed several times in his life. He practiced civil disobedience against segregation laws throughout the southern United States. In April 1963, he spent several days in jail in Birmingham, Alabama. While in prison, a group of white ministers criticized King's method of peaceful protest as unwise and untimely, and they called him a political extremist. The ministers agreed that there was unjust treatment of African Americans, but they believed that change should come through the legal system. Until then, they thought that laws should be obeyed. Some African Americans, such as Malcolm X, opposed King's philosophy. He believed that unjust laws should be opposed not only by peaceful means, but also by violent means if necessary.

## Civil Rights Act of 1964 Lesson

On June 6, 1963, President John F. Kennedy advocated for action to be taken to guarantee equal treatment of every American regardless of race. He asked Congress to write a civil rights law that would deal with voting rights, discrimination in public accommodations, desegregation of schools, and more.

In November of 1963, President Kennedy was assassinated. President Lyndon B. Johnson signed the Civil Rights Act of 1964 into law on July 2, 1964. The act outlawed segregation in theaters, restaurants, and hotels. It also ended segregation in public places, such as swimming pools, libraries, and public schools. The act banned job discrimination by employers who were hiring.

Passage of the act was not easy. In the House of Representatives, they tried to kill the bill in the House Rules Committee. In the Senate, they used the filibuster to try and kill the bill. A filibuster is when Senators try to talk the bill to death. In early 1964, it was clear that strong leadership and political will was going to be necessary to pass the bill. Senator Hubert Humphrey of Minnesota played a major role in overcoming the filibuster. Senate Minority Leader Everett Dirksen of Illinois also helped by convincing Republicans to pass the bill. However, the most important supporter of the bill was President Lyndon Johnson, and because of his efforts and courage, the bill passed.

**Advanced DBAs**

# Teacher Resources *(cont.)*

## Answer Key

### Examine the Police Report (page 273)

1. The offense was committed on December 1, 1955 at 6:06 p.m.
2. The offense was that an African American woman was sitting in the white section of a bus and would not move back. Rosa Parks committed the offense.
3. Answers may include that Rosa Parks was a member and secretary of her local NAACP, and the boycott lasted and gained recognition because the NAACP supported it and inspired others in the South to join it.

### Examine Protests (page 275)

1. They are marching for freedom, equal rights, integrated schools, decent housing, and to end bias.
2. B
3. Answers may include that the sit-ins had more of an impact because they led to the desegregation of lunch counters, which resulted in nation-wide attention and led to the civil rights movement.

### Examine Literacy Tests (page 277)

1. These questions refer to different aspects of the government and the law.
2. Answers may include that the questions were written by people who did not want African Americans to vote or to treat them equally.
3. It is unfair because most citizens do not know this information. Only privileged citizens or those who have studied law would know the answers. Many African Americans had not had the opportunities to learn the answers as others did.

### Examine a Letter to the President (page 279)

1. C
2. The fact that Robinson mentions that he is sitting in a meeting of Negro leaders is a clue that he is probably an African American.
3. Although they had gained freedom after the Civil War, and it was almost 100 years later, they still did not have the freedom to go wherever they wanted or to do whatever they wanted as white people could. This showed the patience of African Americans.

### Examine Freedom Riders (page 281)

1. The quotation suggests that the Freedom Riders were well organized. He mentions the planning done ahead of time and even an orientation meeting.
2. They risked going to jail, paying a fine, and even possible violence against them.
3. B

### Examine Dr. King (page 283)

1. A
2. Answers may include that King was not saying that anyone who did not join him in his protests was acting unjustly, but he did expect people to stand up against unjust treatment even if it was not in one of his protests. People who did not join his protests because they could not travel that distance could still be activists at home.
3. Answers may include that King is expressing his "highest respect" for the law because he wants just laws to be valued and wants to distinguish unjust laws from just laws.

### Examine the Civil Rights Act of 1964 (page 285)

1. It enforced people's right to vote, prevented discrimination in public places, such as schools and other public facilities, and it made employment discrimination illegal.
2. B
3. Answers could include that this law was passed in the middle of the civil rights movement and signed into law and supported by a president who was from the South.

### Civil Rights Movement Document-Based Question (page 286)

Refer to pages 306–307 for the DBQ Rubrics.

# Teacher Resource Appendix

## Document-Analysis Sheets

Name: _____ Date: _____

# Document Deep Dive – Venn Diagram

**Directions:** Fill out as much of the top of the page as you can. Then, follow your teacher's directions to label and complete the Venn diagram.

|  | Document A | Document B |
|---|---|---|
| **Title or Description** |  |  |
| **Type of Document** (map, letter, photo, etc.) |  |  |
| **Document Creator** |  |  |
| **Date Created** |  |  |
| **Purpose** |  |  |

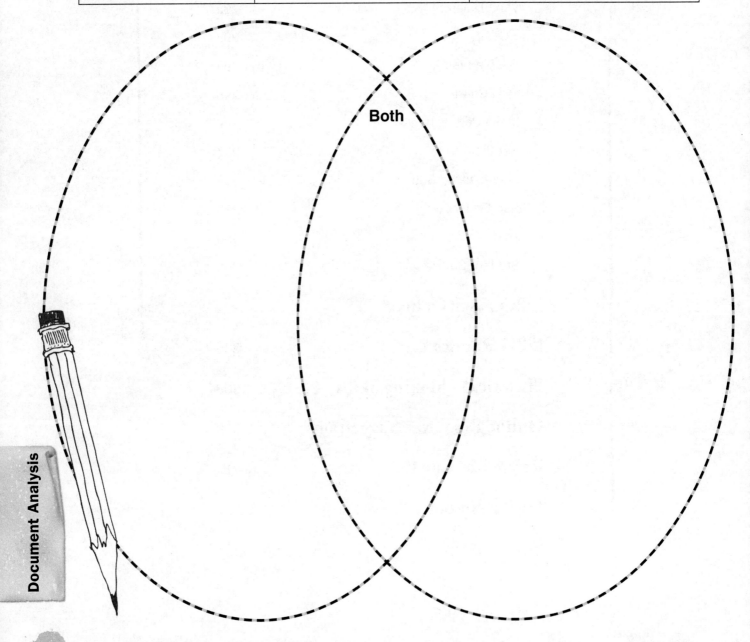

Both

© Shell Education

Document Analysis

Name: _____ Date: _____

# Document Deep Dive – T-Chart

**Directions:** Fill out as much of the top of the page as you can. Then, follow your teacher's directions to label and complete each column.

|  | Document A | Document B |
|---|---|---|
| **Title or Description** |  |  |
| **Type of Document** (map, letter, photo, etc.) |  |  |
| **Document Creator** |  |  |
| **Date Created** |  |  |
| **Purpose** |  |  |

|  |  |
|---|---|
|  |  |

Document Analysis

# Document Deep Dive – Bubble Map

**Directions:** Fill out as much of the top of the page as you can. If there is only one document, cross out the right column. Follow your teacher's directions to label and complete each column.

|  | Document A | Document B |
|---|---|---|
| **Title or Description** |  |  |
| **Type of Document** (map, letter, photo, etc.) |  |  |
| **Document Creator** |  |  |
| **Date Created** |  |  |
| **Purpose** |  |  |

Name: _____ Date: _____

# Document Deep Dive – Flow Chart

**Directions:** Fill out as much of the top of the page as you can.  If there is only one document, cross out the right column.  Follow your teacher's directions to label and complete each column.

| | Document A | Document B |
|---|---|---|
| **Title or Description** | | |
| **Type of Document** (map, letter, photo, etc.) | | |
| **Document Creator** | | |
| **Date Created** | | |
| **Purpose** | | |

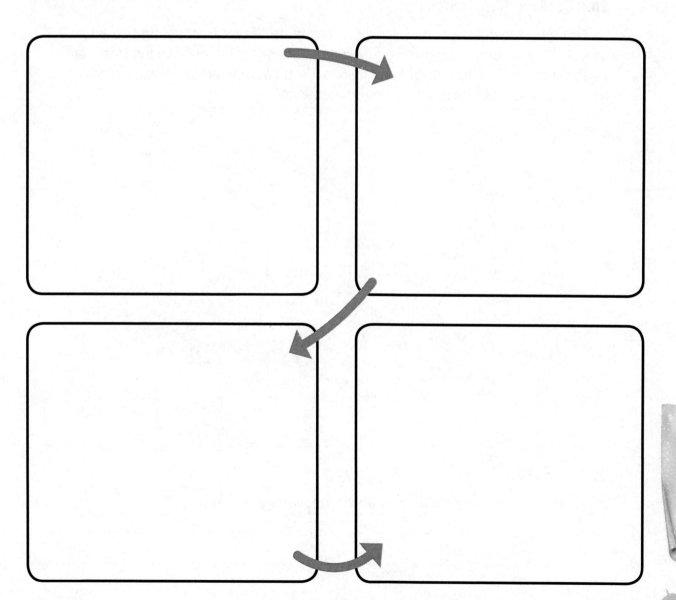

© Shell Education

Document Analysis

Name: _____ Date: _____

# Document Analysis–Make Connections

**Directions:** Complete as much of this page as you can to better understand the document.

## Step 1: Just the Facts

**Title or description:** _____

**Type of document:** _____
(map, letter, photo, etc.)

**Date:** _____ **Place:** _____ **Creator:** _____

**Circle one:**     primary source     secondary source

## Step 2: Make Connections

Use the chart to make connections (e.g., compare and/or contrast, cause and effect). Your teacher may give you directions or ask you to choose the best way to label the sections to record connections. You can use colors, lines, or other marks as needed to help show your connections.

## Step 3: Reflect

What did you learn or notice from the connections you made?

_____

_____

Name: _____ Date: _____

# Document Analysis—Set the Scene

**Directions:** Complete as much of this page as you can to better understand the document.

## Step 1: Just the Facts

**Title or description:** _____

**Type of document:** _____
(map, letter, photo, etc.)

**Date:** _____ **Place:** _____ **Creator:** _____

**Circle one:**    primary source    secondary source

## Step 2: Set the Scene

Record what you know about the time and place the document was created.

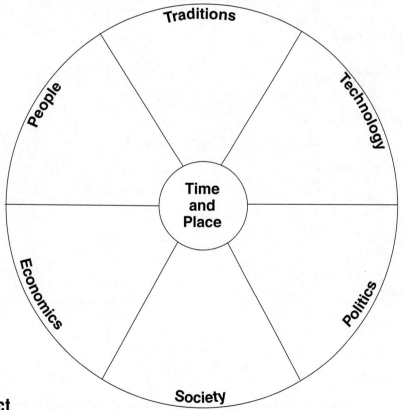

## Step 3: Reflect

How did the historical setting, or context, influence the events, ideas, and/or purpose of the document?

_____

_____

Document Analysis

Name: _____ Date: _____

# Document Analysis–Consider the Source

**Directions:** Complete as much of this page as you can to better understand the document.

## Step 1: Just the Facts

**Title or description:** _____

**Type of document:** _____
(map, letter, photo, etc.)

**Date:** _____ **Place:** _____ **Creator:** _____

**Circle one:**     primary source        secondary source

## Step 2: Consider the Source

| Consider This | Answer (including how you know) | Does this make it more or less reliable? Why? |
|---|---|---|
| Primary or secondary source | | |
| Fact or opinion | | |
| Intended audience | | |
| Creator's viewpoint | | |
| Purpose | | |
| Creator's level of authority/ experience | | |
| Bias | | |

## Step 3: Reflect

Summarize your overall impression of the source, its reliability, and what can be learned from it.

_____

_____

_____

**Document Analysis**

     © Shell Education

Name: _____ Date: _____

# Document Analysis–Use Evidence

**Directions:** Complete as much of this page as you can to better understand the document.

## Step 1: Just the Facts

**Title or description:** _____

**Type of document:** _____
(map, letter, photo, etc.)

**Date:** _____ **Place:** _____ **Creator:** _____

**Circle one:**      primary source      secondary source

## Step 2: Use Evidence

List any claims you can make and conclusions you can draw. They might be about the document, the creator of it, or the historical context around it. Then, list the evidence from the document and/or your background knowledge to support your statements.

| Claims and Conclusions | Evidence |
|---|---|
|  |  |

## Step 3: Reflect

Does this primary source support or dispute other things that you know about the topic? Provide examples.

_____

_____

_____

© Shell Education

Document Analysis

Name: _____ Date: _____

# Document Analysis–Think Across Time

**Directions:** Complete as much of this page as you can to better understand the document.

## Step 1: Just the Facts

**Title or description:** _____

**Type of document:** _____
(map, letter, photo, etc.)

**Date:** _____ **Place:** _____ **Creator:** _____

**Circle one:**     primary source     secondary source

## Step 2: Think Across Time

1.  What are the defining characteristics of the time period this document is from or about?

    _____

    _____

2.  Create a time line to show how the document relates to events across time. Not sure where to start?  Try this: Identify two events related to the time period and write them on opposite ends of the time line.  Then, add 2–3 more events from the time period on the time line.  Finally, put the document in the correct point on the time line.

## Step 3: Reflect

What did you notice, learn, or confirm from the time line you created?

_____

_____

_____

Document Analysis

116869—Document-Based Assessment Activities                              © Shell Education

# Bonus Document Analysis–Student Choice ❓

**Directions:** Complete as much of this page as you can to better understand the document.

## Step 1: Just the Facts

**Title or description:** _____

**Type of document:** _____
(map, letter, photo, etc.)

**Date:** _____ **Place:** _____ **Creator:** _____

**Circle one:**     primary source     secondary source

## Step 2: Student Choice

Choose a historical-thinking skill to focus on as you analyze the document. Then, create and complete a graphic organizer in the space below (time line, chart, Venn diagram, etc.) to support your analysis.

**Historical-Thinking Skill Focus:** _____

## Step 3: Reflect

What did you learn or notice from your thinking in step 2?

_____

_____

_____

© Shell Education

Document Analysis

# DBQ Essay Planner

**Directions:** Complete steps 1–7 to help you plan your essay.

## Step 1—Understand

Read and annotate your chosen essay task.

➤ Circle the type of essay you are being asked to write.

compare/contrast          historical context

cause and effect          periodization

continuity and change

➤ Write your initial answer to the DBQ in one sentence: _____

_____

_____

## Step 2—Prepare

What evidence will you look for in the documents to help you plan your essay? Write your notes.

## Step 3—Use Outside Information

What other information can you include in your essay (information you learned in class or read about)? Write your notes.

## Step 4—Draft a Thesis

Write a first draft of your thesis before you analyze the documents. Make a claim that you can defend. Respond to all parts of the question.

_____

_____

_____

© Shell Education

# DBQ Essay Planner *(cont.)*

### Step 5—Analyze Documents

Analyze the documents to connect them to your thesis.

| | Summarize the document. | Identify one or more of the following: <br>• author's point of view <br>• intended audience <br>• historical context <br>• author's purpose | How does your analysis support your thesis? |
|---|---|---|---|
| 1 | | | |
| 2 | | | |
| 3 | | | |
| 4 | | | |
| 5 | | | |
| 6 | | | |
| 7 | | | |

### Step 6—Revised Thesis

Revise your thesis to make it clear and concise. Make sure you can support your thesis with evidence from the documents.

_____

_____

_____

# DBQ Essay Planner *(cont.)*

## Step 7—Outline

Use the outline guide to create an outline for your essay. Write notes or sentences on the paper, or create your outline on a separate sheet of paper.

**I.** Introduction

   **A.** Topic sentence—Establish the topic of your essay in a clear and engaging way.

   **B.** Additional relevant information to introduce your topic and set the scene

   **C.** Final Thesis Statement

**II.** Body of the Essay

   **A.** Body Paragraph 1

      a. Topic Sentence

      b. Evidence from a document

      c. Evidence from a document

      d. Outside information

      e. Transition Sentence–Connect the evidence to the thesis in your own words.

 © Shell Education

# DBQ Essay Planner *(cont.)*

**Step 7—Outline** *(cont.)*

    **B.** Body Paragraph 2

        a. Topic Sentence

        b. Evidence from a document

        c. Evidence from a document

        d. Outside information

        e. Transition Sentence

    **C.** Body Paragraph 3

        a. Topic Sentence

        b. Evidence from a document

        c. Evidence from a document

        d. Outside information

        e. Transition Sentence

        *Add additional body paragraphs as needed

**III.** Conclusion

    **A.** Summary

    **B.** Restate your argument/purpose with clear understanding and emphasis.

# DBQ Rubric

**Directions:** Use this rubric to evaluate student responses.

**Student Name:** _____

**DBQ Unit:** _____

| | Excellent (4 points) | Great Job (3 points) | Good Work (2 points) | Keep Trying (1 point) |
|---|---|---|---|---|
| **Analysis** | Documents are thoroughly examined and clearly understood. | Documents are examined and understood. | A fair attempt to study and understand the documents is made. | Documents are not examined or properly understood. |
| **Answers** | Responses address the question(s) thoroughly. | Responses address the question(s) clearly. | Responses address the question(s) briefly. | Responses do not address the question(s). |
| **Details** | Responses are supported by strong facts and/or evidence. | Responses are supported by facts and/or evidence. | Responses are supported by at least one fact. | Responses are not supported by facts and/or evidence. |
| **Vocabulary** | Strong, precise content vocabulary is used within the response. | Precise content vocabulary is used within the response. | Some content vocabulary is used within the response. | No content vocabulary is used within the response. |
| **Language Conventions** | There are no errors and writing shows strength in this area. | There are no errors in capitalization, punctuation, or spelling. | There are a few errors in capitalization, punctuation, or spelling. | There are many errors in capitalization, punctuation, or spelling. |

**Comments:** _____

_____

_____

_____

_____

© Shell Education

# DBQ Single-Point Rubric

**Directions:** Use this alternative rubric format to evaluate student responses and provide specific feedback as needed.

**Student Name:** _____

**DBQ Unit:** _____

| | Growth Opportunities *(how student can improve)* | Target Criteria | Highlights *(how student excelled)* |
|---|---|---|---|
| **Analysis** | | Documents are examined and understood. | |
| **Answers** | | Responses address the question(s) clearly. | |
| **Details** | | Responses are supported by facts and/or evidence. | |
| **Vocabulary** | | Precise content vocabulary is used within the response. | |
| **Language Conventions** | | There are no errors in capitalization, punctuation, or spelling. | |

**Comments:** _____

_____

_____

_____

_____

# Historical-Thinking Skills

 **Make Connections**

 **Use Evidence**

 **Consider the Source**

 **Set the Scene**

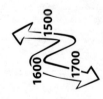 **Think Across Time**

    © Shell Education

# Online Resources Suggestions

There are many great online resources to help teachers create even more document-based assessment activities. The document-analysis sheets (pages 292–301) in this resource are designed to work with other documents. This chart includes resources for finding engaging historical documents and classroom activities. They are also great resources for students to use when trying to find or corroborate evidence.

| Resource | Website Address | Twitter Handle |
|---|---|---|
| American Anitquarian Society | www.americanantiquarian.org | @AmAntiquarian |
| Library of Congress | www.loc.gov<br>www.loc.gov/teachers | @librarycongress |
| Life Magazine Photo Archive | images.google.com/hosted/life | @LIFE |
| National Archives | www.archives.gov | @USNatArchives<br>@TodaysDocument |
| Smithsonian | www.si.edu<br>historyexplorer.si.edu<br>learninglab.si.edu | @smithsonian<br>@amhistorymuseum |
| Stanford History Education Group | www.sheg.stanford.edu | @SHEG_Stanford |
| The Gilder Lehrman Institute of American History | www.gilderlehrman.org | @Gilder_Lehrman |
| Yale Law School: The Avalon Project | avalon.law.yale.edu | n/a |

# References Cited

Cohen, D.W. 1994. *The Combing of History*. Chicago: University of Chicago Press.

Herodotus. 1996. *Histories*. Hertfordshire, England: Wordsworth Editions Limited.

Krug, Mark M. 1967. *History and the Social Sciences*. Waltham, Massachusetts: Blaisdell Publishing Company.

Levstik, Linda, and Keith Barton. 2005. *Doing History: Investigating with Children in Elementary and Middle Schools*. Mahwah, New Jersey: Lawrence Erlbaum Associates.

National Council for the Social Studies (NCSS). 2016. "A Vision of Powerful Teaching and Learning in the Social Studies: A Position Statement of the National Council for the Social Studies." *Social Education* 80 (3): 180–182.

Novik, P. 1988. *That Noble Dream: The "Objectivity Question" and the American Historical Profession*. New York: Cambridge University Press.

Online Library of Liberty. 2019. "1787: Jay, Address to the People of N.Y. (Pamphlet)." Liberty Fund, Inc.oll.libertyfund.org/pages/1787-jay-address-to-the-people-of-n-y-pamphlet.

Patrick Henry Memorial Foundation. 2019. "Liberty or Empire?" www.redhill.org/speech/liberty-or-empire.

Public History Initiative at UCLA. n.d. "1. CHRONOLOGICAL THINKING." UCLA. phi.history.ucla.edu/nchs/historical-thinking-standards-/1-chronological-thinking/.

Thelen, David. 1989. "Memory and American History." *The Journal of American History*, 4: 1117–1129.

Wineburg, Sam. 1991. "On the Reading of Historical Texts: Notes on the Breach Between School and Academy." *American Educational Research Journal* 28: 495–519.

———. 2001. *Historical Thinking and Other Unnatural Acts: Charting the Future of Teaching the Past*. Philadelphia: Temple University Press.

———. 2018. *Why Learn History (When It's Already on Your Phone)*. Chicago, IL: University of Chicago Press.

© Shell Education

# Digital Resources

## Accessing the Digital Resources

The digital resources can be downloaded by following these steps:

1. Go to **www.tcmpub.com/digital**

2. Sign in or create an account.

3. Click Redeem Content and enter the located on page 2 and the back cover, into appropriate field on the website.

4. Respond to the prompts using the book to view your account and available digital content.

5. Choose the digital resources you would like to download. You can download all the files at once, or you can download a specific group of files.

**Please note:** Some files provided for download have large file sizes. Download times for these larger files will vary based on your download speed.

© Shell Education